Eikonoklastes. In Answer To A Book Intitled, Eikon Basilike, The Portraiture of His Sacred Majesty In His Solitudes and Sufferings. By John Milton, Printed In 1650. To Which Is Added, An Original Letter To Milton

John Milton

Eikonoklastes. In answer to a book intitled, Eikon Basilike, the portraiture of his sacred Majesty in his solitudes and sufferings. By John Milton. Now first published from the author's second edition, printed in 1650: with many enlargements: by Richard B
Milton, John
ESTCID: T032467
Reproduction from British Library
The first, eighth and ninth words are in Greek characters.
London : printed for A. Millar, 1756.
vii,[1],96p. ; 4°

ECCO

Eighteenth Century Collections Online Print Editions

Gale ECCO Print Editions

Relive history with *Eighteenth Century Collections Online*, now available in print for the independent historian and collector. This series includes the most significant English-language and foreign-language works printed in Great Britain during the eighteenth century, and is organized in seven different subject areas including literature and language; medicine, science, and technology; and religion and philosophy. The collection also includes thousands of important works from the Americas.

The eighteenth century has been called "The Age of Enlightenment." It was a period of rapid advance in print culture and publishing, in world exploration, and in the rapid growth of science and technology – all of which had a profound impact on the political and cultural landscape. At the end of the century the American Revolution, French Revolution and Industrial Revolution, perhaps three of the most significant events in modern history, set in motion developments that eventually dominated world political, economic, and social life.

In a groundbreaking effort, Gale initiated a revolution of its own: digitization of epic proportions to preserve these invaluable works in the largest online archive of its kind. Contributions from major world libraries constitute over 175,000 original printed works. Scanned images of the actual pages, rather than transcriptions, recreate the works ***as they first appeared.***

Now for the first time, these high-quality digital scans of original works are available via print-on-demand, making them readily accessible to libraries, students, independent scholars, and readers of all ages.

For our initial release we have created seven robust collections to form one the world's most comprehensive catalogs of 18th century works.

Initial Gale ECCO Print Editions collections include:

History and Geography
Rich in titles on English life and social history, this collection spans the world as it was known to eighteenth-century historians and explorers. Titles include a wealth of travel accounts and diaries, histories of nations from throughout the world, and maps and charts of a world that was still being discovered. Students of the War of American Independence will find fascinating accounts from the British side of conflict.

Social Science

Delve into what it was like to live during the eighteenth century by reading the first-hand accounts of everyday people, including city dwellers and farmers, businessmen and bankers, artisans and merchants, artists and their patrons, politicians and their constituents. Original texts make the American, French, and Industrial revolutions vividly contemporary.

Medicine, Science and Technology

Medical theory and practice of the 1700s developed rapidly, as is evidenced by the extensive collection, which includes descriptions of diseases, their conditions, and treatments. Books on science and technology, agriculture, military technology, natural philosophy, even cookbooks, are all contained here.

Literature and Language

Western literary study flows out of eighteenth-century works by Alexander Pope, Daniel Defoe, Henry Fielding, Frances Burney, Denis Diderot, Johann Gottfried Herder, Johann Wolfgang von Goethe, and others. Experience the birth of the modern novel, or compare the development of language using dictionaries and grammar discourses.

Religion and Philosophy

The Age of Enlightenment profoundly enriched religious and philosophical understanding and continues to influence present-day thinking. Works collected here include masterpieces by David Hume, Immanuel Kant, and Jean-Jacques Rousseau, as well as religious sermons and moral debates on the issues of the day, such as the slave trade. The Age of Reason saw conflict between Protestantism and Catholicism transformed into one between faith and logic -- a debate that continues in the twenty-first century.

Law and Reference

This collection reveals the history of English common law and Empire law in a vastly changing world of British expansion. Dominating the legal field is the *Commentaries of the Law of England* by Sir William Blackstone, which first appeared in 1765. Reference works such as almanacs and catalogues continue to educate us by revealing the day-to-day workings of society.

Fine Arts

The eighteenth-century fascination with Greek and Roman antiquity followed the systematic excavation of the ruins at Pompeii and Herculaneum in southern Italy; and after 1750 a neoclassical style dominated all artistic fields. The titles here trace developments in mostly English-language works on painting, sculpture, architecture, music, theater, and other disciplines. Instructional works on musical instruments, catalogs of art objects, comic operas, and more are also included.

'ΕΙΚΟΝΟΚΛΑΣΤΗΣ.

In Anſwer to a Book Intitled,

'ΕΙΚΩΝ ΒΑΣΙΛΙΚΗ,

The PORTRAITURE of his SACRED MAJESTY in his Solitudes and Sufferings.

By JOHN MILTON.

Now firſt publiſhed from the Author's SECOND EDITION, Printed in *1650*:

WITH MANY ENLARGEMENTS:

By RICHARD BARON.

WITH

A PREFACE ſhewing the tranſcendent Excellency of MILTON's Proſe Works.

To which is added,

An ORIGINAL LETTER to MILTON, never before publiſhed.

——— Morpheus, *on thy dewy wing*
Such fair auſpicious viſions bring,
As ſooth'd great MILTON's *injur'd age,*
When in prophetic dreams he ſaw
The Tribes unborn with pious awe
Imbibe each virtue from his heavenly page.

DR. AKINSIDE.

LONDON:

Printed for A. MILLAR, in the Strand.

MDCCLVI.

THE

EDITOR's PREFACE.

WHEN the last impression of MILTON'*s prose works was committed to my care, I executed that trust with the greatest fidelity. Not satisfied with printing from any copy at hand, as Editors are generally wont, my affection and zeal for the Author induced me to compare every sentence, line by line, with the Original Edition of each treatise that I was able to obtain. Hence, errors innumerable of the former impression were corrected; besides what improvements were added from the Author's Second Edition of* The Tenure of Kings and Magistrates, *which Mr.* TOLAND *had either not seen, or had neglected to commit to the press* *.

After I had endeavoured to do this justice to my favourite Author, the last summer I discovered a Second Edition *of his* EIKONOKLASTES, *with many large and curious additions, printed in the year* 1650. *which Edition had escaped the notice both of Mr.* TOLAND *and myself.*

In communicating this discovery to a few friends, I found that This Edition was not unknown to some others, tho' from low and base motives secreted from the Public But I, who from my soul love Liberty, and for that reason openly and boldly assert its principles at all times, resolved that the Public should no longer be with-held from the possession of such a treasure.

* Mr *Toland* first collected and published the Author's prose works in 3 vol folio, 1697, or 1698; for which all lovers of Liberty owe grateful praise to his name . but thro' hurry, or perhaps not having seen the different copies, he printed from the *first* Edition of some Tracts, which the Author had afterwards published with considerable additions

In 1738 *Milton*'s prose works were again published in 2 vol folio of which impression all I shall say is, That no person being employed to inspect the press, the Printer took the liberty to alter what he did not understand, and thereby defaced the Author, and marred the beauty of many passages.

I therefore now give a new impression of this work, with the additions † *and improvements made by the Author: and I deem it a singular felicity to be the instrument of restoring to my country so many excellent lines, long lost, —— and in danger of being for ever lost, —— of a Writer who is a lasting honour to our language and nation; —— and of a Work, wherein the principles of tyranny are confuted and overthrown, and all the arts and cunning of a* Great Tyrant *and his adherents detected and laid open.*

The love of Liberty is a public affection, of which those men must be altogether void, that can suppress or smother any thing written in its defence, and tending to serve its glorious Cause. What signify professions, when the actions are opposite and contradictory? Could any High-Churchman, any partizan of Charles I. *have acted a worse, or a different part, than some pretended friends of Liberty have done in this instance? Many High Church Priests and Doctors have laid out considerable Sums to destroy the prose works of* Milton, *and have purchased Copies of his particular writings for the infernal pleasure of consuming them* ‡. *This practice however detestable, was yet consistent with principle. But no Apology can be made for men that espouse a cause, and at the same time conceal aught belonging to its support. Such men may tell us that they love Liberty, but I tell them that they love their bellies, their ease, their pleasures, their profits in the first place. A man that will not hazard* All *for Liberty, is unworthy to be named among its Votaries, unworthy to participate its blessings.*

Many circumstances at present loudly call upon us to exert ourselves. Venality and corruption have well-nigh extinguished all principles of Liberty. The bad Books also that this age hath produced, have ruined our youth. The Novels and Romances which are eagerly purchased and read, emasculate the mind, and banish every thing grave and manly. One remedy for these evils, is to revive the reading of our old Writers, of which we have good store, and the study whereof would fortify our youth against the blandishments of pleasure and the arts of Corruption.

MILTON *in particular ought to be read and studied by all our young Gentlemen as an* Oracle. *He was a great and noble Genius, perhaps the greatest that ever appeared among men, and his learning was equal to his Genius. He had the highest Sense of Liberty, glorious thoughts, with a strong and nervous style. His works are full of wisdom, a treasure of knowledge. In them the Divine, the Statesman, the Historian, the Philologist, may be all instructed and entertained. It is to be lamented that his divine writings are so little known. Very few are acquainted with them, many have never heard of them. The same is true with respect to another great writer, Contemporary with* Milton *and an advocate for the same glorious Cause, I mean* ALGERNON SYDNEY, *whose Discourses on Government are the most precious legacy to these nations.*

† The additions are all printed in *Italic* character; wherein I have been careful to note even a single word different from the first Edition.

‡ This hath been practised with such zeal by many of that cursed tribe, that it is a wonder, there are any Copies left. *John Swale* a Bookseller of *Leeds* in *Yorkshire*, an honest man tho' of High-Church, told me, that he could have more money for burning *Milton's Defence of Liberty and the People of England*, than I would give for the purchase of it. Some Priests in that neighbourhood used to meet once a year, and after they were well warmed with strong Beer, they sacrificed to the flames the Author's *Defensio pro populo Anglicano*, as also This treatise against the ΕΙΚΩΝ. I have it in my power to produce more instances of the like sacerdotal Spirit, with which in some future publication I may entertain the World.

All

All Antiquity cannot ſhew two writers equal to theſe. They were both great maſters of Reaſon, both great maſters of Expreſſion. They had the ſtrongeſt thoughts, and the boldeſt images, and are the beſt models that can be followed. The ſtyle of SYDNEY *is always clear and flowing, ſtrong and maſculine. The Great* MILTON *has a ſtyle of his own, one fit to expreſs the aſtoniſhing ſublimity of his thoughts, the mighty vigour of his ſpirit, and that* copia *of invention, that redundancy of imagination, which no writer before or ſince hath equalled. In ſome places it is confeſſed that his periods are too long, which renders him intricate, if not altogether unintelligible to vulgar readers; but theſe places are not many. In the Book before us his ſtyle is for the moſt part free and eaſy, and it abounds both in eloquence and wit and argument. I am of opinion that the ſtyle of this work is the beſt and moſt perfect of all his proſe writings. Other men have commended the ſtyle of his* Hiſtory *as matchleſs and incomparable, whoſe malice could not ſee or would not acknowledge the Excellency of his other works. It is no ſecret whence their averſion to* MILTON *proceeds; and whence their caution of naming him as any other writer than a Poet.* MILTON *combated Superſtition and Tyranny of every form, and in every degree. Againſt them he employed his mighty Strength, and, like a* Battering Ram, *beat down all before him. But notwithſtanding theſe mean arts either to hide or to diſparage him, a little time will make him better known; and the more he is known the more he will be admired. His works are not like the fugitive ſhort-lived things of this age, few of which ſurvive their authors: they are ſubſtantial, durable, eternal writings; which will never die, never periſh whilſt Reaſon, Truth, and Liberty have a Being in theſe Nations.*

Thus much I thought proper to ſay on occaſion of this publication, wherein I have no reſentment to gratify, no private intereſt to ſerve: all my aim is to ſtrengthen and ſupport that Good old Cauſe *which in my youth I embraced, and the principles whereof I will aſſert and maintain whilſt I live.*

The following Letter to Milton *being very curious, and no where publiſhed perfect and entire, may be fitly preſerved in this place.*

A Letter from Mr. Wall *to* John Milton *Eſquire.*

SIR,

I Received yours the day after you wrote, and do humbly thank you that you are pleaſed to honour me with your letters. I confeſs I have (even in my privacy in the country) oft had thoughts of you, and that with much reſpect, for your friendlineſs to truth in your early years, and in bad times. But I was uncertain whether your relation to the Court *, (tho' I think a Commonwealth was more friendly to you than a Court) had not clouded your former light, but your laſt Book reſolved that doubt. You complain of the Non-proficiency of the Nation, and of its retrograde motion of late, in liberty and ſpiritual truths. It is much to be bewailed; but yet let us pity human frailty. When thoſe who made deep proteſtations of their zeal for our Liberty both ſpiritual and civil, and made the faireſt offers to be aſſertors thereof, and whom we

* *Milton* was Latin Secretary.

there-

thereupon trusted; when those being instated in power, shall betray the good thing committed to them, and lead us back to *Egypt*, and by that force which we gave them to win us Liberty, hold us fast in chains; what can poor people do? You know who they were that watched our Saviour's Sepulchre to keep him from rising †.

Besides, whilst people are not free but straitned in accommodations for life, their Spirits will be dejected and servile and conducing to that end, there should be an improving of our native commodities, as our Manufactures, our Fishery, our Fens, Forests, and Commons, and our Trade at Sea, *&c.* which would give the body of the nation a comfortable Subsistence; and the breaking that *cursed yoke of Tythes*, would much help thereto.

Also another thing I cannot but mention, which is, that the *Norman* conquest and tyranny is continued upon the nation, without any thought of removing it; I mean the tenure of lands by *copy-hold*, and holding for life under a Lord, or rather Tyrant of a Manour, whereby people care not to improve their land by cost upon it, not knowing how soon themselves or theirs may be outed it; nor what the house is in which they live, for the same reason and they are far more inslaved to the Lord of the Manour, than the rest of the nation is to a King or supreme Magistrate.

We have waited for Liberty, but it must be God's work and not Man's, who thinks it sweet to maintain his pride and worldly interest to the gratifying of the flesh, whatever becomes of the precious Liberty of mankind.

But let us not despond, but do our duty; and God will carry on that blessed work in despite of all opposites, and to their ruin if they persist therein.

Sir, my humble request is, that you would proceed, and give us that other member of the distribution mentioned in your Book; *viz* that *Hire* doth greatly impede Truth and Liberty: it is like if you do, you shall find opposers: but remember that Saying, *Beatius est pati quam frui:* or, in the Apostle's words, James v. 11. *We count them happy that endure.*

I have sometimes thought (concurring with your assertion of that storied voice that should speak from Heaven) when Ecclesiastics were endowed with worldly preferments, *Hodie venenum infunditur in Ecclesiam* for to use the speech of Genesis iv. ult. according to the sense which it hath in the *Hebrew*, *Then began men to corrupt the worship of God.* I shall tell you a supposal of mine, which is this Mr *Dury* has bestowed about thirty years time in travell, conference and writings, to reconcile *Calvinists* and *Lutherans*, and that with little or no success. But the shortest way were, —— Take away Ecclesiastical dignities, honours, and preferments, on both sides, and all would soon be hushed;

† Soldiers; this is a severe insinuation against a standing army

the Ecclesiastics would be quiet, and then the people would come forth into truth and liberty. But I will not engage in this quarrel; yet I shall lay this Engagement upon myself to remain

Your faithful friend and servant

JOHN WALL.

Causham, May 26, 1659.

From this Letter the reader may see in what way wise and good men of that age employed themselves: in studying to remove every grievance, to break every yoke. And it is matter of astonishment that this age, which boasts of greatest light and knowledge, should make no effort toward a Reformation in things acknowledged to be wrong; but both in Religion and in Civil Government be Barbarian!

Below Blackheath,
June 20, 1756.

RICHARD BARON.

’ΕΙΚΟΝΟΚΛΑΣΤΗΣ.

In Anſwer to a Book Intitled,

’ΕΙΚΩΝ ΒΑΣΙΛΙΚΗ,

The PORTRAITURE of his SACRED MAJESTY in his Solitudes and Sufferings.

Prov. xxviii. 15. As a roaring lion and a ranging bear, ſo is a wicked ruler over the poor people.
16 The prince that wanteth underſtanding, is alſo a great oppreſſor; but he that hateth covetouſneſs, ſhall prolong his days.
17. A man that doth violence to the blood of any perſon, ſhall fly to the pit, let no man ſtay him.

Saluſt. Conjurat. Catalin.

Regium imperium, quod initio, conſervandæ libertatis, atque augendæ reipub. causâ fuerat, in ſuperbiam, dominationemque ſe convertit.
Regibus boni, quam mali, ſuſpectiores ſunt, ſemperque his aliena virtus formidoloſa eſt.
Impunè quælibet facere, id eſt regem eſſe. Idem Bell. Jugurth.

Publiſhed by AUTHORITY.

The PREFACE.

TO deſcant on the misfortunes of a perſon *fallen* from ſo high a dignity, who hath alſo paid his final debt both to nature and his faults, is neither of itſelf a thing commendable, nor the intention of this diſcourſe. Neither was it fond ambition, or the vanity to get a name, preſent or with poſterity, by writing againſt a king I never was ſo thirſty after fame, nor ſo deſtitute of other hopes and means, better and more certain to attain it: for kings have gained glorious titles from their favourers by writing againſt private men, as Henry the VIIIth did againſt Luther, but no man ever gained much honour by writing againſt a king, as not uſually meeting with that force of argument in ſuch courtly antagoniſts, which to convince might add to his reputation Kings moſt commonly, though ſtrong in legions, are but weak at arguments, as they who ever have accuſtomed from the cradle to uſe their will only as their right hand, their reaſon always as their left. Whence unexpectedly conſtrained to that kind of combat, they prove but weak and puny adverſaries. Neverthele ſs, for their ſakes who thro' cuſtom, ſimplicity, or want of better teaching, have not more ſeriouſly conſidered

B kings,

kings, than in the gaudy name of majeſty, and admire them and their doings as if they breathed not the ſame breath with other mortal men, I ſhall make no ſcruple to take up (for it ſeems to be the challenge both of him and all his party) to take up this gauntlet, though a king's, in the behalf of liberty and the commonwealth.

And further, ſince it appears manifeſtly the cunning drift of a factious and defeated party, to make the ſame advantage of his book, which they did before of his regal name and authority, and intend it not ſo much the defence of his former actions, as the promoting of their own future deſigns; (making thereby the book their own rather than the king's, as the benefit now muſt be their own more than his:) now the third time to corrupt and diſorder the minds of weaker men, by new ſuggeſtions and narrations, either falſly or fallaciouſly repreſenting the ſtate of things to the diſhonour of this preſent government, and the retarding of a general peace, ſo needful to this afflicted nation, and ſo nigh obtained; I ſuppoſe it no injury to the dead, but a good deed rather to the living, if by better information given them, or, which is enough, by only remembring them the truth of what they themſelves know to be here miſaffirmed, they may be kept from entering the third time unadviſedly into war and bloodſhed: for as to any moment of ſolidity in the book itſelf, (*ſave only that a king is ſaid to be the author, a name, than which there needs no more among the blockiſh vulgar, to make it wiſe, and excellent, and admired, nay to ſet it next the Bible, though otherwiſe containing little elſe but the common grounds of tyranny and popery, dreſſed up, the better to deceive, in a new proteſtant guiſe, trimly garniſhed over,*) or as to any need of anſwering, in reſpect of ſtaid and well-principled men, I take it on me as a work aſſigned rather, than by me choſen or affected: which was the cauſe both of beginning it ſo late, and finiſhing it ſo leiſurely in the midſt of other employments and diverſions *And though well it might have ſeemed in vain to write at all, conſidering the envy and almoſt infinite prejudice likely to be ſtirred up among the common ſort, againſt whatever can be written or gain-ſaid to the king's book, ſo advantageous to a book it is, only to be a king's; and though it be an irkſome labour to write with induſtry and judicious pains, that which neither weighed nor well read, ſhall be judged without induſtry or the pains of well-judging, by faction and the eaſy literature of cuſtom and opinion; it ſhall be ventured yet, and the truth not ſmothered, but ſent abroad, in the native confidence of her ſingle ſelf, to earn, how ſhe can, her entertainment in the world, and to find out her own readers, few perhaps, but thoſe few of ſuch value and ſubſtantial worth, as truth and wiſdom, not reſpecting numbers and big names, have been ever wont in all ages to be contented with.* And if the late king had thought ſufficient thoſe anſwers and defences made for him in his life-time, they who on the other ſide accuſed his evil government, judging that on their behalf enough alſo hath been replied, the heat of this controverſy was in all likelihood drawing to an end; and the further mention of his deeds, not ſo much unfortunate as faulty, had in tenderneſs to his late ſufferings been willingly forborn; and perhaps for the preſent age might have ſlept with him unrepeated, while his adverſaries, calmed and aſſuaged with the ſucceſs of their cauſe, had been the leſs unfavourable to his memory. But ſince he himſelf, making new appeal to truth and the world, hath left behind him this book, as the beſt advocate and interpreter of his own actions, and that his friends by publiſhing, diſperſing, commending, and almoſt adoring it, ſeem to place therein the chief ſtrength and nerves of their cauſe, it would argue doubtleſs in the other party great deficience and diſtruſt of themſelves, not to meet the force of his reaſon in any field whatſoever, the force and equipage of whoſe arms they have ſo often met victoriouſly. And he who at the bar ſtood excepting againſt the form and manner of his judicature, and complained that he was not heard, neither he nor his friends ſhall have that cauſe now to find fault, being met and debated with in this open and monumental court of his own erecting; and not only heard uttering his whole mind at large, but anſwered: which to do effectually, if it be neceſſary that to his book nothing the more reſpect be had for being his, they of his own party can have no juſt reaſon to exclaim. For it were too unreaſonable that he, becauſe

becauſe dead, ſhould have the liberty in his book to ſpeak all evil of the parliament; and they, becauſe living, ſhould be expected to have leſs freedom, or any for them, to ſpeak home the plain truth of a full and pertinent reply. As he, to acquit himſelf, hath not ſpared his adverſaries to load them with all ſorts of blame and accuſation, ſo to him, as in his book alive, there will be uſed no more courtſhip than he uſes; but what is properly his own guilt, not imputed any more to his evil counſellors (a ceremony uſed longer by the parliament than he himſelf deſired) ſhall be laid here without circumlocutions at his own door. That they who from the firſt beginning, or but now of late, by what unhappineſs I know not, are ſo much affatuated, not with his perſon only, but with his palpable faults, and doat upon his deformities, may have none to blame but their own folly, if they live and die in ſuch a ſtrooken blindneſs, as next to that of Sodom hath not happened to any ſort of men more groſs, or more miſleading. *Yet neither let his enemies expect to find recorded here all that hath been whiſpered in the court, or alledged openly, of the king's bad actions; it being the proper ſcope of this work in hand, not to rip up and relate the miſdoings of his whole life, but to anſwer only and refute the miſ-ſayings of his book*

Firſt then, that ſome men (whether this were by him intended, or by his friends) have by policy accompliſhed after death that revenge upon their enemies which in life they were not able, hath been oft related. And among other examples we find that the laſt will of Cæſar being read to the people, and what bounteous legacies he had bequeathed them, wrought more in that vulgar audience to the avenging of his death, than all the art he could ever uſe to win *their* favour in his life-time. And how much their intent, who publiſhed theſe over-late apologies and meditations of the dead king, drives to the ſame end of ſtirring up the people to bring him that honour, that affection, and by conſequence that revenge to his dead corpſe, which he himſelf living could never gain to his perſon, it appears both by the conceited portraiture before his book, drawn out to the full meaſure of a maſking ſcene, and ſet there to catch fools and ſilly gazers; and by thoſe Latin words after the end, Vota dabunt quæ bella negarunt; intimating that what he could not compaſs by war, he ſhould atchieve by his meditations for in words which admit of various ſenſe, the liberty is ours to chuſe that interpretation which may beſt mind us of what our reſtleſs enemies endeavour, and what we are timely to prevent. And here may be well obſerved the looſe and negligent curioſity of thoſe who took upon them to adorn the ſetting out of this book, for though the picture ſet in front would martyr him and ſaint him to befool the people, yet the Latin motto in the end, which they underſtand not, leaves him, as it were, a politic contriver to bring about that intereſt by fair and plauſible words, which the force of arms denied him. But quaint emblems and devices begged from the old pageantry of ſome twelfth-nights entertainment at Whitehall, will do but ill to make a ſaint or martyr and if the people reſolve to take him ſainted at the rate of ſuch a canonizing, I ſhall ſuſpect their calendar more than the Gregorian. In one thing I muſt commend his openneſs who gave the title to this book, Εἰκὼν Βασιλική, that is to ſay, The King's Image, and by the ſhrine he dreſſes out for him, certainly would have the people come and worſhip him For which reaſon this anſwer alſo is intitled, Iconoclaſtes, the famous ſurname of many greek emperors, who in their zeal to the command of God, after long tradition of idolatry in the church, took courage and broke all ſuperſtitious images to pieces But the people, exorbitant and exceſſive in all their motions, are prone oft-times not to a religious only, but to a civil kind of idolatry in idolizing their kings: though never more miſtaken in the object of their worſhip, heretofore being wont to repute for ſaints thoſe faithful and courageous barons who loſt their lives in the field, making glorious war againſt tyrants for the common liberty; as Simon de Momfort Earl of Leiceſter, againſt Henry the IIId, Thomas Plantagenet Earl of Lancaſter, againſt Edward the IId. But now, with a beſotted and degenerate baſeneſs of ſpirit, except ſome few who yet retain in them the old Engliſh fortitude and love of freedom, and have teſtified it by their matchleſs deeds,

 the

the reſt, imbaſtardized from the ancient nobleneſs of their anceſtors, are ready to fall flat and give adoration to the image and memory of this man, who hath offered at more cunning fetches to undermine our liberties, and put tyranny into an art, than any Britiſh king before him: which low dejection and debaſement of mind in the people, I muſt confeſs I cannot willingly aſcribe to the natural diſpoſition of an Engliſhman, but rather to two other cauſes: firſt, to the prelates and their fellow-teachers, though of another name and ſect*, whoſe pulpit-ſtuff, both firſt and laſt, hath been the doctrine and perpetual infuſion of ſervility and wretchedneſs to all their hearers, and *whoſe* lives the type of worldlineſs and hypocriſy, without the leaſt true pattern of virtue, righteouſneſs, or ſelf-denial in their whole practice. I attribute it next to the factious inclination of moſt men divided from the public by ſeveral ends and humours of their own. At firſt no man leſs beloved, no man more generally condemned than was the king; from the time that it became his cuſtom to break parliaments at home, and either wilfully or weakly to betray proteſtants abroad, to the beginning of theſe combuſtions. All men inveighed againſt him; all men, except court-vaſſals, oppoſed him and his tyrannical proceedings; the cry was univerſal, and this full parliament was at firſt unanimous in their diſlike and proteſtation againſt his evil government. But when they who ſought themſelves and not the public, began to doubt that all of them could not by one and the ſame way attain to their ambitious purpoſes, then was the king, or his name at leaſt, as a fit property firſt made uſe of, his doings made the beſt of, and by degrees juſtified; which begot him ſuch a party, as after many wiles and ſtrugglings with his inward fears, emboldened him at length to ſet up his ſtandard againſt the parliament· Whenas before that time, all his adherents, conſiſting moſt of diſſolute ſwordſmen and ſuburb-royſters, hardly amounted to the making up of one ragged regiment ſtrong enough to aſſault the unarmed houſe of commons. After which attempt, ſeconded by a tedious and bloody war on his ſubjects, wherein he hath ſo far exceeded thoſe his arbitrary violences in time of peace, they who before hated him for his high miſgovernment, nay, fought againſt him with diſplayed banners in the field, now applaud him and extol him for the wiſeſt and moſt religious prince that lived. By ſo ſtrange a method amongſt the mad multitude is a ſudden reputation won, of wiſdom by wilfulneſs and ſubtile ſhifts, of goodneſs by multiplying evil, of piety by endeavouring to root out true religion.

But it is evident that the chief of his adherents never loved him, never honoured either him or his cauſe, but as they took him to ſet a face upon their own malignant deſigns, nor bemoan his loſs at all, but the loſs of their own aſpiring hopes. like thoſe captive women, whom the poet notes in his Iliad, to have bewailed the death of Patroclus in outward ſhow, but indeed their own condition.

Πάτροχλον πρόφασιν, σφῶν δ᾽αὐτῶν κήδε ἑκάςη
Hom Iliad τ.

And it needs muſt be ridiculous to any judgment uninthralled, that they who in other matters expreſs ſo little fear either of God or man, ſhould in this one particular outſtrip all preciſianiſm with their ſcruples and caſes, and fill men's ears continually with the noiſe of their conſcientious loyalty and allegiance to the king, rebels in the mean while to God in all their actions beſides much leſs that they whoſe profeſſed loyalty and allegiance led them to direct arms againſt the king's perſon, and thought him nothing violated by the ſword of hoſtility drawn by them againſt him, ſhould now in earneſt think him violated by the unſparing ſword of juſtice, which undoubtedly ſo much the leſs in vain ſhe bears among men, by how much greater and in higheſt place the offender Elſe juſtice, whether moral or political, were not juſtice, but a falſe counterfeit of that impartial and godlike virtue. The only grief is, that the head was not ſtrook off to the beſt advantage and

* The Preſbyterians.

commodity

commodity of them that held it by the hair*. *An ingrateful and perverſe generation, who having firſt cried to God to be delivered from their king, now murmur againſt God that heard their prayers, and cry as loud for their king againſt thoſe that delivered them.* But as to the author of theſe ſoliloquies, whether it were *undoubtedly* the late king, as is vulgarly believed, or any ſecret Coadjutor, and ſome ſtick not to name him; it can add nothing, nor ſhall take from the weight, if any be, of reaſon which he brings. But allegations, not reaſons, are the main contents of this book, and need no more than other contrary allegations to lay the queſtion before all men in an even ballance, though it were ſuppoſed that the teſtimony of one man, in his own cauſe affirming, could be of any moment to bring in doubt the authority of a parliament denying. But if theſe his fair-ſpoken words ſhall be here fairly confronted and laid parallel to his own far differing deeds, manifeſt and viſible to the whole nation, then ſurely we may look on them who notwithſtanding ſhall perſiſt to give to bare words more credit than to open deeds, as men whoſe judgment was not rationally evinced and perſuaded, but fatally ſtupified and bewitched into ſuch a blind and obſtinate belief: for whoſe cure it may be doubted, not whether any charm, though never ſo wiſely murmured, but whether any prayer can be available. *This however would be remembered and well noted, that while the king inſtead of that repentance which was in reaſon and in conſcience to be expected from him, without which we could not lawfully readmit him, perſiſts here to maintain and juſtify the moſt apparent of his evil doings, and waſhes over with a court-fucus the worſt and fouleſt of his actions, diſables and uncreates the parliament itſelf, with all our laws and native liberties that aſk not his leave, diſhonours and attaints all proteſtant churches not prelatical, and what they piouſly reformed, with the ſlander of rebellion, ſacrilege and hypocriſy; they who ſeemed of late to ſtand up hotteſt for the covenant, can now ſit mute and much pleaſed to hear all theſe opprobrious things uttered againſt their faith, their freedom, and themſelves in their own doings made traitors to boot: The divines alſo, their wizards, can be ſo brazen as to cry Hoſanna to this his book, which cries louder againſt them for no diſciples of Chriſt, but of Iſcariot; and to ſeem now convinced with theſe withered arguments and reaſons here, the ſame which in ſome other writings of that party, and in his own former declarations and expreſſes, they have ſo often heretofore endeavoured to confute and to explode; none appearing all this while to vindicate church or ſtate from theſe calumnies and reproaches, but a ſmall handful of men whom they defame and ſpit at with all the odious names of ſchiſm and ſectariſm. I never knew that time in England, when men of trueſt religion were not counted ſectaries: but wiſdom now, valor, juſtice, conſtancy, prudence united and imbodied to defend religion and our liberties, both by word and deed, againſt tyranny, is counted ſchiſm and faction. Thus in a graceleſs age things of higheſt praiſe and imitation under a right name, to make them infamous and hateful to the people, are miſcalled. Certainly, if ignorance and perverſeneſs will needs be national and univerſal, then they who adhere to wiſdom and to truth, are not therefore to be blamed, for being ſo few as to ſeem a ſect or faction. But in my opinion it goes not ill with that people where theſe virtues grow ſo numerous and well joined together, as to reſiſt and make head againſt the rage and torrent of that boiſtrous folly and ſuperſtition that poſſeſſes and hurries on the vulgar ſort. This therefore we may conclude to be a high honour done us from God, and a ſpecial mark of his favour, whom he hath ſelected as the ſole remainder, after all theſe changes and commotions, to ſtand upright and ſtedfaſt in his cauſe, dignified with the defence of truth and public liberty, while others who aſpired to be the top of zealots, and had almoſt brought religion to a kind of trading monopoly, have not only by their late ſilence and neutrality belied their profeſſion, but foundered themſelves and their conſciences, to comply with enemies in that wicked cauſe and intereſt, which they have too often curſed in others, to proſper now in the ſame themſelves.*

* The author adds in the firſt edition, Which obſervation, tho' made by a common enemy, may for the truth of it hereafter become a proverb.

I. Upon

I. Upon the king's calling this laſt parliament.

THAT which the king lays down here as his firſt foundation, and as it were the head ſtone of *his* whole ſtructure, that, "He called this laſt parliament, not more by others advice, and the neceſſity of his affairs, than by his own choice and inclination;" is to all knowing men ſo apparently not true, that a more unlucky and inauſpicious ſentence, and more betokening the downfal of his whole fabric, hardly could have come into his mind. For who knows not that the inclination of a prince is beſt known either by thoſe next about him, and moſt in favour with him, or by the current of his own actions. Thoſe neareſt to this king, and moſt his favourites, were courtiers and prelates; men whoſe chief ſtudy was to find out which way the king inclined, and to imitate him exactly. How theſe men ſtood affected to parliaments, cannot be forgotten. No man but may remember it was their continual exerciſe to diſpute and preach againſt them; and in their common diſcourſe nothing was more frequent, than that "they hoped the king ſhould now have no need of parliaments any more." And this was but the copy which his paraſites had induſtriouſly taken from his own words and actions, who never called a parliament but to ſupply his neceſſities, and having ſupplied thoſe, as ſuddenly and ignominiouſly diſſolved it, without redreſſing any one grievance of the people. Sometimes chooſing rather to miſs of his ſubſidies, or to raiſe them by illegal courſes, than that the people ſhould not ſtill miſs of their hopes to be relieved by parliaments.

The firſt he broke off at his coming to the crown, for no other cauſe than to protect the duke of Buckingham againſt them who had accuſed him, beſides other heinous crimes, of no leſs than poiſoning the deceaſed king his father, *concerning which matter the declaration of No more addreſſes, hath ſufficiently informed us.* And ſtill the latter breaking was with more affront and indignity put upon the houſe and her worthieſt members, than the former. Inſomuch that in the fifth year of his reign, in a proclamation he ſeems offended at the very rumour of a parliament divulged among the people, as if he had taken it for a kind of ſlander that men ſhould think him that way exorable, much leſs inclined: and forbids it as a preſumption to preſcribe him any time for parliaments, that is to ſay, either by perſuaſion or petition, or ſo much as the reporting of ſuch a rumour: for other manner of preſcribing was at that time not ſuſpected. By which fierce edict, the people, forbidden to complain, as well as forced to ſuffer, began from thenceforth to deſpair of parliaments. Whereupon ſuch illegal actions, and eſpecially to get vaſt ſums of money, were put in practice by the king and his new officers, as monopolies, compulſive knighthoods, coat, conduct and ſhip-money, the ſeizing not of one Naboth's vineyard, but of whole inheritances under the pretence of forreſt, or crown-lands, corruption and bribery compounded for, with impunities granted for the future, as gave evident proof that the king never meant, nor could it ſtand with the reaſon of his affairs, ever to recall parliaments: having brought by theſe irregular courſes the people's intereſt and his own to ſo direct an oppoſition, that he might foreſee plainly, if nothing but a parliament could ſave the people, it muſt neceſſarily be his undoing.

Till eight or nine years after, proceeding with a high hand in theſe enormities, and having the ſecond time levied an injurious war againſt his native country Scotland, and finding all thoſe other ſhifts of raiſing money, which bore out his firſt expedition, now to fail him, not "of his own choice and inclination," as any child may ſee, but urged by ſtrong neceſſities, and the very pangs of ſtate, which his own violent proceedings had brought him to, he calls a parliament, firſt in Ireland, which only was to give him four ſubſidies, and ſo to expire; then in England, where his firſt demand was but twelve ſubſidies, to maintain a Scots war, condemned and abominated by the whole kingdom: promiſing their grievances ſhould be conſidered afterwards. Which when the parliament, who

who judged that war it ſelf one of their main grievances, made no haſte to grant, not enduring the delay of his impatient will, or elſe fearing the conditions of their grant, he breaks off the whole ſeſſion, and diſmiſſes them and their grievances with ſcorn and fruſtration.

Much leſs therefore did he call this laſt parliament by his own choice and inclination; but having firſt tried in vain all undue ways to procure money, his army of their own accord being beaten in the north, the lords petitioning, and the general voice of the people almoſt hiſſing him and his ill-acted regality off the ſtage, compelled at length both by his wants, and by his fears, upon mere extremity he ſummoned this laſt parliament. And how is it poſſible that he ſhould willingly incline to parliaments, who never was perceived to call them but for the greedy hope of a whole national bribe, his ſubſidies; and never loved, never fulfilled, never promoted the true end of parliaments, the redreſs of grievances; but ſtill put them off, and prolonged them, whether gratified or not gratified; and was indeed the author of all thoſe grievances? To ſay therefore that he called this parliament of his own choice and inclination, argues how little truth we can expect from the ſequel of this book, which ventures in the very firſt period to affront more than one nation with an untruth ſo remarkable, and preſumes a more implicit faith in the people of England, than the pope ever commanded from the Romiſh laity; or elſe a natural ſottiſhneſs fit to be abuſed and ridden. While in the judgment of wiſe men, by laying the foundation of his defence on the avouchment of that which is ſo manifeſtly untrue, he hath given a worſe foil to his own cauſe, than when his whole forces were at any time overthrown. They therefore who think ſuch great ſervice done to the king's affairs in publiſhing this book, will find themſelves in the end miſtaken, if ſenſe and right mind, or but any mediocrity of knowledge and remembrance hath not quite forſaken men.

But to prove his inclination to parliaments, he affirms here, "to have always thought the right way of them moſt ſafe for his crown, and beſt pleaſing to his people." What he thought we know not, but that he ever took the contrary way, we ſaw; and from his own actions we felt long ago what he thought of parliaments or of pleaſing his people: a ſurer evidence than what we hear now too late in words.

He alledges, that "the cauſe of forbearing to convene parliaments was the ſparks which ſome men's diſtempers there ſtudied to kindle." They were indeed not tempered to his temper; for it neither was the law, nor the rule by which all other tempers were to be tried; but they were eſteemed and choſen for the fitteſt men, in their ſeveral counties, to allay and quench thoſe diſtempers which his own inordinate doings had inflamed. And if that were his refuſing to convene, till thoſe men had been qualified to his temper, that is to ſay, his will, we may eaſily conjecture what hope there was of parliaments, had not fear and his inſatiate poverty, in the midſt of his exceſſive wealth, conſtrained him.

"He hoped by his freedom and their moderation to prevent miſunderſtandings." And wherefore not by their freedom and his moderation? But freedom he thought too high a word for them, and moderation too mean a word for himſelf: this was not the way to prevent miſunderſtandings. He ſtill "feared paſſion and prejudice in other men," not in himſelf: "and doubted not by the weight of his "own" reaſon to counterpoiſe any faction," it being ſo eaſy for him, and ſo frequent, to call his obſtinacy reaſon, and other men's reaſon, faction. We in the mean while muſt believe, that wiſdom and all reaſon came to him by title with his crown; paſſion, prejudice, and faction came to others by being ſubjects.

"He was ſorry to hear with what popular heat elections were carried in many places." Sorry rather that court-letters and intimations prevailed no more, to divert, or to deter the people from their free election of thoſe men, whom they thought beſt affected to religion and their country's liberty, both at that time in danger to be loſt.

And

And ſuch men they were, as by the kingdom were ſent to adviſe him, not ſent to be cavilled at, becauſe elected, or to be entertained by him with an undervalue and miſpriſion of their temper, judgment, or affection. In vain was a parliament thought fitteſt by the known laws of our nation, to adviſe and regulate unruly kings, if they, inſtead of hearkening to advice, ſhould be permitted to turn it off, and refuſe it by vilifying and traducing their adviſers, *or* by accuſing of a popular heat thoſe that lawfully elected them.

"His own and his children's intereſt obliged him to ſeek, and to preſerve the love and welfare of his ſubjects." Who doubts it? But the ſame intereſt, common to all kings, was never yet available to make them all ſeek that, which was indeed beſt for themſelves and their poſterity. All men by their own and their children's intereſt are obliged to honeſty and juſtice. but how little that conſideration works in private men, how much leſs in kings, their deeds declare beſt.

"He intended to oblige both friends and enemies, and to exceed their deſires, did they but pretend to any modeſt and ſober ſenſe;" miſtaking the whole buſineſs of a parliament, which met not to receive from him obligations, but juſtice; nor he to expect from them their modeſty, but their grave advice, uttered with freedom in the public cauſe His talk of modeſty in their deſires of the common welfare, argues him not much to have underſtood what he had to grant, who miſconceived ſo much the nature of what they had to deſire And for "ſober ſenſe," the expreſſion was too mean, and recoils with as much diſhonour upon himſelf, to be a king where ſober ſenſe could poſſibly be ſo wanting in a parliament

"The odium and offences which ſome men's rigour, or remiſſneſs in Church and ſtate, had contracted upon his government, he reſolved to have expiated with better laws and regulations." And yet the worſt of miſdemeanors committed by the worſt of all his favourites in the height of their dominion, whether acts of rigor or remiſſneſs, he hath from time to time continued, owned, and taken upon himſelf by public declarations, as often as the clergy, or any other of his inſtruments felt themſelves overburdened with the people's hatred. And who knows not the ſuperſtitious rigour of his Sunday's chapel, and the licentious remiſſneſs of his Sunday's theatre; accompanied with that reverend ſtatute for Dominical jigs and maypoles, publiſhed in his own name, and derived from the example of his father James? Which teſtifies all that rigor in ſuperſtition, all that remiſſneſs in religion to have iſſued out originally from his own houſe, and from his own authority. Much rather then may thoſe general miſcarriages in ſtate, his proper ſphere, be imputed to no other perſon chiefly than to himſelf. And which of all thoſe oppreſſive acts or impoſitions did he ever diſclaim or diſavow, till the fatal awe of this parliament hung ominouſly over him? Yet here he ſmoothly ſeeks to wipe off all the envy of his evil government upon his ſubſtitutes and under-officers, and promiſes, though much too late, what wonders he purpoſed to have done in the reforming of religion, a work wherein all his undertakings heretofore declare him to have had little or no judgment. Neither could his breeding, or his courſe of life acquaint him with a thing ſo ſpiritual. Which may well aſſure us what kind of reformation we could expect from him, either ſome politic form of an impoſed religion, or elſe perpetual vexation and perſecution to all thoſe that complied not with ſuch a form. The like amendment he promiſes in ſtate; not a ſtep further "than his reaſon and conſcience told him was fit to be deſired;" wiſhing "he had kept within thoſe bounds, and not ſuffered his own judgment to have been over-born in ſome things," of which things one was the Earl of Strafford's execution And what ſignifies all this, but that ſtill his reſolution was the ſame, to ſet up an arbitrary government of his own, and that all Britain was to be tied and chained to the conſcience, judgment, and reaſon of one man, as if thoſe gifts had been only his peculiar and prerogative, intailed upon him with his fortune to be a king? Whenas doubtleſs no man ſo obſtinate, or ſo much a tyrant,

tyrant, but profeſſes to be guided by that which he calls his reaſon and his judgment, tho' never ſo corrupted; and pretends alſo his conſcience. In the mean while, for any parliament or the whole nation to have either reaſon, judgment, or conſcience, by this rule was altogether in vain, if it thwarted the king's will; which was eaſy for him to call by any other plauſible name. *He himſelf hath many times acknowledged to have no right over us but by law; and by the ſame law to govern us: but law in a free nation hath been ever public reaſon, the enacted reaſon of a parliament; which he denying to enact, denies to govern us by that which ought to be our law; interpoſing his own private reaſon, which to us is no law.* And thus we find theſe fair and ſpecious promiſes, made upon the experience of many hard ſufferings, and his moſt mortified retirements, being throughly ſifted, to contain nothing in them much different from his former practices, ſo croſs, and ſo averſe to all his parliaments, and both the nations of this iſland. What fruits they could in likelihood have produced in his reſtorement, is obvious to any prudent foreſight.

And this is the ſubſtance of his firſt ſection, till we come to the devout of it, modelled into the form of a private pſalter. Which they who ſo much admire, *either for the matter or the manner, may as well admire* the arch-biſhop's late breviary, and many other as good Manuals and Hand-maids of Devotion, the lip-work of every prelatical liturgiſt, clapt together and quilted out of ſcripture-phraſe, with as much eaſe, and as little need of chriſtian diligence or judgment, as belongs to the compiling of any ordinary and ſaleable piece of Engliſh divinity that the ſhops value. But he who from ſuch a kind of pſalmiſtry, or any other verbal devotion, without the pledge and earneſt of ſuitable deeds, can be perſuaded of a zeal and true righteouſneſs in the perſon, hath much yet to learn; and knows not that the deepeſt policy of a tyrant hath been ever to counterfeit religious. And Ariſtotle in his Politics hath mentioned that ſpecial craft among twelve other tyrannical Sophiſms. Neither want we examples. Andronicus Comnenus the Byzantine emperor, though a moſt cruel tyrant, is reported by Nicetas to have been a conſtant reader of Saint Paul's epiſtles; and by continual ſtudy had ſo incorporated the phraſe and ſtile of that tranſcendant apoſtle into all his familiar letters, that the imitation ſeemed to vie with the original. Yet this availed not to deceive the people of that empire, who notwithſtanding his ſaint's vizard, tore him to pieces for his tyranny. From ſtories of this nature both ancient and modern which abound, the poets alſo, and ſome Engliſh, have been in this point ſo mindful of Decorum, as to put never more pious words in the mouth of any perſon, than of a tyrant. I ſhall not inſtance an abſtruſe author, wherein the king might be leſs converſant, but one whom we well know was the cloſet companion of theſe his ſolitudes, William Shakeſpeare, who introduces the perſon of Richard the Third, ſpeaking in as high a ſtrain of piety and mortification as is uttered in any paſſage of this book, and ſometimes to the ſame ſenſe and purpoſe with ſome words in this place, "I intended," ſaith he, "*not only* "to oblige my friends, but my enemies." The like ſaith Richard, Act II. Scen. 1

> I do not know that Engliſhman alive,
> With whom my ſoul is any jot at odds,
> More than the infant that is born to-night,
> I thank my God for my humility.

Other ſtuff of this ſort may be read throughout the whole tragedy, wherein the poet uſed not much licence in departing from the truth of hiſtory, which delivers him a deep diſſembler, not of his affections only, but of religion.

In praying therefore, and in the outward work of devotion, this king we ſee hath not at all exceeded the worſt of kings before him. But herein the worſt of kings, profeſſing Chriſtianiſm, have by far exceeded him. They, for aught we know, have ſtill prayed their own, or at leaſt borrowed from fit authors. But this king, not content with that which, although in a thing holy, is no holy theſt, to attribute to his own making other men's whole prayers, hath as it were unhallowed and unchriſtened the very duty of prayer itſelf, by borrowing to a chriſtian uſe prayers offered to a heathen god. Who would have imagined ſo little fear in him of the true all-ſeeing deity, ſo little reverence of the Holy Ghoſt, whoſe office is to dictate and preſent our chriſtian prayers, ſo little care of truth in his laſt words, or honour to himſelf, or to his friends, or ſenſe of his afflictions, or of that ſad hour which was upon him, as immediately before his death to pop into the hand of that grave biſhop who attended him, for a ſpecial relique of his ſaintly exerciſes, a Prayer ſtolen word for word from the mouth of a heathen * woman praying to a heathen god; and that in no ſerious book, but the vain amatorious poem of Sir Philip Sidney's Arcadia; a book in that kind full of worth and wit, but among religious thoughts and duties not worthy to be named, nor to be read at any time without good caution, much leſs in time of trouble and affliction to be a chriſtian's prayer-book? *They who are yet incredulous of what I tell them for a truth, that this philippic prayer is no part of the king's goods, may ſatisfy their own eyes at leiſure, in the 3d book of Sir Philip's Arcadia, p 248. comparing Pamela's prayer with the firſt prayer of his majeſty, delivered to Dr. Juxton immediately before his death, and entitled a Prayer in time of Captivity, printed in all the beſt editions of his book. And ſince there be a crew of lurking railers, who in their libels, and their fits of railing up and down, as I hear from others, take it ſo curriſhly that I ſhould dare to tell abroad the ſecrets of their Ægyptian Apis, to gratify their gall in ſome meaſure yet more, which to them will be a kind of alms, (for it is the weekly vomit of their gall which to moſt of them is the ſole means of their feeding) that they may not ſtarve for me, I ſhall gorge them once more with this digreſſion ſomewhat larger than before nothing troubled or offended at the working upward of their ſale venom thereupon, tho' it happen to aſperſe me, being, it ſeems, their beſt livelyhood, and the only uſe or good digeſtion that their ſick and periſhing minds can make of truth charitably told them However, to the benefit of others much more worth the gaining, I ſhall proceed in my aſſertion, that if only but to taſte wittingly of meat or drink offered to an idol, be in the doctrine of St. Paul judged a pollution, much more muſt be his ſin, who takes a prayer ſo dedicated into his mouth, and offers it to God Yet hardly it can be thought upon (tho' how ſad a thing!) without ſome kind of laughter at the manner, and ſolemn tranſaction of ſo groſs a couſenage, that he who had trampled over us ſo ſtately and ſo tragically, ſhould leave the world at laſt ſo ridiculouſly in his exit, as to bequeath among his deifying friends that ſtood about him ſuch a precious piece of mockery to be publiſhed by them, as muſt needs cover both his and their heads with ſhame, if they have any left. Certainly they that will, may now ſee at length how much they were deceived in him, and were ever like to be hereafter, who cared not, ſo near the minute of his death, to deceive his beſt and deareſt friends with the trumpery of ſuch a prayer, not more ſecretly than ſhamefully purloined, yet given them as the royal iſſue of his own proper zeal* And ſure it was the hand of God *to* let them fall, and be taken in ſuch a fooliſh trap, as hath expoſed them to all deriſion, if for nothing elſe, to throw contempt and diſgrace in the ſight of all men, upon this his idolized book, and the whole roſary of his prayers, thereby teſtifying how little he accepted them from thoſe who thought no better of the living God than of a buzzard idol, *fit to be ſo ſerved and worſhipped in reverſion, with the polluted orts and refuſe of Arcadias and Romances, without being able to diſcern the affront rather than the worſhip of ſuch an ethnic prayer. But leaving what might juſtly be offenſive to God, it was a treſpaſs alſo more than uſual againſt human right, which commands that every author ſhould have the property of his own work reſerved to him after death as well as living Many princes have been rigorous in laying taxes on their ſubjects by the head, but of any king heretofore that made a levy upon their wit, and ſeized it as his own legitimate, I*

* The ſecond edition for woman, has *fiction*

have

have not whom beſide to inſtance. True it is, I looked rather to have found him gleaning out of books written purpoſely to help devotion. And if in likelihood he have borrowed much more out of prayer-books than out of paſtorals, then are theſe painted feathers, that ſet him off ſo gay among the people, to be thought few or none of them his own. But if from his divines he have borrowed nothing, nothing out of all the magazine, and the rheum of their mellifluous prayers and meditations, let them who now mourn for him as for Tamuz, them who howl in their pulpits, and by their howling declare themſelves right wolves, remember and conſider in the midſt of their hideous faces, when they do only not cut their fleſh for him like thoſe rueful prieſts whom Elijah mocked; that he who was once their Ahab, now their Joſiah, though feigning outwardly to reverence churchmen, yet here hath ſo extremely ſet at nought both them and their praying faculty, that being at a loſs himſelf what to pray in captivity, he conſulted neither with the liturgy, nor with the directory, but neglecting the huge ſardell of all their honeycomb devotions, went directly where he doubted not to find better praying to his mind with Pamela, in the Counteſſes Arcadia. What greater argument of diſgrace and ignominy could have been thrown with cunning upon the whole clergy, than that the king among all his prieſtery, and all thoſe numberleſs volumes of their theological diſtillations, not meeting with one man or book of that coat that could befriend him with a prayer in captivity, was forced to rob Sir Philip and his captive ſhepherdeſs of their heathen oriſons, to ſupply in any faſhion his miſerable indigence, not of bread, but of a ſingle prayer to God? I ſay therefore not of bread, for that want may befal a good man, and yet not make him totally miſerable: but he who wants a prayer to beſeech God in his neceſſity, 'tis inexpreſſible how poor he is; far poorer within himſelf than all his enemies can make him. And the unfitneſs, the indecency of that pitiful ſupply which he ſought, expreſſes yet further the deepneſs of his poverty

Thus much be ſaid in general to his prayers, and in ſpecial to that Arcadian prayer uſed in his captivity, enough to undeceive us what eſteem we are to ſet upon the reſt

For he certainly whoſe mind could ſerve him to ſeek a chriſtian prayer out of a pagan legend, and aſſume it for his own, might gather up the reſt God knows from whence; one perhaps out of the French Aſtræa, another out of the Spaniſh Diana, Amadis and Palmerin could hardly 'ſcape him. Such a perſon we may be ſure had it not in him to make a prayer of his own, or at leaſt would excuſe himſelf the pains and coſt of his invention, ſo long as ſuch ſweet Rapſodies of heatheniſm and knighterrantry could yield him prayers. How diſhonourable then, and how unworthy of a chriſtian king, were theſe ignoble ſhifts to ſeem holy and to get a ſaintſhip among the ignorant and wretched people; to draw them by this deception, worſe than all his former injuries, to go a whoring after him? And how unhappy, how forſook of grace, and unbeloved of God that people who reſolve to know no more of piety or of goodneſs, than to account him their chief ſaint and martyr, whoſe bankrupt devotion came not honeſtly by his very prayers, but having ſharked them from the mouth of a heathen worſhipper, (deteſtable to teach him prayers!) ſold them to thoſe that ſtood and honoured him next to the Meſſiah, as his own heavenly compoſitions in adverſity, for hopes no leſs vain and preſumptuous (and death at that time ſo imminent upon him) than by theſe goodly relics to be held a ſaint and martyr in opinion with the cheated people!

And thus far in the whole chapter we have ſeen and conſidered, and it cannot but be clear to all men, how, and for what ends, what concernments and neceſſities, the late king was no way induced, but every way conſtrained to call this laſt parliament; yet here in his firſt prayer he trembles not to avouch as in the ears of God, "That he did it with an upright intention to his glory, and his people's good" of which dreadful atteſtation how ſincerely meant, God, to whom it was avowed, can only judge; and he hath judged already, and hath written his impartial ſentence in characters legible to all chriſtendom; and beſides hath taught us, that there be ſome, whom he hath given over to deluſion, whoſe very mind and conſcience is defiled; of whom St. Paul to Titus makes mention.

II. Upon the Earl of STRAFFORD's Death.

THIS next chapter is a penitent confeſſion of the king, and the ſtrangeſt, if it be well weighed, that ever was auricular. For he repents here of giving his conſent, though moſt unwillingly, to the moſt ſeaſonable and ſolemn piece of juſtice that had been done of many years in the land · but his ſole conſcience thought the contrary. And thus was the welfare, the ſafety, and within a little, the unanimous demand of three populous nations to have attended ſtill on the ſingularity of one man's opinionated conſcience, if men had always been ſo tame and ſpiritleſs, and had not unexpectedly found the grace to underſtand, that if his conſcience were ſo narrow and peculiar to itſelf, it was not fit his authority ſhould be ſo ample and univerſal over others for certainly a private conſcience ſorts not with a public calling, but declares that perſon rather meant by nature for a private fortune And this alſo we may take for truth, that he whoſe conſcience thinks it ſin to put to death a capital offender, will as oft think it meritorious to kill a righteous perſon But let us hear what the ſin was that lay ſo ſore upon him, and, as *one of* his prayers given to Dr Juxon teſtifies, to the very day of his death, it was his ſigning the bill of Strafford's execution. a man whom all men looked upon as one of the boldeſt and moſt impetuous inſtruments that the king had, to advance any violent or illegal deſign He had ruled Ireland and ſome parts of England, *in an arbitrary manner*, had endeavoured to ſubvert fundamental laws, to ſubvert parliaments, and to incenſe the king againſt them, he had alſo endeavoured to make hoſtility between England and Scotland he had counſelled the king to call over that Iriſh army of papiſts, which he had cunningly raiſed, to reduce England, as appeared by good teſtimony then preſent at the conſultation for which, and many other crimes alledged and proved againſt him in twenty-eight articles, he was condemned of high treaſon by the parliament. The commons by far the greater number caſt him, the lords, after they had been ſatisfied in a full diſcourſe by the king's ſolicitor, and the opinions of many judges delivered in their houſe, agreed likewiſe to the ſentence of treaſon. The people univerſally cried out for juſtice. None were his friends but courtiers and clergymen, the worſt at that time, and moſt corrupted ſort of men, and court ladies, not the beſt of women, who when they grow to that inſolence as to appear active in ſtate-affairs, are the certain ſign of a diſſolute, degenerate, and puſillanimous common-wealth Laſt of all the king, or rather firſt, for theſe were but his apes, was not ſatisfied in conſcience to condemn him of high treaſon, and declared to both houſes, "That no fears or reſpects whatſoever ſhould make him alter that reſolution founded upon his conſcience" either then his reſolution was indeed not founded upon his conſcience, or his conſcience received better information, or elſe both his conſcience and this his ſtrong reſolution ſtruck ſail, notwithſtanding theſe glorious words, to his ſtronger fear for within a few days after, when the judges at a privy council, and four of his elected biſhops had picked the thorn out of his conſcience, he was at length perſuaded to ſign the bill for Strafford's execution. And yet perhaps that it wrung his conſcience to condemn the earl of high treaſon is not unlikely, not becauſe he thought him guiltleſs of higheſt treaſon, had half thoſe crimes been committed againſt his own private intereſt or perſon, as appeared plainly by his charge againſt the ſix members, but becauſe he knew himſelf a principal in what the earl was but his acceſſory, and thought nothing treaſon againſt the commonwealth, but againſt himſelf only

Had he really ſcrupled to ſentence that for treaſon which he thought not treaſonable, why did he ſeem reſolved by the judges and the biſhops? and if by them reſolved, how comes the ſcruple here again? It was not then, as he now pretends, "The importunities of ſome, and the fear of many," which made him ſign, but the ſatisfaction given him

him by thoſe judges and ghoſtly fathers of his own chuſing. Which of him ſhall we believe? for he ſeems not one, but double; either here we muſt not believe him profeſſing that his ſatisfaction was but ſeemingly received and out of fear, or elſe we may as well believe that the ſcruple was no real ſcruple, as we can believe him here againſt himſelf before, that the ſatisfaction then received was no real ſatisfaction. Of ſuch a variable and fleeting conſcience, what hold can be taken? But that indeed it was a facil conſcience, and could diſſemble ſatisfaction when it pleaſed, his own enſuing actions declared; being ſoon after found to have the chief hand in a moſt deteſted conſpiracy againſt the parliament and kingdom, as by letters and examinations of Percy, Goring, and other conſpirators came to light; that his intention was to reſcue the earl of Strafford, by ſeizing on the Tower of London; to bring up the Engliſh army out of the North, joined with eight thouſand Iriſh papiſts raiſed by Strafford, and a French army to be landed at Portſmouth againſt the parliament and their friends. For which purpoſe the king, though requeſted by both houſes to diſband thoſe Iriſh Papiſts, refuſed to do it, and kept them ſtill in arms to his own purpoſes. No marvel then, if being as deeply criminous as the earl himſelf, it ſtung his conſcience to adjudge to death thoſe miſdeeds whereof himſelf had been the chief author: no marvel though inſtead of blaming and deteſting his ambition, his evil counſel, his violence and oppreſſion of the people, he fall to praiſe his great Abilities, and with ſcholaſtic flouriſhes beneath the decency of a king, compares him to the Sun, which in all figurative uſe and ſignificance bears alluſion to a king, not to a ſubject: no marvel though he knit contradictions as cloſe as words can lie together, "not approving in his judgment," and yet approving in his ſubſequent reaſon all that Strafford did, as "driven by the neceſſity of times, and the temper of that people," for this excuſes all his miſdemeanours. Laſtly, no marvel that he goes on building many fair and pious concluſions upon falſe and wicked premiſes, which deceive the common reader, not well diſcerning the antipathy of ſuch connexions: but this is the marvel, and may be the aſtoniſhment of all that have a conſcience, how he durſt in the ſight of God (and with the ſame words of contrition wherewith David repents the murdering of Uriah) repent his lawful compliance to that juſt act of not ſaving him, whom he ought to have delivered up to ſpeedy puniſhment, though himſelf the guiltier of the two. If the deed were ſo ſinful to have put to death ſo great a malefactor, it would have taken much doubtleſs from the heavineſs of his ſin, to have told God in his confeſſion, how he laboured, what dark plots he had contrived, into what a league entred, and with what conſpirators againſt his parliament and kingdoms, to have reſcued from the claim of juſtice ſo notable and ſo dear an inſtrument of tyranny, which would have been a ſtory, no doubt, as pleaſing in the ears of Heaven, as all theſe equivocal repentances. For it was fear, and nothing elſe, which made him feign before both the ſcruple and the ſatiſfaction of his conſcience, that is to ſay, of his mind: his firſt fear pretended conſcience, that he might be borne with to refuſe ſigning; his latter fear being more urgent, made him find a conſcience both to ſign, and to be ſatiſfied. As for repentance, it came not on him till a long time after; when he ſaw "he could have ſuffered nothing more, though he had denied that Bill." For how could he underſtandingly repent of letting that be treaſon, which the parliament and whole nation ſo judged? This was that which repented him, to have given up to juſt puniſhment ſo ſtout a champion of his deſigns, who might have been ſo uſeful to him in his following civil broils. It was a worldly repentance, not a conſcientious, or elſe it was a ſtrange tyranny which his conſcience had got over him, to vex him like an evil ſpirit for doing one act of juſtice, and by that means to "fortify his reſolution" from ever doing ſo any more. That mind muſt needs be irrecoverably depraved, which either by chance or importunity, taſting but once of one juſt deed, ſpatters at it, and abhors the reliſh ever after. To the ſcribes and phariſees, woe was denounced by our Saviour, for ſtraining at a gnat and ſwallowing

ing a camel, though a gnat were to be ſtrained at: But to a conſcience with whom one good deed is ſo hard to paſs down as to endanger almoſt a choaking, and bad deeds without number, though as big and bulky as the ruin of three kingdoms, go down currently without ſtraining, certainly a far greater woe appertains. If his conſcience were come to that unnatural Dyſcraſy, as to digeſt poiſon and to keck at wholeſome food, it was not for the parliament, or any of his kingdoms to feed with him any longer. Which to conceal he would perſuade us that the parliament alſo in their conſcience eſcaped not "ſome touches of remorſe" for putting Strafford to death, in forbidding it by an after-act to be a precedent for the future But in a fairer conſtruction, that act implied rather a deſire in them to pacify the king's mind, whom they perceived by this means quite alienated in the mean while not imagining that this after-act ſhould be retorted on them to tie up juſtice for the time to come upon like occaſion, whether this were made a precedent or not, no more than the want of ſuch a precedent, if it had been wanting, had been available to hinder this

But how likely is it that this after-act argued in the parliament their leaſt repenting for the death of Strafford, when it argued ſo little in the king himſelf. who notwithſtanding this after act, which had his own hand and concurrence, if not his own inſtigation, within the ſame year accuſed of high treaſon no leſs than ſix members at once for the ſame pretended crimes which his conſcience would not yield to think treaſonable in the earl So that this his ſubtle argument to faſten a repenting, and by that means a guiltineſs of Strafford's death upon the parliament, concludes upon his own head, and ſhews us plainly that either nothing in his judgment was treaſon againſt the commonwealth, but only againſt the king's perſon, (a tyrannical principle!) or that his conſcience was a perverſe and prevaricating conſcience, to ſcruple that the commonwealth ſhould puniſh for treaſonous in one eminent offender, that which he himſelf ſought ſo vehemently to have puniſhed in ſix guiltleſs perſons. If this were "that touch of conſcience which he bore with greater regret" than for any ſin committed in his life, whether it were that proditory aid ſent to Rochel and religion abroad, or that prodigality of ſheding blood at home, to a million of his ſubjects lives not valued in compariſon of one Strafford, we may conſider yet at laſt, what true ſenſe and feeling could be in that conſcience, and what fitneſs to be the maſter-conſcience of three kingdoms.

But the reaſon why he labours that we ſhould take notice of ſo much "tenderneſs and regret in his ſoul for having any hand in Strafford's death," is worth the marking e'er we conclude: "He hoped it would be ſome evidence before God and man to all poſterity, that he was far from bearing that vaſt load and guilt of blood" laid upon him by others. Which hath the likeneſs of a ſubtle diſſimulation; bewailing the blood of one man, his commodious inſtrument, put to death moſt juſtly, though by him unwillingly, that we might think him too tender to ſhed willingly the blood of thoſe thouſands, whom he counted rebels. And thus by dipping voluntarily his fingers end, yet with ſhew of great remorſe, in the blood of Strafford, whereof all men clear him, he thinks to ſcape that ſea of innocent blood wherein his own guilt inevitably hath plunged him all over. And we may well perceive to what eaſy ſatisfactions and purgations he had inured his ſecret conſcience, who *thought* by ſuch weak policies and oſtentations as theſe, to gain belief and abſolution from underſtanding men.

III. Upon

III. Upon his going to the Houſe of Commons.

CONcerning his unexcuſable and hoſtile march from the court to the houſe of commons, there needs not much be ſaid; for he confeſſes it to be an act which moſt men, whom he calls "his enemies," cried ſhame upon, "indifferent men grew jealous of and fearful, and many of his friends reſented, as a motion ariſing rather from paſſion than reaſon." He himſelf, in one of his anſwers to both houſes, made profeſſion to be convinced that it was a plain breach of their privilege; yet here like a rotten building newly trimmed over, he repreſents it ſpeciouſly and fraudulently, to impoſe upon the ſimple reader; and ſeeks by ſmooth and ſupple words not here only, but through his whole book, to make ſome beneficial uſe or other even of his worſt miſcarriages.

"Theſe men," ſaith he, meaning his friends, "knew not the juſt motives and pregnant grounds with which I thought myſelf furniſhed," to wit, againſt the five members whom he came to drag out of the houſe. His beſt friends indeed knew not, nor could ever know his motives to ſuch a riotous act; and had he himſelf known any juſt grounds, he was not ignorant how much it might have tended to his juſtifying, had he named them in this place, and not concealed them. But ſuppoſe them real, ſuppoſe them known, what was this to that violation and diſhonour put upon the whole houſe, whoſe very door forcibly kept open, and all the paſſages near it he beſet with ſwords and piſtols cokt and menaced in the hands of about three hundred ſwaggerers and ruffians, who but expected, nay audibly called for, the word of onſet to begin a ſlaughter?

"He had diſcovered, as he thought, unlawful correſpondencies which they had uſed, and engagements to embroil his kingdoms," and remembers not his own unlawful correſpondencies and conſpiracies with the Iriſh army of papiſts, with the French to land at Portſmouth, and his tampering both with the Engliſh and Scots army to come up againſt the parliament: the leaſt of which attempts by whomſoever, was no leſs than manifeſt treaſon againſt the commonwealth.

If to demand juſtice on the five members were his Plea, for that which they with more reaſon might have demanded juſtice upon him (I uſe his own argument) there needed not ſo rough aſſiſtance. If he had "reſolved to bear that repulſe with patience," which his queen by her words to him at his return little thought he would have done, wherefore did he provide againſt it with ſuch an armed and unuſual force? but his heart ſerved him not to undergo the hazard that ſuch a deſperate ſcuffle would have brought him to. But wherefore did he go at all, it behoving him to know there were two ſtatutes that declared he ought firſt to have acquainted the parliament, who were the accuſers, which he refuſed to do, though ſtill profeſſing to govern by law, and ſtill juſtifying his attempts againſt law? And when he ſaw it was not permitted him to attaint them but by a fair trial, as was offered him from time to time, for want of juſt matter which yet never came to light, he let the buſineſs fall of his own accord, and all thoſe Pregnancies and juſt Motives came to juſt nothing.

"He had no temptation of diſpleaſure or revenge againſt thoſe men:" None but what he thirſted to execute upon them, for the conſtant oppoſition which they made againſt his tyrannous proceedings, and the love and reputation which they therefore had among the people; *but moſt immediately, for that they were ſuppoſed the chief by whoſe activity those twelve proteſting biſhops were but a week before committed to the Tower.*

"He miſt but little to have produced writings under ſome men's own hands." But yet he miſt, though their chambers, trunks, and ſtudies were ſealed up and ſearched, yet not found guilty. "Providence would not have it ſo." Good Providence! that curbs the raging of proud monarchs, as well as of mad multitudes. "Yet he wanted not ſuch probabilities" (for his pregnant is come now to probable) "as were ſufficient to to raiſe jealouſies in any king's heart." And thus his pregnant motives are at laſt proved nothing but a tympany, or a queen Mary's cuſhion, for in any king's heart, as kings go now, what ſhadowy conceit or groundleſs toy will not create a jealouſy?

"That he had deſigned to aſſault the houſe of commons," taking God to witneſs, he utterly denies, yet in his anſwer to the city, maintains that "any courſe of violence had been very juſtifiable." And we may then gueſs how far it was from his deſign. However, it diſcovered in him an exceſſive eagerneſs to be avenged on them that croſſed him, and that to have his will, he ſtood not to do things never ſo much below him. What a becoming ſight it was, to ſee the king of England one while in the houſe of commons, and by and by in the Guildhall among the liveries and manufactures, proſecuting ſo greedily the track of five or ſix fled ſubjects; himſelf not the ſollicitor only but the purſivant, and the apparitor of his own partial cauſe! And although in his anſwers to the parliament, he hath confeſſed, firſt that his manner of proſecution was illegal, next "that as he once conceived he had ground enough to accuſe them, ſo at length that he found as good cauſe to deſert any proſecution of them;" yet here he ſeems to reverſe all, and againſt promiſe takes up his old deſerted accuſation, that he might have ſomething to excuſe himſelf, inſtead of giving due reparation, which he always refuſed to give them, whom he had ſo diſhonoured.

"That I went," ſaith he of his going to the houſe of commons, "attended with ſome gentlemen," Gentlemen indeed! the ragged infantry of ſtews, and brothels, the ſpawn and ſhipwreck of taverns and dicing-houſes. and then he pleads, "it was no unwonted thing for the majeſty and ſafety of a king to be ſo attended, eſpecially in diſcontented times." An illuſtrious majeſty no doubt, ſo attended! a becoming ſafety for the king of England, placed in the fidelity of ſuch guards and champions! happy times, when braves and hackſters, the only contented members of his government, were thought the fitteſt and the faithfulleſt to defend his perſon againſt the diſcontents of a parliament and all good men! Were thoſe the choſen ones to "preſerve reverence to him," while he entered "unaſſured," and full of ſuſpicions, into his great and faithful counſel? Let God then and the world judge, whether the cauſe were not in his own guilty and unwarrantable doings. The houſe of commons upon ſeveral examinations of this buſineſs, declared it ſufficiently proved, that the coming of thoſe ſoldiers, papiſts and others with the king, was to take away ſome of their members, and in caſe of oppoſition or denial, to have fallen upon the houſe in a hoſtile manner. This the king here denies, adding a fearful imprecation againſt his own life, "if he purpoſed any violence or oppreſſion againſt the innocent, then," ſaith he, "let the enemy perſecute my ſoul, and tread my life to the ground, and lay my honour in the duſt." What need then more diſputing? He appealed to God's tribunal, and behold! God hath judged and done to him in the ſight of all men according to the verdict of his own mouth. To be a warning to all kings hereafter, how they uſe preſumptuouſly the words and proteſtations of David, without the ſpirit and conſcience of David. And the king's admirers may here ſee their madneſs, to miſtake this book for a monument of his worth and wiſdom, whenas indeed it is his Doomſday-Book, not like that of William the Norman his predeceſſor, but the record and memorial of his condemnation, and diſcovers whatever hath befallen him, to have been haſtened on from divine juſtice by the raſh and inconſiderate appeal of his own lips. But what evaſions, what pretences, though never ſo unjuſt and empty, will he refuſe in matters more unknown, and more involved in the miſts and intricacies of ſtate, who, rather than not juſtify himſelf in a thing ſo generally odious, can flatter his integrity with ſuch frivolous excuſes againſt the manifeſt diſſent of all men, whether enemies, neuters, or friends. But God and his judgments have not been mocked, and good men may well perceive what a diſtance there was ever like to be between him and his parliament, and perhaps between him and all amendment, who for one good deed, tho' but conſented to, aſks God forgiveneſs, and from his worſt deeds done, takes occaſion to inſiſt upon his righteouſneſs!

IV. Upon

IV. Upon the Inſolency of the Tumults:

WE have here, I muſt confeſs, a neat and well-couched invective againſt tumults, expreſſing a true fear of them in the author; but yet ſo handſomely compoſed, and withal ſo feelingly, that, to make a royal compariſon, I believe Rehoboam the ſon of Solomon, could not have compoſed it better. Yet Rehoboam had more cauſe to inveigh againſt them; for they had ſtoned his tribute gatherer, and perhaps had as little ſpared his own perſon, had he not with all ſpeed betaken him to his chariot. But this king hath ſtood the worſt of them in his own houſe without danger, when his coach and horſes, in a panic fear, have been to ſeek: which argues that the tumults at Whitehall, were nothing ſo dangerous as thoſe at Sechem.

But the matter here conſiderable is not whether the king, or his houſhold Rhetorician have made a pithy declamation againſt tumults, but firſt whether theſe were tumults or not: next if they were, whether the king himſelf did not cauſe them. Let us examine therefore how things at that time ſtood. The king, as before hath been proved, having both called this parliament unwillingly, and as unwillingly from time to time condeſcended to their ſeveral acts, carrying on a disjoint and private intereſt of his own, and not enduring to be ſo croſſed and overſwayed, eſpecially in the executing of his chief and boldeſt inſtrument, the deputy of Ireland, firſt tempts the Engliſh army, with no leſs reward than the ſpoil of London, to come up and deſtroy the parliament. That being diſcovered by ſome of the officers, who, though bad enough, yet abhorred ſo foul a deed; the king hardened in his purpoſe, *tempts them the ſecond time at Burrowbridge, promiſes to pawn his jewels for them, and that they ſhould be met and aſſiſted (would they but march on) with a groſs body of horſe under the earl of Newcaſtle. He tempts them yet the third time, though after diſcovery, and his own abjuration to have ever tempted them, as is affirmed in the declaration of* "No more addreſſes." *Neither this ſucceeding,* he turns him next to the Scotch army, and *by his own credential letters given to Oneal and Sir John Henderſon,* baits his temptation with a richer reward, not only to have the ſacking of London, but four northern counties to be made Scotiſh, with jewels of great value to be given in pawn the while. But neither would the Scots, for any promiſe of reward be brought to ſuch an execrable and odious treachery; but with much honeſty gave notice of the king's deſign both to the parliament and city of London. The parliament moreover had intelligence, and the people could not but diſcern, that there was a bitter and malignant party grown up now to ſuch a boldneſs, as to give out inſolent and threatning ſpeeches againſt the parliament itſelf. Beſides this, the rebellion in Ireland was now broke out, and a conſpiracy in Scotland had been made, while the king was there, againſt ſome chief members of that parliament, great numbers here of unknown and ſuſpicious perſons reſorted to the city. The king being returned from Scotland, preſently diſmiſſes that guard which the parliament thought neceſſary in the midſt of ſo many dangers to have about them, and puts another guard in their place, contrary to the privilege of that high court, and by ſuch a one commanded, as made them no leſs doubtful of the guard itſelf. Which they therefore, upon ſome ill effects thereof firſt found, diſcharge; deeming it more ſafe to ſit free, though without a guard, in open danger, than incloſed with a ſuſpected ſafety. The people therefore, leſt their worthieſt and moſt faithful patriots, who had expoſed themſelves for the public, and whom they ſaw now left naked, ſhould want aid, or be deſerted in the midſt of theſe dangers, came in multitudes, though unarmed, to witneſs their fidelity and readineſs in caſe of any violence offered to the parliament. The king both envying to ſee the people's love thus devolved on another object, and doubting leſt it might utterly diſable him to do with parliaments as he was wont, ſent a meſſage into the city forbidding ſuch reſorts. The parliament alſo, both by what was diſcovered to them, and what they ſaw in a malignant party (ſome of which had already drawn blood in a fray or two at the court-gate, and even at their own gate in Weſtminſter-hall) conceiving themſelves to be ſtill in danger where they ſate, ſent a moſt reaſonable and juſt petition to the king, that a guard might be allowed them out of the city, whereof the king's own chamberlain, the earl of Eſſex, might have command; it being the right of inferior courts to make choice of their own guard This the king refuſed to do, and why he refuſed, the very next day made manifeſt: For on that day it was, that he ſallied out from Whitehall, with thoſe truſty Myrmidons, to block up, or give aſſault to the houſe of commons. He had, beſides all this, begun to fortify his court, and entertained armed men not a few; who ſtanding at his palace-gate, reviled, and with drawn ſwords wounded many of the people, as they went by unarmed, and in a peaceable manner, whereof ſome died. The paſſing by of a multitude, though neither to St. George's feaſt, nor to a tilting, certainly of itſelf was no tumult; the expreſſion of their loyalty and ſtedfaſtneſs to the parliament, whoſe lives and ſafeties by more than ſlight rumours they doubted to be in danger, was no tumult. If it grew to be ſo, the cauſe was in the king himſelf and his injurious retinue, who both by hoſtile preparations in the court, and by actual aſſailing of the people, gave them juſt cauſe to defend themſelves

Surely thoſe unarmed and petitioning people, needed not have been ſo formidable to any, but to ſuch whoſe conſciences miſgave them how ill they had deſerved of the people, and firſt began to injure them, becauſe they juſtly feared it from them; and then aſcribe that to popular tumult, which was occaſioned by their own provoking.

And that the king was ſo emphatical and elaborate on this theme againſt tumults, and expreſſed with ſuch a vehemence his hatred of them, will redound leſs perhaps than he was aware to the commendation of his government. For beſides that in good governments they happen ſeldomeſt, and riſe not without cauſe, if they prove extreme and pernicious, they were never counted ſo to monarchy, but to monarchical tyranny, and extremes one with another are at moſt antipathy. If then the king ſo extremely ſtood in fear of tumults, the inference will endanger him to be the other extreme. Thus far the occaſion of this diſcourſe againſt tumults: now to the diſcourſe itſelf, voluble enough, and full of ſentence, but that, for the moſt part, either ſpecious rather than ſolid, or to his cauſe nothing pertinent.

"He never thought any thing more to preſage the miſchiefs that enſued, than thoſe tumults" Then was his foreſight but ſhort, and much miſtaken. Thoſe tumults were but the mild effects of an evil and injurious reign; not ſigns of miſchiefs to come, but ſeeking relief for miſchiefs paſt: thoſe ſigns were to be read more apparent in his rage and purpoſed revenge of thoſe free expoſtulations, and clamours of the people againſt his lawleſs government "Not any thing," ſaith he, "portends more God's diſpleaſure againſt a nation, than when he ſuffers the clamours of the vulgar to paſs all bounds of law and reverence to authority." It portends rather his diſpleaſure againſt a tyrannous king, whoſe proud throne he intends to overturn by that contemptible vulgar; the ſad cries and oppreſſions of whom his royalty regarded not. As for that ſupplicating people, they did no hurt either to law or authority, but ſtood for it rather in the parliament againſt whom they feared would violate it.

"That they invaded the honour and freedom of the two houſes;" is his own officious accuſation, not ſeconded by the parliament, who, had they ſeen cauſe, were themſelves beſt able to complain. And if they "ſhook and menaced" any, they were ſuch as had more relation to the court than to the commonwealth, enemies, not patrons of the people. But if their petitioning unarmed were an invaſion of both houſes, what was his entrance into the houſe of commons, beſetting it with armed men? In what condition then was the honour and freedom of that houſe?

"They

" They forbore not rude deportments, contemptuous words and actions to himſelf and his court."

It was more wonder, having heard what treacherous hoſtility he had deſigned againſt the city and his whole kingdom, that they forbore to handle him as people in their rage have handled tyrants heretofore for leſs offences.

" They were not a ſhort ague, but a fierce quotidian fever." He indeed may beſt ſay it, who moſt felt it; for the ſhaking was within him, and it ſhook him by his own deſcription " worſe than a ſtorm, worſe than an earthquake," Belſhazzar's palſy. Had not worſe fears, terrors, and envies made within him that commotion, how could a multitude of his ſubjects, armed with no other weapon than petitions, have ſhaken all his joints with ſuch a terrible ague? Yet that the parliament ſhould entertain the leaſt fear of bad intentions from him or his party, he endures not; but would perſuade us that " men ſcare themſelves and others without cauſe:" for he thought fear would be to them a kind of armour, and his deſign was, if it were poſſible, to diſarm all, eſpecially of a wiſe fear and ſuſpicion; for that he knew would find weapons.

He goes on therefore with vehemence to repeat the miſchiefs done by theſe tumults. " They firſt petitioned, then proteſted; dictate next, and laſtly over-awe the parliament. They removed obſtructions, they purged the houſes, caſt out rotten members." If there were a man of iron, ſuch as Talus, by our poet Spencer, is feigned to be the page of juſtice, who with his iron flail could do all this, and expeditiouſly, without thoſe deceitful forms and circumſtances of law, worſe than ceremonies in religion, I ſay, God ſend it done, whether by one Talus, or by a thouſand.

" But they ſubdued the men of conſcience in parliament, backed and abetted all ſeditious and ſchiſmatical propoſals againſt government eccleſiaſtical and civil."

Now we may perceive the root of his hatred, whence it ſprings. It was not the king's grace or princely goodneſs, but this iron flail, the people, that drove the biſhops out of their baronies, out of their cathedrals, out of the lord's houſe, out of their copes and ſurplices, and all thoſe papiſtical innovations, threw down the high-commiſſion and ſtar-chamber, gave us a triennial parliament, and what we moſt deſired, in revenge whereof he now ſo bitterly inveighs againſt them: theſe are thoſe ſeditious and ſchiſmatical propoſals then by him condeſcended to as acts of grace, now of another name, which declares him, touching matters of church and ſtate, to have been no other man in the deepeſt of his ſolitude, than he was before at the higheſt of his ſovereignty.

But this was not the worſt of theſe tumults, they played the haſty " midwives, and would not ſtay the ripening, but went ſtreight to ripping up, and forcibly cut out abortive votes."

They would not ſtay perhaps the Spaniſh demurring, and putting off ſuch wholeſome acts and counſels, as the politic cabinet at Whitehall had no mind to. But all this is complained here as done to the parliament, and yet we heard not the parliament at that time complain of any violence from the people, but from him Wherefore intrudes he to plead the cauſe of parliament againſt the people, while the parliament was pleading their own cauſe againſt him, and againſt him were forced to ſeek refuge of the people? It is plain then that thoſe confluxes and reſorts interrupted not the parliament, nor by them were thought tumultuous, but by him only and his court-faction.

" But what good man had not rather want any thing he moſt deſired for the public good, than attain it by ſuch unlawful and irreligious means?" As much as to ſay, had not rather ſit ſtill, and let his country be tyrannized, than that the people, finding no other remedy, ſhould ſtand up like men, and demand their rights and liberties This is the artificialeſt piece of fineſſe to perſuade men *into ſlavery*, that the wit of court could have invented. But hear how much better the moral of this leſſon would befit the teacher. What good man had not rather want a boundleſs and arbitrary power, and thoſe fine flowers of the crown, called prerogatives, than for them to uſe force and perpetual vexation to his faithful ſubjects, nay to wade for them through blood and civil war? So that this and the whole bundle of thoſe following ſentences may be applied better to the convincement of his own violent courſes, than of thoſe pretended tumults.

"Who were the chief demagogues to ſend for thoſe tumults, ſome alive are not ignorant." Setting aſide the affrightment of this goblin word, for the king, by his leave, cannot coin Engliſh, as he could money, to be current (and it is believed this wording was above his known ſtile and orthography, and accuſes the whole compoſure to be conſcious of ſome other author) yet if the people were ſent for, emboldened and directed by thoſe Demagogues, who, ſaving his Greek, were good patriots, and by his own confeſſion "men of ſome repute for parts and piety," it helps well to aſſure us there was both urgent cauſe, and the leſs danger of their coming.

"Complaints were made, yet no redreſs could be obtained." The parliament alſo complained of what danger they ſate in from another party, and demanded of him a guard, but it was not granted. What marvel then if it cheared them to ſee ſome ſtore of their friends, and in the Roman, not the pettifogging ſenſe, their clients ſo near about them, a defence due by nature both from whom it was offered, and to whom, as due as to their parents; tho' the court ſtormed and fretted to ſee ſuch honour given to them, who were then beſt fathers of the commonwealth. And both the parliament and people complained, and demanded juſtice fŏr thoſe aſſaults, if not murders done at his own doors by that crew of rufflers, but he, inſtead of doing juſtice on them, juſtified and abetted them in what they did, as in his public anſwer to a petition from the city may be read. Neither is it ſlightly to be paſſed over, that in the very place where blood was firſt drawn in this cauſe, at the beginning of all that followed, there was his own blood ſhed by the executioner: According to that ſentence of divine juſtice, "in the place where dogs licked the blood of Naboth, ſhall dogs lick thy blood, even thine."

From hence he takes occaſion to excuſe that improvident and fatal error of his abſenting from the parliament. "When he found that no declaration of the biſhops could take place againſt thoſe tumults." Was that worth his conſidering, that fooliſh and ſelf-undoing declaration of twelve cypher biſhops, who were immediately appeached of treaſon for that audacious declaring? The biſhops peradventure were now and then pulled by the rochets, and deſerved another kind of pulling, but what amounted this to "the fear of his own perſon in the ſtreets?" Did he not the very next day after his irruption into the houſe of commons, than which nothing had more exaſperated the people, go in his coach unguarded into the city? Did he receive the leaſt affront, much leſs violence, in any of the ſtreets, but rather humble demeanors and ſupplications? Hence may be gathered, that however in his own guiltineſs he might have juſtly feared, yet that he knew the people ſo full of awe and reverence to his perſon, as to dare commit himſelf ſingle among the thickeſt of them, at a time when he had moſt provoked them. Beſides, in Scotland they had handled the biſhops in a more robuſtious manner; Edinburgh had been full of tumults, two armies from thence had entered England againſt him: yet after all this he was not fearful, but very forward to take ſo long a journey to Edinburgh, which argues firſt, as did alſo his rendition afterward to the Scots army, that to England he continued ſtill, as he was indeed, a ſtranger, and full of diffidence, to the Scots only a native king, in his confidence, though not in his dealing towards them. It ſhews us next beyond doubting, that all this his fear of tumults was but a mere colour and occaſion taken of his reſolved abſence from the parliament, for ſome other end not difficult to be gueſſed. And thoſe inſtances wherein valour is not to be queſtioned for not "ſcuffling with the ſea, or an undiſciplined rabble," are but ſubſervient to carry on the ſolemn jeſt of his fearing tumults, if they diſcover not withal the true reaſon why he departed, only to turn his ſlaſhing at the court-gate to ſlaughtering in the field, his diſorderly bickering to an orderly invading, which was nothing elſe but a more orderly diſorder.

"Some

" Some ſuſpected and affirmed that he meditated a war, when he went firſt from Whitehall." And they were not the worſt heads that did ſo, nor did any of his former acts weaken him to that, as he alledges for himſelf; or if they had, they clear him only for the time of paſſing them, not for whatever thoughts might come after into his mind. Former actions of improvidence or fear, not with him unuſual, cannot abſolve him of all after-meditations.

He goes on proteſting his " no intention to have left Whitehall," had theſe horrid tumults given him but fair quarter; as if he himſelf, his wife and children had been in peril. But to this enough hath been anſwered.

" Had this parliament, as it was in its firſt election," namely with the lord and baron biſhops, " ſate full and free," he doubts not but all had gone well. What warrant this of his to us, whoſe not doubting was all good men's greateſt doubt?

" He was reſolved to hear reaſon, and to conſent ſo far as he could comprehend." A hopeful reſolution: what if his reaſon were found by oft experience to comprehend nothing beyond his own advantages; was this a reaſon fit to be intruſted with the common good of three nations?

But, faith he, " as ſwine are to gardens, ſo are tumults to parliaments." This the parliament, had they found it ſo, could beſt have told us. In the mean while, who knows not that one great hog may do as much miſchief in a garden as many little ſwine?

" He was ſometimes prone to think, that had he called this laſt parliament to any other place in England, the ſad conſequences might have been prevented." But change of air changes not the mind. Was not his firſt parliament at Oxford diſſolved after two ſubſidies given him, and no juſtice received? Was not his laſt in the ſame place, where they ſate with as much freedom, as much quiet from tumults as they could deſire; a parliament, both in his account and their own, conſiſting of all his friends, that fled after him, and ſuffered for him, and yet by him nicknamed, and caſhiered for a " mungrel parliament, that vext his queen with their baſe and mutinous motions," as his cabinet-letter tells us? Whereby the world may ſee plainly, that no ſhifting of place, no ſifting of members to his own mind, no number, no paucity, no freedom from tumults could ever bring his arbitrary wilfulneſs, and tyrannical deſigns to brook the leaſt ſhape or ſimilitude, the leaſt counterfeit of a parliament.

Finally, inſtead of praying for his people as a good king ſhould do, he prays to be delivered from them, as " from wild beaſts, inundations, and raging ſeas, that had overborn all loyalty, modeſty, laws, juſtice, and religion." God ſave the people from ſuch interceſſors!

V. Upon the bill for triennial parliaments, and for ſettling this, &c.

THE bill for a triennial parliament was *but the third part of one good ſtep toward that which in times paſt was our annual right. The other bill for ſettling this parliament was new indeed, but at that time very neceſſary; and in the king's own words no more than what the world* " was fully confirmed he might in juſtice, reaſon, honour and conſcience grant them," *for to that end he affirms to have done it.*

But whereas he attributes the paſſing of them to his own act of grace and willingneſs, (as his manner is to make virtues of his neceſſities) and giving to himſelf all the praiſe, heaps ingratitude upon the parliament, a little memory will ſet the clean contrary before us, that for thoſe beneficial acts we owe what we owe to the parliament: but to his granting them neither praiſe nor thanks. The firſt bill granted much leſs than two former ſtatutes yet in force by Edward the third, that a parliament ſhould be called every year, or oftener, if need were: nay, from a far ancienter law-book called the " Mirror," it is affirmed in a late treatife called "Rights of the kingdom *," that parliaments by our old laws ought twice a year to be at London. *From twice in one year to once in three years, it may be foon caft up how great a lofs we fell into of our ancient liberty by that act, which in the ignorant and flavifh minds we then were, was thought a great purchafe. Wifeft men perhaps were contented (for the prefent at leaft) by this act to have recovered parliaments, which were then upon the brink of danger to be for ever loft. And this is that which the king preaches here for a fpecial token of his princely favour, to have abridged and over-reached the people five parts in fix of what their due was, both by ancient ftatute and originally. And thus the taking from us all but a triennial remnant of that Englifh freedom which our fathers left us double, in a fair annuity enrolled, is fet out, and fold to us here for the gracious, and over-liberal giving of a new enfranchifement How little, may we think, did he ever give us, who in the bill of his pretended givings writes down* imprimis *that benefit or privilege once in three year given us, which by fo giving, he more than twice every year illegally took from us; fuch givers as give fingle to take away fix-fold, be to our enemies! For certainly this commonwealth, if the ftatutes of our anceftors be worth aught, would have found it hard and hazardous to thrive under the damage of fuch a guileful liberality.* The *other act* was fo neceffary, that nothing in the power of man, more feemed to be the ftay and fupport of all things from that fteep ruin to which he had nigh brought them, than that act obtained. He had by his ill ftewardfhip, and, to fay no worfe, the needlefs raifing of two armies intended for a civil war, beggared both himfelf and the public, and befides had left us upon the fcore of his needy enemies for what it coft them in their own defence againft him To difengage him and the kingdom great fums were to be borrowed, which would never have been lent, nor could ever be *repaid*, had the king chanced to diffolve this parliament as heretofore The errors alfo of his government had brought the kingdom to fuch extremes, as were incapable of all recovery without the abfolute continuance of *a* parliament. It had been elfe in vain to go about the fettling of fo great diftempers, if he who firft caufed the malady, might, when he pleafed, reject the remedy. Notwithftanding all which, that he granted both thefe acts unwillingly, and as a mere paffive inftrument, was then vifible even to moft of thofe men who now will fee nothing.

At paffing of the former act he himfelf concealed not his unwillingnefs; and teftifying a general diflike of their actions, which they then proceeded in with great approbation of the whole kingdom, he told them with a mafterly brow, that "by this act he had obliged them above what they had deferved," and gave a piece of juftice to the commonwealth *fix* times fhort of his predeceffors, as if he had been giving fome boon or begged office to a fort of his defertlefs grooms.

That he paffed the latter act againft his will, no man in reafon can hold it queftionable For if the February before he made fo dainty, and were fo loth to beftow a parliament once in three year upon the nation, becaufe this had fo oppofed his courfes, was it likely that the May following he fhould beftow willingly on this parliament an indiffoluble fitting, when they had offended him much more, by cutting fhort and impeaching of high treafon his chief favourites? It was his fear then, not his favour, which drew from him that act, left the parliament, incenfed by his confpiracies againft them about the fame time difcovered, fhould with the people have refented too heinoufly thofe his doings, if to the fufpicion of their danger from him, he had alfo added the denial of this only means to fecure themfelves

From thefe acts therefore in which he glories, and wherewith fo oft he upbraids the parliament, he cannot juftly expect to reap aught but difhonour and difpraife; as being both unwillingly granted, and the one granting much lefs than was before allowed by ftatute, the other being a teftimony of his violent and lawlefs cuftom, not only to

* Written by Mr *Sadler*, of which the beft edition is that of 1649, in quarto; the edition of 1687 being curtailed. It is an excellent book.

5 break

break privileges, but whole parliaments; from which enormity they were conftrained to bind him firft of all his predeceffors; never any before him having given like caufes of diftruft and jealoufy to his people. As for this parliament, how far he was from being advifed by them as he ought, let his own words exprefs.

He taxes them with "undoing what they found well done:" and yet knows they undid nothing in the Church but lord bifhops, liturgies, ceremonies, high commiffion, judged worthy by all true proteftants to be thrown out of the Church. They undid nothing in the ftate but irregular and grinding courts, the main grievances to be removed; and if thefe were the things which in his opinion they found well done, we may again from hence be informed with what unwillingnefs he removed them: and that thofe gracious acts whereof fo frequently he makes mention, may be englifhed more properly acts of fear and diffimulation againft his mind and confcience.

The bill preventing diffolution of this parliament he calls "an unparalleled act, out of the extreme confidence that his fubjects would not make ill ufe of it." But was it not a greater confidence of the people to put into one man's hand fo great a power, till heabufed it, as to fummon and diffolve parliaments? He would be thanked for trufting them, and ought to thank them rather for trufting him: the truft iffuing firft from them, not from him.

And that it was a mere truft, and not his prerogative, to call and diffolve parliaments at his pleafure; and that parliaments were not to be diffolved, till all petitions were heard, all grievances redreffed, is not only the affertion of this parliament, but of our ancient law-books, which aver it to be an unwritten law of common right, fo ingraven in the hearts of our anceftors, and by them fo conftantly enjoyed and claimed, as that it needed not enrolling. And if the Scots in their declaration could charge the king with breach of their laws for breaking up that parliament without their confent, while matters of greateft moment were depending, it were unreafonable to imagine that the wifdom of England fhould be fo wanting to itfelf through all ages, as not to provide by fome known law, written or unwritten, againft the not calling, or the arbitrary diffolving of parliaments, or that they who ordained their fummoning twice a year, or as oft as need required, did not tacitly enact alfo, that as neceffity of affairs called them, fo the fame neceffity fhould keep them undiffolved till that were fully fatisfied. Were it not for that, parliaments, and all the fruit and benefit we receive by having them, would turn foon to mere abufion. It appears then that if this bill of not diffolving were an unparalleled act, it was a known and common right which our anceftors under other kings enjoyed as firmly as if it had been graven in marble; and that the infringement of this king firft brought it into a written act who now boafts that as a great favour done us, which his own lefs fidelity than was in former kings, conftrained us only of an old undoubted right to make a new written act But what needed written acts, whenas anciently it was efteemed part of his crown-oath not to diffolve parliaments till all grievances were confidered? whereupon the old "Modi of Parliament," calls it flat perjury, if he diffolve them before: as I find cited in a book mentioned at the beginning of this chapter, to which and other law-tractats I refer the more lawyerly mooting of this point, which is neither my element, nor my proper work here, fince the book which I have to anfwer, pretends reafon, not authorities and quotations. and I hold reafon to be the beft arbitrator, and the law of law itfelf

It is true, that "good fubjects think it not juft that the king's condition fhould be worfe by bettering theirs." But then the king muft not be at a fuch a diftance from the people in judging what is better and what worfe; which might have been agreed, had he known (for his own words condemn him) "as well with moderation to ufe, as with earneftnefs to defire his own advantages."

"A continual parliament he thought would keep the commonwealth in tune." Judge, commonwealth, what proofs he gave that this boafted profeffion was ever in his thought, "Some,

"Some," ſaith he, "gave out that I repented me of that ſettling act." His own actions gave it out beyond all ſuppoſition; for doubtleſs it repented him to have eſtabliſhed that by law, which he went about ſo ſoon after to abrogate by the ſword.

He calls thoſe acts which he confeſſes "tended to their good, not more princely than friendly contributions." As if to do his duty were of courteſy, and the diſcharge of his truſt a parcel of his liberality; ſo nigh loſt in his eſteem was the birth-right of our liberties, that to give them back again upon demand, ſtood at the mercy of his contribution.

"He doubts not but the affections of his people will compenſate his ſufferings for thoſe acts of confidence:" And imputes his ſufferings to a contrary cauſe. Not his confidence, but his diſtruſt was that which brought him to thoſe ſufferings, from the time that he forſook his parliament, and truſted them never the ſooner for what he tells "of their piety and religious ſtrictneſs," but rather hated them as puritans, whom he always ſought to extirpate.

He would have it believed that "to bind his hands by theſe acts, argued a very ſhort foreſight of things, and extreme fatuity of mind in him," if he had meant a war If we ſhould conclude ſo, that were not the only argument neither did it argue that he meant peace, knowing that what he granted for the preſent out of fear, he might as ſoon repeal by force, watching his time; and deprive them the fruit of thoſe acts, if his own deſigns wherein he put his truſt, took effect.

Yet he complains, "that the tumults threatened to abuſe all acts of grace, and turn them into wantonneſs" I would they had turned his wantonneſs into the grace of not abuſing Scripture Was this becoming ſuch a ſaint as they would make him, to adulterate thoſe ſacred words from the grace of God to the acts of his own grace? Herod was eaten up of worms for ſuffering others to compare his voice to the voice of God, but the borrower of his phraſe gives much more cauſe of jealouſy, that he likened his own acts of grace to the acts of God's grace.

From prophaneneſs he ſcarce comes off with perfect ſenſe "I was not then in a capacity to make war," therefore I intended not. "I was not in a capacity," therefore "I could not have given my enemies greater advantage than by ſo unprincely inconſtancy to have ſcattered them by arms, whom but lately I had ſettled by parliament" What place could there be for his inconſtancy in that thing whereto he was in no capacity? Otherwiſe his inconſtancy was not ſo unwonted, or ſo nice, but that it would have eaſily found pretences to ſcatter thoſe in revenge, whom he ſettled in fear

"It had been a courſe full of ſin as well as of hazard and diſhonour." True; but if thoſe conſiderations withheld him not from other actions of like nature, how can we believe they were of ſtrength ſufficient to withhold him from this? And that they withheld him not, the event ſoon taught us

"His letting ſome men go up to the pinacle of the temple, was a temptation to them to caſt him down headlong" In this ſimile we have himſelf compared to Chriſt, the parliament to the Devil, and his giving them that act of ſettling, to his letting them go up to the "Pinacle of the Temple" A tottering and giddy act rather than a ſettling This was goodly uſe made of Scripture in his ſolitudes: But it was no pinacle of the temple, it was a pinacle of Nebuchadnezzar's palace, from whence he and monarchy fell headlong together.

He would have others ſee that "all the kingdoms of the world are not worth gaining by ways of ſin which hazard the ſoul," and hath himſelf left nothing unhazarded to keep three He concludes with ſentences that rightly ſcanned, make not ſo much for him as againſt him, and confeſſes that "the act of ſettling was no ſin of his will;" and we eaſily believe him, for it hath been clearly proved a ſin of his unwillingneſs

With his oriſons I meddle not, for he appeals to a high audit. This yet may be noted, that at his prayers he had before him the ſad preſage of his ill ſucceſs, "as of a dark and

and dangerous ſtorm, which never admitted his return to the port from whence he ſet out. Yet his prayer-book no ſooner ſhut, but other hopes flattered him; and their flattering was his deſtruction.

VI. Upon his retirement from Weſtminſter.

THE ſimile wherewith he begins, I was about to have found fault with, as in a garb ſomewhat more poetical than for a ſtatiſt: but meeting with many ſtrains of like dreſs in other of his eſſays, and hearing him reported a more diligent reader of poets, than of politicians, I begun to think that the whole book might perhaps be intended a piece of poetry. The words are good, the fiction ſmooth and cleanly; there wanted only rhyme, and that they ſay, is beſtowed upon it lately. But to the argument.

"I ſtaid at Whitehall, till I was driven away by ſhame more than fear." I retract not what I thought of the fiction, yet here, I muſt confeſs, it lies too open. In his meſſages and declarations, nay in the whole chapter next but one before this, he affirms that "the danger wherein his wife, his children, and his own perſon" were by thoſe tumults, was the main cauſe that drove him from Whitehall, and appeals to God as witneſs: he affirms here that it was "ſhame more than fear." And Digby, who knew his mind as well as any, tells his new-liſted guard, "that the principal cauſe of his majeſty's going thence, was to ſave them from being trod in the dirt." From whence we may diſcern what falſe and frivolous excuſes are avowed for truth, either in thoſe declarations, or in this penitential book. Our forefathers were of that courage and ſeverity of zeal to juſtice and their native liberty, againſt the proud contempt and miſrule of their kings, that when Richard the Second departed but from a committee of lords who ſate preparing matter for the parliament not yet aſſembled, to the removal of his evil counſellors, they firſt vanquiſhed and put to flight Robert de Vere his chief favourite, and then coming up to London with a huge army, required the king then withdrawn for fear, but no further off than the Tower, to come to Weſtminſter. Which he refuſing, they told him flatly, that unleſs he came they would chuſe another. So high a crime it was accounted then for kings to abſent themſelves, not from a parliament, which none ever durſt, but from any meeting of his peers and counſellors which did but tend towards a parliament. Much leſs would they have ſuffered that a king for ſuch trivial and various pretences, one while for fear of tumults, another while "for ſhame to ſee them," ſhould leave his regal ſtation, and the whole kingdom bleeding to death of thoſe wounds which his own unſkilful and perverſe government had inflicted.

Shame then it was that drove him from the parliament, but the ſhame of what? Was it the ſhame of his manifold errors and miſdeeds, and to ſee how weakly he had played the king? No, "but to ſee the barbarous rudeneſs of thoſe tumults to demand any thing." We have ſtarted here another, and I believe the trueſt cauſe of his deſerting the parliament. The worſt and ſtrangeſt of that "Any-thing" which the people then demanded, was but the unlording of biſhops, and expelling them the houſe, and the reducing of Church diſcipline to a conformity with other proteſtant churches, this was the barbariſm of thoſe tumults and that he might avoid the granting of thoſe honeſt and pious demands, as well demanded by the parliament as the people, for this very cauſe more than for fear, by his own confeſſion here, he left the city, and in a moſt tempeſtuous ſeaſon forſook the helm and ſteerage of the commonwealth. This was that terrible "Any-thing" from which his Conſcience and his Reaſon choſe to run rather than not deny. To be importuned the removing of evil counſellors, and other grievances in Church and ſtate, was to him "an intolerable oppreſſion." If the people's demanding were ſo burdenſome to him, what was his denial and delay of juſtice to them?

But as the demands of his people were to him a burden and oppreſſion, ſo was the advice of his parliament eſteemed a bondage; "Whoſe agreeing votes," as he affirms, "were not by any law or reaſon concluſive to his judgment." For the law, it ordains a parliament to adviſe him in his great affairs; but if it ordain alſo that the ſingle judgment of a king ſhall out-ballance all the wiſdom of his parliament, it ordains that which fruſtrates the end of its own ordaining. For where the king's judgment may diſſent, to the deſtruction, as it may happen, both of himſelf and the kingdom, there advice, and no further, is a moſt inſufficient and fruſtraneous means to be provided by law in caſes of ſo high concernment. *And where the main and principal law of common preſervation againſt tyranny is left ſo fruitleſs and infirm, there it muſt needs follow, that all leſſer laws are to their ſeveral ends and purpoſes much more weak and ineffectual. For that nation would deſerve to be renowned and chronicled for folly and ſtupidity, that ſhould by law provide force againſt private and petty wrongs, advice only againſt tyranny and public ruin.* It being therefore moſt unlike a law, to ordain a remedy ſo ſlender and unlawlike, to be the utmoſt means of all public ſafety or prevention,* as advice is, which may at any time be rejected by the ſole judgment of one man, the king, and ſo unlike the law of England, which lawyers ſay is the quinteſſence of reaſon *and mature wiſdom*; we may conclude that the king's negative voice was never any law, but an abſurd and reaſonleſs cuſtom, begotten and grown up either from the flattery of baſeſt times, or the uſurpation of immoderate princes. Thus much to the law of it, by a better evidence than rolls and records, reaſon.

But is it poſſible he ſhould pretend alſo to reaſon, that the judgment of one man, not as a wiſe or good man, but as a king, and oft-times a wilful, proud, and wicked king, ſhould outweigh the prudence and all the virtue of an elected parliament? What an abuſive thing were it then to ſummon parliaments, that by the major part of voices greateſt matters may be there debated and reſolved, whenas one ſingle voice after that ſhall daſh all their reſolutions?

He attempts to give a reaſon why it ſhould, "Becauſe the whole parliament repreſents not him in any kind." But mark how little he advances, for if the parliament repreſent the whole kingdom, as is ſure enough they do, then doth the king repreſent only himſelf; and if a king without his kingdom be in a civil ſenſe nothing, then without or againſt the repreſentative of his whole kingdom, he himſelf repreſents nothing, and by conſequence his judgment and his negative is as good as nothing. and though we ſhould allow him to be ſomething, yet not equal † or comparable to the whole kingdom, and ſo neither to them *who* repreſent it *much leſs that one ſyllable of his breath put into the ſcales ſhould be more ponderous than the joint voice and efficacy of a whole parliament, aſſembled by election, and endued with the plenipotence of a free nation, to make laws, not to be denied laws, and with no more, but no, a ſleeveleſs reaſon in the moſt preſſing times of danger and diſturbance to be ſent home fruſtrate and remedileſs*

Yet here he maintains, "to be no further bound to agree with the votes of both houſes, than he ſees them to agree with the will of God, with his juſt rights as a king, and the general good of his people." As to the freedom of his agreeing or not agreeing, limited with due bounds, no man reprehends it, this is the queſtion here, or the miracle rather, why his only not agreeing ſhould lay a negative bar and inhibition upon that which is agreed to by a whole parliament, though never ſo conducing to the public good or ſafety? To know the will of God better than his whole kingdom, whence ſhould he have it? Certainly court breeding and his perpetual converſation with flatterers, was but a bad ſchool To judge of his own rights could not belong to him, who had no right by law in any court to judge of ſo much as felony or treaſon, being

* Second edition has it *Of all our ſafety or prevention.* † Second edition has *equivalent*

held

held a party in both theſe caſes, much more in this; and his rights however ſhould give place to the general good, for which end all his rights were given him. Laſtly, to ſuppoſe a clearer inſight and diſcerning of the general good, allotted to his own ſingular judgment, than to the parliament and all the people, and from that ſelf-opinion of diſcerning, to deny them that good which they, being all freemen, ſeek earneſtly and call for, is an arrogance and iniquity beyond imagination rude and unreaſonable; they undoubtedly having moſt authority to judge of the public good, who for that purpoſe are choſen out and ſent by the people to adviſe him. And if it may be in him to ſee oft "the major part of them not in the right," had it not been more his modeſty to have doubted their ſeeing him more often in the wrong?

He paſſes to another reaſon of his denials, "becauſe of ſome men's hydropic unſatiableneſs, and thirſt of aſking, the more they drank, whom no fountain of regal bounty was able to overcome." A compariſon more properly beſtowed on thoſe that came to guzzle in his wine-cellar, than on a freeborn people that came to claim in parliament their rights and liberties, which a king ought therefore to grant, becauſe of right demanded; not to deny them for fear his bounty ſhould be exhauſted, which in theſe demands (to continue the ſame metaphor) was not ſo much as broached, it being his duty, not his bounty to grant theſe things. *He who thus refuſes to give us law, in that refuſal gives us another law, which is his will, another name alſo, and another condition, of freemen to become his vaſſals*

Putting off the courtier, he now puts on the philoſopher, and ſententiouſly diſputes to this effect, "That reaſon ought to be uſed to men, force and terror to beaſts; that he deſerves to be a ſlave, who captivates the rational ſovereignty of his ſoul and liberty of his will to compulſion, that he would not forfeit that freedom which cannot be denied him as a king, becauſe it belongs to him as a man and a chriſtian, though to preſerve his kingdom, but rather die enjoying the empire of his ſoul, than live in ſuch a vaſſalage, as not to uſe his reaſon and conſcience to like or diſlike as a king" Which words, of themſelves, as far as they are ſenſe, good and philoſophical, yet in the mouth of him who to engroſs this common liberty to himſelf, would tread down all other men into the condition of ſlaves and beaſts, they quite loſe their commendation. He confeſſes a rational ſovereignty of ſoul, and freedom of will in every man, and yet with an implicit repugnancy would have his reaſon the ſovereign of that ſovereignty, and would captivate and make uſeleſs that natural freedom of will in all other men but himſelf But them that yield him this obedience he ſo well rewards, as to pronounce them worthy to be ſlaves They who have loſt all to be his ſubjects, may ſtoop and take up the reward What that freedom is, which "cannot be denied him as a king, becauſe it belongs to him as a man and a chriſtian," I underſtand not. If it be his negative voice, it concludes all men who have not ſuch a negative as his againſt a whole parliament, to be neither men nor chriſtians And what was he himſelf then, all this while that we denied it him as a king? Will he ſay that he enjoyed within himſelf the leſs freedom for that? Might not he, both as a man and as a chriſtian, have reigned within himſelf in full ſovereignty of ſoul, no man repining, but that his outward and imperious will muſt invade the civil liberties of a nation? Did we therefore not permit him to uſe his reaſon or his conſcience, not permitting him to bereave us the uſe of ours? And might not he have enjoyed both as a king, governing us as free-men by what laws we ourſelves would be governed? It was not the inward uſe of his reaſon and *of* his conſcience that would content him, but to uſe them both as a law over all his ſubjects, "in whatever he declared as a king to like or diſlike" Which uſe of reaſon, moſt reaſonleſs and unconſcionable, is the utmoſt that any tyrant ever pretended over his vaſſals.

In all wiſe nations the legiſlative power, and the judicial execution of that power, have been moſt commonly diſtinct, and in ſeveral hands; but yet the former ſupreme, the other ſubordinate. If then the king be only ſet up to execute the law, which is indeed the higheſt of his office, he ought no more to make or forbid the making of any law agreed upon in parliament, than other inferior judges, who are his deputies. Neither can he more reject a law offered him by the commons, than he can new make a law which they reject. And yet the more to credit and uphold his cauſe, he would ſeem to have philoſophy on his ſide, ſtraining her wiſe dictates to unphiloſophical purpoſes. But when kings come ſo low, as to fawn upon philoſophy, which before they neither valued nor underſtood, it is a ſign that fails not, they are then put to their laſt trump. And philoſophy as well requites them, by not ſuffering her golden ſayings either to become their lips, or to be uſed as maſks and colours of injurious and violent deeds. So that what they preſume to borrow from her ſage and virtuous rules, like the riddle of Sphinx not underſtood, breaks the neck of their own cauſe.

But now again to politics. "He cannot think the Majeſty of the crown of England to be bound by any coronation oath in a blind and brutiſh formality, to conſent to whatever its ſubjects in parliament ſhall require." What tyrant could preſume to ſay more, when he meant to kick down all law, government, and bond of oath? But why he ſo deſires to abſolve himſelf the oath of his coronation, would be worth the knowing. It cannot but be yielded that the oath which binds him to performance of his truſt, ought in reaſon to contain the ſum of what his chief truſt and office is. But if it neither do enjoin, nor mention to him, as a part of his duty, the making or the marring of any law, or ſcrap of law, but requires only his aſſent to thoſe laws which the people have already choſen, or ſhall chuſe (for ſo both the Latin of that oath, and the old Engliſh, and all reaſon admits, that the people ſhould not loſe under a new king what freedom they had before) then that negative voice ſo contended for, to deny the paſſing of any law, which the commons chuſe, is both againſt the oath of his coronation, and his kingly office. And if the king may deny to paſs what the parliament hath choſen to be a law, then doth the king make himſelf ſuperior to his whole kingdom; which not only the general maxims of policy gainſay, but even our own ſtanding laws, as hath been cited to him in remonſtrances heretofore, that "the king hath two ſuperiors, the law, and his court of parliament." But this he counts to be a blind and brutiſh formality, whether it be law, or oath, or his duty, and thinks to turn it off with wholeſome words and phraſes, which he then firſt learnt of the honeſt people, when they were ſo often compelled to uſe them againſt thoſe more truly blind and brutiſh formalities thruſt upon us by his own command, *not in civil matters only, but in ſpiritual. And if his oath to perform what the people require, when they crown him, be in his eſteem a brutiſh formality, then doubtleſs theſe other oaths of allegiance and ſupremacy, taken abſolute on our part, may moſt juſtly appear to us in all reſpects as brutiſh and as formal, and ſo by his own ſentence no more binding to us than his oath to him*.

As for his inſtance, in caſe "He and the Houſe of Peers attempted to enjoin the Houſe of Commons, it bears no equality, for he and the peers repreſent but themſelves, the commons are the whole kingdom.

Thus he concludes "his oath to be fully diſcharged in governing by laws already made," as being not bound to paſs any new, "if his reaſon bids him deny." And ſo may infinite miſchiefs grow, *and he with a pernicious negative may deny us all things good, or juſt, or ſafe, whereof our anceſtors in times much differing from ours, had either no foreſight, or no occaſion to foreſee*, while our general good and ſafety ſhall depend upon the private and overweening reaſon of one obſtinate man, who againſt all the kingdom, if he liſt, will interpret both the law and his oath of coronation by the tenor of his own will. Which he himſelf confeſſes to be an arbitrary power, yet doubts not in his argument to imply, as if he thought it more fit the parliament ſhould be ſubject to his will, than he to their advice, a man neither by nature nor by nurture wiſe. How is it poſſible that he in whom ſuch principles as theſe were ſo deep rooted, could ever, though reſtored again, have reigned otherwiſe than tyrannically?

He

He objects, "That force was but a ſlaviſh method to diſpel his error." But how often ſhall it be anſwered him, that no force was uſed to diſpel the error out of his head, but to drive it from off our necks? for his error was imperious, and would command all other men to renounce their own reaſon and underſtanding, till they periſhed under the injunction of his all-ruling error.

He alledges the uprightneſs of his intentions to excuſe his poſſible failings, a poſition falſe both in law and divinity: yea, contrary to his own better principles, who affirms in the twelfth chapter, that "the goodneſs of a man's intention will not excuſe the ſcandal and contagion of his example." His not knowing, through the corruption of flattery and court-principles, what he ought to have known, will not excuſe his not doing what he ought to have done; no more than the ſmall ſkill of him who undertakes to be a Pilot, will excuſe him to be miſled by any wandring ſtar miſtaken for the Pole. But let his intentions be never ſo upright, what is that to us? what anſwer for the reaſon and the national rights which God hath given us, if having parliaments, and laws, and the power of making more to avoid miſchief, we ſuffer one man's blind intentions to lead us all with our eyes open to manifeſt deſtruction?

And if arguments prevail not with ſuch a one, force is well uſed, not "to carry on the weakneſs of our counſels, or to convince his error," as he ſurmiſes, but to acquit and reſcue our own reaſon, our own conſciences from the force and prohibition laid by his uſurping error upon our liberties and underſtandings.

"Never any thing pleaſed him more, than when his judgment concurred with theirs." That was to the applauſe of his own judgment, and would as well have pleaſed any ſelf-conceited man.

"Yea, in many things he choſe rather to deny himſelf than them." That is to ſay, in trifles. For "of his own intereſts" and perſonal rights he conceives himſelf "Maſter." To part with, if he pleaſe, not to conteſt for, againſt the kingdom, which is greater than he, whoſe rights are all ſubordinate to the kingdom's good: and "in what concerns truth, juſtice, the right of church, or his crown, no man ſhall gain his conſent againſt his mind." What can be left then for a parliament, but to ſit like images, while he ſtill thus either with incomparable arrogance aſſumes to himſelf the beſt ability of judging for other men what is truth, juſtice, goodneſs, what his own *and* the church's right, or with unſufferable tyranny reſtrains all men from the enjoyment of any good, which his judgment, though erroneous, thinks not fit to grant them, notwithſtanding that the law and his coronal oath requires his undeniable aſſent to what laws the parliament agree upon.

"He had rather wear a crown of thorns with our Saviour." Many would be all one with our Saviour, whom our Saviour will not know. They who govern ill thoſe kingdoms which they had a right to, have to our Saviour's crown of thorns no right at all. Thorns they may find enow of their own gathering, and their own twiſting; for thorns and ſnares, ſaith Solomon, are in the way of the froward: but to wear them, as our Saviour wore them, is not given to them that ſuffer by their own demerits. Nor is a crown of gold his due, who cannot firſt wear a crown of lead, not only for the weight of that great office, but for the compliance which it ought to have with them who are to counſel him, which here he terms in ſcorn "An imbiſeel flexibleneſs to the various and oft contrary dictates of any factions," meaning his parliament; for the queſtion hath been all this while between them two. And to his parliament, though a numerous and choice aſſembly of whom the land thought wiſeſt, he imputes, rather than to himſelf, "want of reaſon, neglect of the public, intereſt of parties, and particularity of private will and paſſion," but with what modeſty or likelihood of truth, it will be wearisome to repeat ſo often.

He concludes with a ſentence fair in ſeeming, but fallacious. For if the conſcience be ill edified, the reſolution may more beſit a fooliſh than a chriſtian king, to prefer a ſelf-

ſelf-willed conſcience before a kingdom's good; eſpecially in the denial of that which law and his regal office by oath bids him grant to his parliament and whole kingdom rightfully demanding. For we may obſerve him throughout the diſcourſe to aſſert his negative power againſt the whole kingdom; now under the ſpecious plea of his conſcience and his reaſon, but heretofore in a louder note, "Without us, or againſt our conſent, the votes of either or of both houſes together, muſt not, cannot, ſhall not." Declar. May 4. 1642.

With theſe and the like deceivable doctrines, he levens alſo his prayer.

VII. Upon the Queen's departure.

TO this argument we ſhall ſoon have ſaid; for what concerns it us to hear a huſband divulge his houſhold privacies, extolling to others the virtues of his wife? an infirmity not ſeldom incident to thoſe who have leaſt cauſe. But how good ſhe was a wife, was to himſelf, and be it left to his own fancy; how bad a ſubject, is not much diſputed. And being ſuch, it need be made no wonder, though ſhe left a proteſtant kingdom with as little honour as her mother left a popiſh.

That this "is the firſt example of any proteſtant ſubjects that have taken up arms againſt their king a proteſtant," can be to proteſtants no diſhonour, when it ſhall be heard that he firſt levied war on them, and to the intereſt of papiſts more than of proteſtants. He might have given yet the precedence of making war upon him to the ſubjects of his own nation, who had twice oppoſed him in the open field long ere the Engliſh found it neceſſary to do the like. And how groundleſs, how diſſembled is that fear, leſt ſhe, who for ſo many years had been averſe from the religion of her huſband, and every year more and more, before theſe diſturbances broke out, ſhould for them be now the more alienated from that to which we never heard ſhe was inclined? But if the fear of her delinquency, and that juſtice which the proteſtants demanded on her, was any cauſe of her alienating the more, to have gained her by indirect means had been no advantage to religion, much leſs then was the detriment to loſe her further off. It had been happy if his own actions had not given cauſe of more ſcandal to the proteſtants, than what they did againſt her could juſtly ſcandalize any papiſt.

Them who accuſed her, well enough known to be the parliament, he cenſures for "Men yet to ſeek their Religion, whether Doctrine, Diſcipline, or Good Manners," the reſt he ſoothes with the name of true Engliſh proteſtants, a meer ſchiſmatical name, yet he ſo great an enemy of ſchiſm.

He aſcribes "rudeneſs and barbarity, worſe than Indian," to the Engliſh parliament, and "all virtue" to his wife, in ſtrains that come almoſt to ſonnetting: how fit to govern men, undervaluing and aſperſing the great council of his kingdom, in compariſon of one woman! Examples are not far to ſeek, how great miſchief and diſhonour hath befallen nations under the government of effeminate and uxorious magiſtrates, who being themſelves governed and overſwayed at home under a feminine uſurpation, cannot but be far ſhort of ſpirit and authority without doors, to govern a whole nation.

"Her tarrying here he could not think ſafe among them who were ſhaking hands with allegiance, to lay faſter hold on religion," and taxes them of a duty rather than a crime, it being juſt to obey God rather than man, and impoſſible to ſerve two maſters. I would they had quite ſhaken off what they ſtood ſhaking hands with, the fault was in their courage, not in their cauſe.

In his prayer he prays that "the diſloyalty of his proteſtant ſubjects may not be a hindrance to her love of the true religion," and never prays, that the diſſoluteneſs of his

his court, the ſcandals of his clergy, the unſoundneſs of his *own* judgment, the luke-warmneſs of his life, his letter of compliance to the pope, his permitting agents at Rome, the pope's Nuncio, *and her jeſuited mother* here, may not be found in the ſight of God far greater hindrances to her converſion.

But this had been a ſubtle prayer indeed, and well prayed, though as duly as a Pater-noſter, if it could have charmed us to ſit ſtill, and have religion and our liberties one by one ſnatched from us, for fear leſt riſing to defend ourſelves, we ſhould fright the Queen, a ſtiff papiſt, from turning proteſtant! As if the way to make his queen a proteſtant, had been to make his ſubjects more than half-way papiſts.

He prays next "that his conſtancy may be an antidote againſt the poiſon of other men's example." His conſtancy in what? Not in religion, for it is openly known that her religion wrought more upon him, than his religion upon her; and his open favouring of papiſts, and his hatred of them called puritans, *(the miniſters alſo that prayed in churches for her converſion, being checked from court)* made moſt men ſuſpect ſhe had quite perverted him. But what is it that the blindneſs of hypocriſy dares not do? It dares pray, and thinks to hide that from the eyes of God, which it cannot hide from the open view of man.

VIII. Upon his Repulſe at Hull, and the Fate of the Hothams.

HULL, a town of great ſtrength and opportunity both to ſea and land-affairs, was at that time the magazine of all thoſe arms which the king had bought with money moſt illegally extorted from his ſubjects of England, to uſe in a cauſeleſs and moſt unjuſt civil war againſt his ſubjects of Scotland. The king in high diſcontent and anger had left the parliament, and was gone toward the North, the queen into Holland, where ſhe pawned and ſet to ſale the crown-jewels (a crime heretofore counted treaſonable in kings) and to what intent theſe ſums were raiſed, the parliament was not ignorant. His going northward in ſo high a chaſe, they doubted was to poſſeſs himſelf of that ſtrength, which the ſtore-houſe and ſituation of Hull might add ſuddenly to his malignant party. Having firſt therefore in many petitions earneſtly prayed him to diſpoſe and ſettle, with conſent of both houſes, the military power in truſty hands, and he as oft refuſing, they were neceſſitated by the turbulence and danger of thoſe times to put the kingdom by their own authority into a poſture of defence; and very timely ſent Sir John Hotham, a member of the houſe, and knight of that county, to take Hull into his cuſtody, and ſome of the trained-bands to his aſſiſtance. *For beſides the general danger, they had, before the king's going to York, notice given them of his private commiſſions to the earl of Newcaſtle, and to colonel Legg, one of thoſe employed to bring the army up againſt the parliament; who had already made ſome attempts, and the former of them under a diſguiſe, to ſurprize that place for the king's party.* And letters of the lord Digby were intercepted, wherein was wiſhed that the king would declare himſelf, and retire to ſome ſafe place, other information came from abroad, that Hull was the place deſigned for ſome new enterprize. *And accordingly Digby himſelf not long after, with many other commanders, and much foreign ammunition, landed in thoſe parts.* But theſe attempts not ſucceeding, and that town being now in cuſtody of the parliament, he ſends a meſſage to them, that he had firmly reſolved to go in perſon into Ireland, to chaſtiſe thoſe wicked rebels (for theſe and worſe words he then gave them) and that towards this work he intended forthwith to raiſe by his commiſſions, in the counties near Weſtcheſter, a guard for his own perſon, conſiſting of 2000 foot, and 200 horſe, that ſhould be armed from his magazine at Hull. On the other ſide, the parliament, foreſeeing the king's drift, about the ſame time ſend him a petition, that they might have leave for neceſſary cauſes to remove the magazine of Hull to the tower of London; to which the king returns his denial; and ſoon after going to Hull, attended with about 400 horſe, requires the governor to deliver him up the town: whereof the governor beſought humbly to be excuſed, till he could ſend notice to the parliament who had intruſted him; whereat the king much incenſed, proclaims him traitor before the town-walls, and gives immediate order to ſtop all paſſages between him and the parliament. Yet he himſelf diſpatches poſt after poſt to demand juſtice, as upon a traitor; uſing a ſtrange iniquity to require juſtice upon him whom he then way-laid and debarred from his appearance. The parliament no ſooner underſtood what had paſſed, but they declare that Sir John Hotham had done no more than was his duty, and was therefore no traitor.

This relation being moſt true, proves that which is affirmed here to be moſt falſe, ſeeing the parliament, whom he accounts his "greateſt Enemies," had "more confidence to abet and own" what Sir John Hotham had done, than the king had confidence to let him anſwer in his own behalf.

To ſpeak of his patience, and in that ſolemn manner, he might better have forborne. "God knows," ſaith he, "it affected me more with ſorrow for others than with anger for myſelf, nor did the affront trouble me ſo much as their ſin." This is read, I doubt not, and believed: and as there is ſome uſe of every thing, ſo is there of this book, were it but to ſhew us, what a miſerable, credulous, deluded thing that creature is, which is called the vulgar, who notwithſtanding what they might know, will believe ſuch vain-glories as theſe. Did not that choleric and vengeful act of proclaiming him traitor before due proceſs of law, having been convinced ſo late before of his illegality with the five members, declare his anger to be incenſed? doth not his own relation confeſs as much? and his ſecond meſſage left him fuming three days after, and in plain words teſtifies "his impatience of delay" till Hotham be ſeverely puniſhed, for that which he there terms an inſupportable affront.

Surely if his ſorrow for Sir John Hotham's ſin were greater than his anger for the affront, it was an exceeding great ſorrow indeed, and wondrous charitable. But if it ſtirred him ſo vehemently to have Sir John Hotham puniſhed, and not at all, that we hear, to have him repent, it had a ſtrange operation to be called a ſorrow for his ſin. He who would perſuade us of his ſorrow for the ſins of other men, as they are ſins, not as they are ſinned againſt himſelf, muſt give us firſt ſome teſtimony of a ſorrow for his own ſins, and next for ſuch ſins of other men as cannot be ſuppoſed a direct injury to himſelf. But ſuch compunction in the king no man hath yet obſerved, and till then, his ſorrow for Sir John Hotham's ſin will be called no other than the reſentment of his repulſe, and his labour to have the ſinner only puniſhed, will be called by a right name, his revenge.

And "the hand of that cloud which caſt all ſoon after into darkneſs and diſorder," was his own hand. For aſſembling the inhabitants of Yorkſhire and other counties, horſe and foot, firſt under colour of a new guard to his perſon, ſoon after, being ſupplied with ammunition from Holland, bought with the crown jewels, he begins an open war by laying ſiege to Hull: which town was not his own, but the kingdom's, and the arms there, public arms, bought with the public money, or not his own. Yet had they been his own by as good right as the private houſe and arms of any man are his own, to uſe either of them in a way not private, but ſuſpicious to the commonwealth, no law permits. But the king had no propriety at all either in Hull or in the magazine: ſo that the following Maxims which he cites "of bold and diſloyal undertakers," may belong more juſtly to whom he leaſt meant them. After this he again relapſes into the praiſe of his patience at Hull, and by his overtalking of it, ſeems to doubt either his own conſcience, or the hardneſs of other men's belief. To me, the more he praiſes it in himſelf, the more he ſeems to ſuſpect that in very deed it was not in him, and that the lookers on ſo likewiſe thought.

Thus much of what he ſuffered by Hotham, and with what patience; now of what Hotham ſuffered, as he judges, for oppoſing him: "He could not but obſerve how God not long after pleaded and avenged his cauſe." Moſt men are too apt, and commonly the worſt of men, ſo to interpret and expound the judgments of God, and all other events of Providence or chance, as makes moſt to the juſtifying of their own cauſe, though never ſo evil; and attribute all to the particular favour of God towards them. Thus when Saul heard that David was in Keilah, "God," ſaith he, "hath delivered him into my hands, for he is ſhut in." But how far that king was deceived in his thought that God was favouring to his cauſe, that ſtory unfolds; and how little reaſon this king had to impute the death of Hotham to God's avengement of his repulſe at Hull, may eaſily be ſeen. For while Hotham continued faithful to his truſt, no man more ſafe, more ſucceſsful, more in reputation than he: But from the time he firſt ſought to make his peace with the king, and to betray into his hands that town, into which before he had denied him entrance, nothing proſpered with him. Certainly had God purpoſed him ſuch an end for his oppoſition to the king, he would not have deferred to puniſh him till then, when of an enemy he was changed to be the king's friend, nor have made his repentance and amendment the occaſion of his ruin. How much more likely is it, ſince he fell into the act of diſloyalty to his charge, that the judgment of God concurred with the puniſhment of man, and juſtly cut him off for revolting to the king? To give the world an example, that glorious deeds done to ambitious ends, find reward anſwerable, not to their outward ſeeming, but to their inward ambition In the mean while, what thanks he had from the king for revolting to his cauſe, and what good opinion for dying in his ſervice, they who have ventured like him, or intend, may here take notice

He proceeds to declare, not only in general wherefore God's judgment was upon Hotham, but undertakes by fancies, and alluſions, to give a criticiſm upon every particular: "That his head was divided from his body, becauſe his heart was divided from the king, two heads cut off in one family for affronting the head of the commonwealth, the eldeſt ſon being infected with the ſin of *his* father, againſt the father of his country." Theſe petty gloſſes and conceits on the high and ſecret judgments of God, beſides the boldneſs of unwarrantable commenting, are ſo weak and ſhallow, and ſo like the quibbles of a court-ſermon, that we may ſafely reckon them either fetched from ſuch a pattern, or that the hand of ſome houſhold prieſt foiſted them in, leſt the world ſhould forget how much he was a diſciple of thoſe cymbal doctors. But that argument by which the author would commend them to us, diſcredits them the more. For if they be ſo "obvious to every fancy," the more likely to be erroneous, and to miſconceive the mind of thoſe high ſecrecies, whereof they preſume to determine. For God judges not by human fancy

But however God judged Hotham, yet he had the king's pity: but mark the reaſon how prepoſterous, ſo far he had his pity, "as he thought he at firſt acted more againſt the light of his conſcience than many other men in the ſame cauſe." Queſtionleſs they who act againſt conſcience, whether at the bar of human, or divine juſtice, are pitied leaſt of all. Theſe are the common grounds and verdicts of nature, whereof when he who hath the judging of a whole nation, is found deſtitute, under ſuch a governor that nation muſt needs be miſerable.

By the way he jerks at "ſome men's reforming to models of religion, and that they think all is gold of piety that doth but gliſter with a ſhew of zeal." We know his meaning, and apprehend how little hope there could be of him from ſuch language as this But are ſure that the piety of his prelatic model, gliſtered more upon the poſts and pillars which their zeal and fervency gilded over, than in the true works of ſpiritual edification.

"He is ſorry that Hotham felt the juſtice of others, and fell not rather into the hands of his mercy." But to clear that, he ſhould have ſhewn us what mercy he had ever uſed to ſuch as fell into his hands before, rather than what mercy he intended to ſuch as never could come to aſk it. Whatever mercy one man might have expected, it is too well known the whole nation found none; though they beſought it often, and ſo humbly, but had been ſwallowed up in blood and ruin, to ſet his private will above the parliament, had not his ſtrength failed him. "Yet clemency he counts a debt, which he ought to pay to thoſe that crave it; ſince we pay not any thing to God for his mercy but prayers and praiſes" By this reaſon we ought as freely to pay all things to all men; for of all that we receive from God, what do we pay for, more than prayers and praiſes? we looked for the diſcharge of his office, the payment of his duty to the kingdom, and are paid court-payment with empty ſentences that have the ſound of gravity, but the ſignificance of nothing pertinent

Yet again after his mercy paſt and granted, he returns back to give ſentence upon Hotham, and whom he tells us he would ſo fain have ſaved alive, him he never leaves killing with *a* repeated condemnation, though dead long ſince. It was ill that ſomebody ſtood not near to whiſper him, that a reiterating judge is worſe than a tormentor. "He pities him, he rejoices not, he pities him" again, but ſtill is ſure to brand him at the tail of his pity with ſome ignominious mark, either of ambition or diſloyalty. And with a kind of cenſorious pity, aggravates rather than leſſens or conceals the fault: To pity thus, is to triumph.

He aſſumes to foreknow, that "after-times will diſpute, whether Hotham were more infamous at Hull, or at Tower-hill." What knew he of after-times, who while he ſits judging and cenſuring without end, the fate of that unhappy father and his ſon at Tower-hill, knew not that the like fate attended him before his own palace-gate, and as little knew whether after times reſerve *not* a greater infamy *to the ſtory of* his own life and reign?

He ſays but over again in his prayer, what his ſermon hath preached. how acceptably to thoſe in Heaven, we leave to be decided by that precept which forbids "vain Repetitions." Sure enough it lies as heavy as he can lay it upon the head of poor Hotham.

Needs he will faſten upon God a piece of revenge as done for his ſake, and takes it for a favour, before he know it was intended him which in his cloſet had been excuſable, but in a written and publiſhed prayer, too preſumptuous. Eccleſiaſtes hath a right name for ſuch kind of ſacrifices.

Going on he prays thus, "Let not thy juſtice prevent the objects and opportunities of my mercy." To folly, or to blaſphemy, or to both ſhall we impute this? Shall the juſtice of God give place, and ſerve to glorify the mercies of a man? All other men who know what they aſk, deſire of God that their doings may tend to his glory, but in this prayer, God is required that his juſtice would forbear to prevent, and as good have ſaid to intrench upon the glory of a man's mercy If God forbear his juſtice, it muſt be, ſure, to the magnifying of his own mercy: *How then can any mortal man, without preſumption little leſs than impious, take the boldneſs to aſk that glory out of his hand?* It may be doubted now by them who underſtand religion, whether the king were more unfortunate in this his prayer, or Hotham in thoſe his ſufferings.

IX. Upon the liſting and raiſing Armies, &c.

IT were an endleſs work to walk ſide by ſide with the verboſity of this chapter; only to what already hath not been ſpoken, convenient anſwer ſhall be given. He begins again with tumults, all demonſtration of the people's love and loyalty to the parliament

ment was tumult; their petitioning, tumult; their defenſive armies were but liſted Tumults; and will take no notice that thoſe about him, thoſe in a time of peace liſted into his own houſe, *were the beginners of all theſe tumults*; abuſing and aſſaulting not only ſuch as came peaceably to the parliament at London, but thoſe that came petitioning to the king himſelf at York. Neither did they abſtain from doing violence and outrage to the meſſengers ſent from parliament; he himſelf either countenancing or conniving at them

He ſuppoſes that "his receſs gave us confidence that he might be conquered." Other men ſuppoſe both that and all things elſe, who knew him neither by nature warlike, nor experienced, nor fortunate; ſo far was any man that diſcerned aught, from eſteeming him unconquerable; yet ſuch are readieſt to imbroil others.

"But he had a ſoul invincible." What praiſe is that? The ſtomach of a child is ofttimes invincible to all correction. The unteachable man hath a ſoul to all reaſon and good advice invincible; and he who is intractable, he whom nothing can perſuade, may boaſt himſelf invincible, whenas *in ſome things to be overcome, is more honeſt and* laudable than to conquer

He labours to have it thought that "his fearing God more than man" was the ground of his ſufferings; but he ſhould have known that a good principle not rightly underſtood may prove as hurtful as a bad; and his fear of God may be as faulty as a blind zeal. He pretended to fear God more than the parliament, who never urged him to do otherwiſe, he ſhould alſo have feared God more than he did his courtiers, and the biſhops, who drew him, as they pleaſed, to things inconſiſtent with the fear of God. Thus boaſted Saul to have "performed the commandment of God," and ſtood in it againſt Samuel; but it was found at length that he had feared the people more than God, in ſaving thoſe fat oxen for the worſhip of God which were appointed for deſtruction. Not much unlike, if not much worſe, was that fact of his, who for fear to diſpleaſe his court and mungrel clergy, with the diſſoluteſt of the people, upheld in the church of God, while his power laſted, thoſe beaſts of Amalec, the prelates, againſt the advice of his parliament and the example of all reformation; in this more inexcuſable than Saul, that Saul was at length convinced, he to the hour of death fixed in his falſe perſuaſion; and ſoothes himſelf in the flattering peace of an erroneous and obdurate conſcience, ſinging to his ſoul vain pſalms of exultation, as if the parliament had aſſailed his reaſon with the force of arms, and not he on the contrary their reaſon with his arms, which hath been proved already, and ſhall be more hereafter.

He twits them with "his Acts of Grace," proud, and un-ſelf-knowing words in the mouth of any king who affects not to be a God, and ſuch as ought to be as odious in the ears of a free nation For if they were unjuſt acts, why did he grant them as of grace? If juſt, it was not of his grace, but of his duty and his oath to grant them.

"A glorious king he would be, though by his ſufferings:" But that can never be to him, whoſe ſufferings are his own doings He feigns "a hard choice" put upon him, "either to kill his ſubjects, or be killed." Yet never was king leſs in danger of any violence from his ſubjects, till he unſheathed his ſword againſt them, nay long after that time, when he had ſpilt the blood of thouſands, they had ſtill his perſon in a fooliſh veneration.

He complains, "That civil war muſt be the fruits of his ſeventeen years reigning with ſuch a meaſure of juſtice, peace, plenty, and religion, as all nations either admired or envied." For the juſtice we had, let the council-table, ſtar-chamber, high-commiſſion ſpeak the praiſe of it; not forgetting the unprincely uſage, and, as far as might be, the aboliſhing of parliaments, the diſplacing of honeſt judges, the ſale of offices, bribery and exaction, not found out to be puniſhed, but to be ſhared in with impunity for the time to come. Who can number the extortions, the oppreſſions, the publick robberies and rapines committed on the ſubject both by ſea and land under various pretences?

tences? their poſſeſſions alſo taken from them, one while as foreſt-land, another while as crown-land, nor were their goods exempted, no not the bullion in the mint, piracy was become a project owned and authorized againſt the ſubject.

For the peace we had, what peace was that which drew out the Engliſh to a needleſs and diſhonourable voyage againſt the Spaniard at Cales? Or that which lent our ſhipping to a treacherous and antichriſtian war againſt the poor proteſtants of Rochel our ſuppliants? What peace was that which fell to rob the French by Sea, to the imbarring of all our merchants in that kingdom? which brought forth that unbleſt expedition to the Iſle of Rhee, doubtful whether more calamitous in the ſucceſs or in the deſign, betraying all the flower of our military youth and beſt commanders to a ſhameful ſurpriſal and execution. This was the peace we had, and the peace we gave, whether to friends or to foes abroad. And if at home any peace *were* intended us, what meant thoſe Iriſh billeted ſoldiers in all parts of the kingdom, and the deſign of German horſe to ſubdue us in our peaceful houſes?

For our religion, where was there a more ignorant, profane, and vitious clergy, learned in nothing but the antiquity of their pride, their covetouſneſs and ſuperſtition? whoſe unſincere and levenous doctrine, corrupting the people, firſt taught them looſeneſs, then bondage, looſening them from all ſound knowledge and ſtrictneſs of life, the more to fit them for the bondage of tyranny and ſuperſtition. So that what was left us for other nations not to pity rather than admire or envy, all thoſe ſeventeen years, no wiſe man could ſee. For wealth and plenty in a land where juſtice reigns not, is no argument of a flouriſhing ſtate, but of a nearneſs rather to ruin or commotion.

Theſe were not "ſome miſcarriages" only of government, "which might eſcape," but a univerſal diſtemper, and reducement of law to arbitrary power, not through the evil counſels of "ſome men," but through the conſtant courſe and practice of all that were in higheſt favour. whoſe worſt actions *frequently avowing he took upon himſelf, and what faults did not yet ſeem in public to be originally his, ſuch care he took by profeſſing, and proclaiming openly, as made them all at length his own adopted ſins. The perſons alſo, when he could no longer protect, he eſteemed* and favoured to the end, but never otherwiſe than by conſtraint, *yielded* any of them to due puniſhment; thereby manifeſting that what they did, was by his own authority and approbation.

Yet here he aſks, "Whoſe innocent blood he hath ſhed, what widows or orphans tears can witneſs againſt him?" After the ſuſpected poiſoning of his father, not enquired into, but ſmothered up, and him protected and advanced to the very half of his kingdom, who was accuſed in parliament to be author of the fact, *(with much more evidence than duke Dudley, that falſe protector, is accuſed upon record to have poiſoned Edward the ſixth) after all his rage and perſecution,* after ſo many years of cruel war on his people in three kingdoms! Whence the author of "Truths manifeſt *," a Scotſman, not unacquainted with affairs, poſitively affirms, "That there hath been more chriſtian blood ſhed by the commiſſion, approbation, and connivance of king Charles, and his father James in the latter end of their reign, than in the ten Roman perſecutions." Not to ſpeak of thoſe many whippings, pillories, and other corporal inflictions wherewith his reign alſo before this war was not unbloody; ſome have died in priſon under cruel reſtraint, others in baniſhment, whoſe lives were ſhortened through the rigour of that perſecution wherewith ſo many years he infeſted the true church. And thoſe ſix members all men judged to have eſcaped no leſs than capital danger, whom he ſo greedily purſuing into the houſe of commons, had not there the forbearance to conceal how much it troubled him, "That the Birds were flown." If ſome vulture in the mountains could have opened his beak intelligibly and ſpoke, what fitter words could he have uttered at the loſs of his prey?

* The title of the treatiſe here referred to, is *Truth its manifeſt, or, a ſhort and true relation of divers main paſſages of things (in ſome whereof the* Scots *are particularly concerned) from the very firſt beginning of theſe unhappy troubles to this day* Publiſhed in 12mo, 1645. A reply to this was publiſhed in quarto, 1646, entitled, *Manifeſt Truths, or, an inverſion of truths manifeſt.*

The

The tyrant Nero, though not yet deſerving that name, ſet his hand ſo unwillingly to the execution of a condemned perſon, as to wiſh "he had not known letters." Certainly for a king himſelf to charge his ſubjects with high treaſon, and ſo vehemently to proſecute them in his own cauſe, as to do the office of a Searcher, argued in him no great averſation from ſhedding blood, were it but to "ſatisfy his anger," and that revenge was no unpleaſing morſel to him, whereof he himſelf thought not much to be ſo diligently his own caterer. But we inſiſt rather upon what was actual, than what was probable.

He now falls to examine the cauſes of this war, as a difficulty which he had long "ſtudied" to find out "It was not," ſaith he, "my withdrawing from Whitehall; for no account in reaſon could be given of thoſe tumults, where an orderly guard was granted." But if it be a moſt certain truth, that the parliament could never yet obtain of him any guard fit to be confided in, then by his own confeſſion ſome account of thoſe pretended tumults "may in reaſon be given," and both concerning them and *the* guards enough hath been ſaid already.

"Whom did he protect againſt the juſtice of parliament?" Whom did he not to his utmoſt power? Endeavouring to have reſcued Strafford from their juſtice, though with the deſtruction of them and the city, to that end expreſly commanding the admittance of new ſoldiers into the tower, raiſed by Suckling and other conſpirators, under pretence for the Portugal, *though that ambaſſador, being ſent to, utterly denied to know of any ſuch commiſſion from his maſter. And yet that liſting continued:* not to repeat his other plot of bringing up the two armies. But what can be diſputed with ſuch a king, in whoſe mouth and opinion the parliament itſelf was never but a Faction, and their juſtice no juſtice, but "the dictates and overſwaying inſolence of tumults and rabbles?" and under that excuſe avouches himſelf openly the general patron of moſt notorious delinquents, and approves their flight out of the land, whoſe crimes were ſuch, as that the juſteſt and the faireſt trial would have ſooneſt condemned them to death. But did not Cataline plead in like manner againſt the Roman ſenate, and the injuſtice of their trial, and the juſtice of his flight from Rome? Cæſar alſo, then hatching tyranny, injected the ſame ſcrupulous demurs to ſtop the ſentence of death in full and free ſenate decreed on Lentulus and Cethegus, two of Cataline's accomplices, which were renewed and urged for Strafford. He vouchſafes to the reformation, by both kingdoms intended, no better name than "Innovation and ruin both in church and ſtate." And what we would have learned ſo gladly of him in other paſſages before, to know wherein, he tells us now of his own accord. The expelling biſhops out of the houſe of peers, this was "ruin to the ſtate," the "removing" them "root and branch," this was "ruin to the church."

How happy could this nation be in ſuch a governor who counted that their ruin, which they thought their deliverance, the ruin both of church and ſtate, which was the recovery and the ſaving of them both?

To the paſſing of thoſe bills againſt biſhops, how is it likely that the houſe of peers gave ſo hardly their conſent, which they gave ſo eaſily before to the attaching them of high treaſon, twelve at once, only for proteſting that the parliament could not act without them? Surely if their rights and privileges were thought ſo undoubted in that houſe, as is here maintained, then was that proteſtation, being meant and intended in the name of their whole ſpiritual order, no treaſon, and ſo that houſe itſelf will become liable to a juſt conſtruction either of injuſtice *to appeach them for ſo conſenting*, or of uſurpation, repreſenting none but themſelves, to expect that their voting or not voting ſhould obſtruct the commons Who not for "five repulſes of the Lords," no not for fifty, were to deſiſt from what in the name of the whole kingdom they demanded, ſo long as thoſe lords were none of our lords. And for the bill againſt root and branch, though it paſſed not in both houſes till many of the lords and ſome few of the commons, either enticed away by the king, or overawed by the ſenſe of their own malignancy not prevailing, deſerted the parliament, and made a fair riddance of themſelves; that

that was no warrant for them who remained faithful, being far the greater number, to lay aſide that bill of root and branch, till the return of their fugitives; a bill ſo neceſſary and ſo much deſired by themſelves as *well as* by the people.

This was the Partiality, this degrading of the biſhops, a thing ſo wholeſome in the ſtate, and ſo orthodoxal in the church both ancient and reformed; which the king rather than aſſent to, " will either hazard both his own and the kingdom's ruin," by our juſt defence againſt his force of arms, or proſtrate our conſciences in a blind obedience to himſelf, and thoſe men, whoſe ſuperſtition, zealous or unzealous, would inforce upon us an antichriſtian tyranny in the church, neither primitive, apoſtolical, nor more anciently univerſal than ſome other manifeſt corruptions.

But " he was bound, beſides his judgment, by a moſt ſtrict and indiſpenſable oath to preſerve that order and the rights of the church " If he mean the oath of his coronation, and that the letter of that oath admit not to be interpreted either by equity, reformation, or better knowledge, then was the king bound by that oath to grant the clergy all thoſe cuſtoms, franchiſes, and canonical privileges granted to them by Edward the Confeſſor, and ſo might one day, under pretence of that oath and his conſcience, have brought us all again to popery: But had he ſo well remembred as he ought, the words to which he ſwore, he might have found himſelf no otherwiſe obliged there, than ' according to the laws of God, and true profeſſion of the Goſpel " For if thoſe following words, " eſtabliſhed in this kingdom," be ſet there to limit and lay preſcription on the laws of God and truth of the goſpel by man's eſtabliſhment, nothing can be more abſurd or more injurious to religion So that however the German emperors, or other kings have levied all thoſe wars on their proteſtant ſubjects under the colour of a blind and literal obſervance to an oath, yet this king had leaſt pretence of all, *both ſworn to the laws of God and evangelic truth, and diſclaiming, as we heard him before,* " *to be bound by any coronation-oath, in a blind and brutiſh formality* " Nor is it to be imagined, if what ſhall be eſtabliſhed come in queſtion, but that the parliament ſhould overſway the king, and not he the parliament And by all law and reaſon that which the parliament will not, is no more eſtabliſhed in this kingdom, neither is the king bound by oath to uphold it as a thing eſtabliſhed. *And that the king (who of his princely grace, as he profeſſes, hath ſo oft aboliſhed things that ſtood firm by law, as the ſtar chamber and high commiſſion) ever thought himſelf bound by oath to keep them up, becauſe eſtabliſhed, he who will believe, muſt at the ſame time condemn him of as many perjuries, as he is well known to have aboliſhed both laws and juriſdictions, that wanted no eſtabliſhment*

" Had he gratified," he thinks, " *their* antiepiſcopal faction with his conſent, and ſacrificed the church-government and revenues to the fury of their covetouſneſs, &c " an army had not been raiſed Whereas it was the fury of his own hatred to the profeſſors of true religion, which firſt incited him to proſecute them with the ſword of war, when whips, pillories, exiles, and impriſonments were not thought ſufficient. To colour which he cannot find wherewithal, but that ſtale pretence of Charles the Vth, and other popiſh kings, that the proteſtants had only an intent to lay hands *upon* the church-revenues, a thing never in the thoughts of this parliament, till exhauſted by his endleſs war upon them, their neceſſity ſeized on that for the commonwealth, which the luxury of prelates had abuſed before to a common miſchief

His conſent to the unlording of biſhops (for to that he himſelf conſented, and at Canterbury the chief ſeat of their pride, ſo God would have it!) " was from his firm perſuaſion of their contentedneſs to ſuffer a preſent diminution of their rights." Can any man, reading this, not diſcern the pure mockery of a royal conſent, to delude us only for " the preſent," meaning, it ſeems, when time ſhould ſerve, to revoke all? By this reckoning, his conſents and his denials come all to one paſs and we may hence perceive the *ſmall* wiſdom and integrity of thoſe votes which voted his conceſſions at the Iſle of Wight, for grounds of a laſting peace. This he alledges, this controverſy about

biſhops,

biſhops, " to be the true ſtate" of that difference between him and the parliament. For he held epiſcopacy " both very ſacred and divine;" with this judgment, and for this cauſe, he withdrew from the parliament, and confeſſes that ſome men knew " he was like to bring again the ſame judgment which he carried with him." A fair and unexpected juſtification from his own mouth afforded to the parliament, who notwithſtanding what they knew of his obſtinate mind, omitted not to uſe all thoſe means and that patience to have gained him!

As for delinquents, " he allows them to be but the neceſſary conſequences of his and their withdrawing and defending," A pretty ſhift! to mince the name of a delinquent into a neceſſary conſequent. what is a traitor, but the neceſſary conſequence of his treaſon? What a rebel, but of his rebellion? From this conceit he would infer a pretext only in the parliament " to fetch in delinquents," as if there had indeed been no ſuch cauſe, but all the delinquency in London tumults Which is the over-worn theme, and ſtuffing of all his diſcourſes

This he thrice repeats to be the true ſtate and reaſon of all that war and devaſtation in the land; and that " of all the treaties and propoſitions" offered him, he was reſolved " never to grant the aboliſhing of epiſcopal, or the eſtabliſhment of preſbyterian government." I would demand now of the Scots and covenanteers (for ſo I call them, as miſobſervers of the covenant) how they will reconcile " the preſervation of religion and their liberties, and the bringing of delinquents to condign puniſhment," with the freedom, honour, and ſafety of this vowed reſolution here, that eſteems all the zeal of their proſtituted covenant no better than " a noiſe and ſhew of piety, a heat for reformation, filling them with prejudice, and obſtructing all equality and clearneſs of judgment in them " With theſe principles who knows but that at length he might have come to take the covenant, as others whom they brotherly admit, have done before him? And then all, no doubt, had gone well, and ended in a happy peace

His prayer is moſt of it borrowed out of David; but what if it be anſwered him as the Jews, who truſted in Moſes, were anſwered by our Saviour, " there is one that accuſeth you, even David, whom you miſapply "

He tells God, " that his enemies are many," but tells the people, when it ſerves his turn, they are but " a faction of ſome few, prevailing over the major part of both houſes "

" God knows he had no paſſion, deſign or preparation to embroil his kingdom in a civil war " True, for he thought his kingdom to be Iſſachar, a " ſtrong aſs that would have couched down between two burthens," the one of prelatical ſuperſtition, the other of civil tyranny but what paſſion and deſign, what cloſe and open preparation he had made, to ſubdue us to both theſe by terror and preventive force, all the nation knows

" The confidence of ſome men had almoſt perſuaded him to ſuſpect his own innocence." As the words of Saint Paul had almoſt perſuaded Agrippa to be a chriſtian. But almoſt in the works of repentance, is as good as not at all

" God, ſaith he, will find out bloody and deceitful men, many of whom have not lived out half their days." It behoved him to have been more cautious how he tempted God's finding out of blood and deceit, till his own years had been further ſpent, or that he had enjoyed longer the fruits of his own violent counſels

But inſtead of warineſs he adds another temptation, charging God " to know that the chief deſign of this war was either to deſtroy his perſon, or to force his judgment." And thus his prayer from the evil practice of unjuſt accuſing men to God, ariſes to the hideous raſhneſs of accuſing God before men, to know that for truth, which all men know to be moſt falſe.

He prays, " that God would forgive the people, for they know not what they do " It is an eaſy matter to ſay over what our Saviour ſaid, but how he loved the people, other arguments than affected ſayings muſt demonſtrate He who ſo oft hath preſumed raſhly

to

to appeal to the knowledge and teſtimony of God in things ſo evidently untrue, may be doubted what belief or eſteem he had of his forgiveneſs, either to himſelf, or thoſe for whom he would * ſo feign that men ſhould hear he prayed.

X. Upon their ſeizing the magazines, forts, &c.

TO put the matter ſooneſt out of controverſy who was the firſt beginner of this civil war, ſince the beginning of all war may be diſcerned not only by the firſt act of hoſtility, but by the counſels and preparations foregoing, it ſhall evidently appear that the king was ſtill foremoſt in all theſe. No king had ever at his firſt coming to the crown more love and acclamation from a people, never any people found worſe requital of their loyalty and good affection: Firſt, by his extraordinary fear and miſtruſt that their liberties and rights were the impairing and diminiſhing of his regal power, the true original of tyranny; next, by his hatred to all thoſe who were eſteemed religious; doubting that *their principles* too much aſſerted liberty. This was quickly ſeen by the vehemence, and the cauſes alledged of his perſecuting, the other by his frequent and opprobrious diſſolution of parliaments; after he had demanded more money of them, and they to obtain their rights had granted him, than would have bought the Turk out of Morea, and ſet free all the Greeks But when he ſought to extort from us, by way of tribute, that which had been offered him conditionally in parliament, as by a free people, and that thoſe extortions were now conſumed and waſted by the luxury of his court, he began then (for ſtill the more he did wrong, the more he feared) before any tumult or inſurrection of the people, to take counſel how he might totally ſubdue them to his own will. Then was the deſign of German horſe, *while the duke reigned*; *and which was worſt of all, ſome thouſands of the Iriſh papiſts were in ſeveral parts billetted upon us, while a parliament was then ſitting.* The pulpits reſounded with no other doctrine than that which gave all property to the king, and paſſive obedience to the ſubject After which, innumerable forms and ſhapes of new exactions and exactors overſpread the land: nor was it enough to be impoveriſhed, unleſs we were diſarmed. Our trained-bands, which are the truſtieſt and moſt proper ſtrength of a free nation *not at war with itſelf*, had their arms in divers counties taken from them; other ammunition by deſign was ingroſſed and kept in the tower, not to be bought without a licence, and at a high rate.

Thus far, and many other ways were his counſels and preparations before-hand with us, either to a civil war, if it ſhould happen, or to ſubdue us without a war, which is all one, until the raiſing of his two armies againſt the Scots, and the latter of them raiſed to the moſt perfidious breaking of a ſolemn pacification *the articles whereof, though ſubſcribed with his own hand, he commanded ſoon after to be burned openly by the hangman. What enemy durſt have done him that diſhonour and affront, which he did therein to himſelf?*

After the beginning of this parliament, whom he ſaw ſo reſolute and unanimous to relieve the commonwealth, and that the earl of Strafford was condemned to die, other of his evil counſellors impeached and impriſoned; to ſhew there wanted not evil counſel within himſelf ſufficient to begin a war upon his ſubjects, though no way by them provoked, he ſends an agent with letters to the king of Denmark, requiring aid againſt the parliament: *and that aid was coming, when divine providence to divert them, ſent a ſudden torrent of Swedes into the bowels of Denmark. He then* endeavours to bring up both armies, firſt the Engliſh, with whom 8000 Iriſh papiſts raiſed by Strafford, and a French army were to join, then the Scots at Newcaſtle, whom he thought to have encouraged by telling them what money and horſe he was to have from Denmark. I mention not the Iriſh conſpiracy till due place. Theſe and many other were his counſels toward a civil war His preparations, after thoſe two armies were diſmiſſed, could not ſuddenly

* The ſecond edition has *ſo fain*. To *feign*, is to diſſemble, but we uſe the word *fain* for fond deſire of a thing.

be too open: nevertheleſs there were 8000 Iriſh papiſts which he refuſed to diſband, though intreated by both houſes, firſt, for reaſons beſt known to himſelf, next, under pretence of lending them to the Spaniard, and ſo kept them undiſbanded till very near the month wherein that rebellion broke forth. He was alſo raiſing forces in London, pretendedly to ſerve the Portugal, but with intent to ſeize the tower; into which divers canoneers were by him ſent *with many fireworks and granadoes, and many great battering pieces were mounted againſt the city.* The court was fortified with ammunition, and ſoldiers new liſted, who followed the king from London, and appeared at Kingſton ſome hundreds of horſe in a warlike manner, with waggons of ammunition after them; the queen in Holland was buying more; *of which the parliament had certain knowledge, and had not yet ſo much as demanded the Militia to be ſettled, till they knew both of her going over ſea, and to what intent. For ſhe had packed up the crown-jewels to have been going long before, had not the parliament, ſuſpecting by the diſcoveries at Burrow-bridge what was intended with the jewels, uſed means to ſtay her journey till the winter. Hull and the magazine there had been ſecretly attempted under the king's hand, from whom (though in his Declarations renouncing all thought of war) notes were ſent over-ſea for ſupply of arms: which were no ſooner come, but* the inhabitants of Yorkſhire and other counties were called to arms, and actual forces raiſed, while the parliament were yet petitioning in peace, and had not one man liſted.

As to the act of hoſtility, though not much material in whom firſt it began, *or by whoſe commiſſions dated firſt,* after ſuch counſels and preparations diſcovered, and ſo far advanced by the king, yet in that act alſo he will be found to have had precedency, if not at London by the aſſault of his armed court upon the naked people, and his attempt upon the houſe of commons, yet certainly at Hull, firſt by his cloſe practices on that town, next by his ſiege. Thus, whether counſels, preparations, or acts of hoſtility be conſidered, it appears with evidence enough, though much more might be ſaid, that the king is truly charged to be the firſt beginner of theſe civil wars. To which may be added as a cloſe, that in the Iſle of Wight he charged it upon himſelf at the public treaty, and acquitted the parliament

But as for the ſecuring of Hull and the public ſtores therein, and in other places, it was no "ſurpriſal of his ſtrength," the cuſtody whereof by authority of parliament was committed into hands moſt fit and moſt reſponſible for ſuch a truſt. It were a folly beyond ridiculous, to count ourſelves a free nation, if the king, not in parliament, but in his own perſon, and againſt them, might appropriate to himſelf the ſtrength of a whole nation as his proper goods What the laws of the land are, a parliament ſhould know beſt, having both the life and death of laws in their law-giving power And the law of England is, at beſt, but the reaſon of parliament The parliament therefore, taking into their hands that whereof moſt properly they ought to have the keeping, committed no ſurpriſal. If they prevented him, that argued not at all either "his innocency or unpreparedneſs," but their timely foreſight to uſe prevention.

But what needed that? "They knew his chiefeſt arms left him were thoſe only which the ancient chriſtians were wont to uſe againſt their proſecutors, prayers and tears" O ſacred reverence of God! reſpect and ſhame of men! whither were ye fled when theſe hypocriſies were uttered? Was the kingdom then at all that coſt of blood, to remove from him none but prayers and tears? What were thoſe thouſands of blaſpheming cavaliers about him, whoſe mouths let fly oaths and curſes by the volley; were thoſe the prayers? and thoſe carouſes drunk to the confuſion of all things good or holy, did thoſe miniſter the tears? Were they prayers and tears that were liſted at York, muſtered on Heworth moore, and laid ſiege to Hull for the guard of his perſon? Were prayers and tears at ſo high a rate in Holland, that nothing could purchaſe them but the crown-jewels? Yet they in Holland (ſuch word was ſent us) ſold them for guns, carabines, mortar-pieces, cannons, and other deadly inſtruments of war; which when they came to York, were all, no doubt, by the merit of ſome great ſaint ſuddenly transformed into prayers and tears; and being divided into regiments and brigades, were the only arms that miſchieved us in all thoſe battles and encounters.

Theſe were his chief arms, whatever we muſt call them, and yet ſuch arms, as they who fought for the commonwealth, have by the help of better prayers vanquiſhed and brought to nothing.

He bewails his want of the militia, " not ſo much in reference to his own protection, as the people's, whoſe many and ſore oppreſſions grieve him." Never conſidering how ill for ſeventeen years together he had protected them, and that theſe miſeries of the people are ſtill his own handy-work, having ſmitten them, like a forked arrow, ſo ſore into the kingdom's ſides, as not to be drawn out and cured without the inciſion of more fleſh

He tells us that " what he wants in the hand of power," he has in " the wings of faith and prayer." But they who made no reckoning of thoſe wings while they had that power in their hands, may eaſily miſtake the wings of faith for the wings of preſumption, and ſo fall headlong

We meet next with a compariſon, how apt let them judge *who* have travelled to Mecca, " that the parliament have hung the majeſty of kingſhip in an airy imagination of regality, between the privileges of both houſes, like the tomb of Mahomet " He knew not that he was propheſying the death and burial of a Turkiſh tyranny, that ſpurned down thoſe laws which gave it life and being, ſo long as it endured to be a regulated monarchy.

He counts it an injury " not to have the ſole power in himſelf to help or hurt any ," and that the " militia, which he holds to be his undoubted right, ſhould be diſpoſed as the parliament thinks fit " And yet confeſſes that if he had it in his actual diſpoſing, he would defend thoſe whom he calls " his good ſubjects from thoſe men's violence and fraud, who would perſuade the world that none but wolves are fit to be truſted with the cuſtody of the ſhepherd and his flock." Surely, if we may gueſs whom he means here, by knowing whom he hath ever moſt oppoſed in this controverſy, we may then aſſure ourſelves that by violence and fraud he means that which the parliament hath done in ſettling the militia, and thoſe the wolves, into whoſe hands it was by them intruſted : which draws a clear confeſſion from his own mouth, that if the parliament had left him ſole power of the militia, he would have uſed it to the deſtruction of them and their friends.

As for ſole power of the militia, which he claims as a right no leſs undoubted than the crown, it hath been oft enough told him, that he hath no more authority over the ſword than over the law; over the law he hath none, either to eſtabliſh or to abrogate, to interpret or to execute, but only by his courts and in his courts, whereof the parliament is higheſt; no more therefore hath he power of the militia, which is the ſword, either to uſe or to diſpoſe, but with conſent of parliament; give him but that, and as good give him *in a lump* all our laws and liberties. For if the power of the ſword were any where ſeparate and undepending from the power of law, which is originally ſeated in the higheſt court, then *would* that power of the ſword *be ſoon maſter of the law* and being at one man's diſpoſal, might, when he pleaſed, controul the law, *and in deriſion of our Magna Charta, which were but weak reſiſtance againſt an armed tyrant, might abſolutely enſlave us. And not to have in ourſelves, though vaunting to be freeborn, the power of our own freedom, and the public ſafety, is a degree lower than not to have the property of our own goods. For liberty of perſon and the right of ſelf-preſervation, is much nearer, much more natural, and more worth to all men, than the propriety of their goods and wealth. Yet ſuch power as all* this did the king in open terms challenge to have over us, and brought thouſands to help him win it; ſo much more good at fighting than at underſtanding, as to perſuade themſelves that they fought then for the ſubject's liberty.

He is contented, becauſe he knows no other remedy, to reſign this power "for his own time, but not for his ſucceſſors:" So diligent and careful he is that we ſhould be ſlaves, if not to him, yet to his poſterity, and fain would leave us the legacy of another war about it. But the parliament have done well to remove that queſtion: whom, as his manner is to dignify with ſome good name or other, he calls now a "many-headed hydra of government, full of factious diſtractions, and not more eyes than mouths." Yet ſurely not more mouths, or not ſo wide, as the diſſolute rabble of all his courtiers had, both hees and ſhees, if there were any males among them.

He would prove that to govern by parliament hath "a monſtroſity rather than perfection," and grounds his argument upon two or three eminent abſurdities: Firſt, by placing counſel in the ſenſes; next, by turning the ſenſes out of the head, and in lieu thereof placing power, ſupreme above ſenſe and reaſon: Which be now the greater monſtroſities? Further to diſpute what kind of government is beſt, would be a long *debate*, it ſufficeth that his reaſons here for monarchy are found weak and inconſiderable.

He bodes much "horror and bad influence after his eclipſe." He ſpeaks his wiſhes; but they who by weighing prudently things paſt, foreſee things to come, the beſt divination, may hope rather all good ſucceſs and happineſs, by removing that darkneſs, which the miſty cloud of his prerogative made between us and a peaceful reformation, which is our true ſun-light, and not he, though he would be taken for our ſun itſelf. And wherefore ſhould we not hope to be governed more happily without a king, whenas all our miſery and trouble hath been either by a king, or by our neceſſary vindication and defence againſt him?

He would be thought "inforced to perjury," by having granted the militia, by which his oath bound him to protect the people. If he can be perjured in granting that, why doth he refuſe for no other cauſe the aboliſhing of epiſcopacy? But never was any oath ſo blind as to ſwear him to protect delinquents againſt juſtice, but to protect all the people in that order, and by thoſe hands which the parliament ſhould adviſe him to, and the protected confide in; not under the ſhew of protection to hold a violent and incommunicable ſword over us, as ready to be let fall upon our own necks, as upon our enemies; nor to make our own hands and weapons fight againſt our own liberties.

By his parting with the militia, he takes to himſelf much praiſe of his "aſſurance in God's protection;" and to the parliament imputes the fear "of not daring to adventure the injuſtice of their actions upon any other way of ſafety." But wherefore came not this aſſurance of God's protection to him, till the militia was wrung out of his hands? It ſhould ſeem by his holding it ſo faſt, that his own actions and intentions had no leſs of injuſtice in them, than what he charges upon others, whom he terms Chaldeans, Sabeans, and the devil himſelf. But Job uſed no ſuch militia againſt thoſe enemies, nor ſuch a magazine as was at Hull, which this king ſo contended for, and made war upon us, that he might have wherewithal to make war againſt us.

He concludes, that "although they take all from him, yet can they not obſtruct his way to heaven." It was no handſome occaſion, by feigning obſtructions where they are not, to tell us whither he was going: he ſhould have ſhut the door, and prayed in ſecret, not here in the high ſtreet. Private prayers in public, aſk ſomething of whom they aſk not, and that ſhall be their reward.

XI. Upon the Nineteen Propoſitions, &c.

OF the nineteen propoſitions he names none in particular, neither ſhall the anſwer: But he inſiſts upon the old plea of "his conſcience, honour and reaſon;" uſing the plauſibility of large and indefinite words, to defend himſelf at ſuch a diſtance as may hinder the eye of common judgment from all diſtinct view and examination of his reaſoning. "He would buy the peace of his people at any rate, ſave only the parting with his conſcience and honour." Yet ſhews not how it can happen that the peace of a people, if otherwiſe to be bought at any rate, ſhould be inconſiſtent or at variance with the conſcience and honour of a king. Till then, we may receive it for a better ſentence, that nothing ſhould be more agreeable to the conſcience and honour of a king, than to preſerve his ſubjects in peace; eſpecially from civil war.

And which of the propoſitions were "obtruded on him with the point of the ſword," till he firſt with the point of the ſword thruſt from him both the propoſitions and the propounders? He never reckons thoſe violent and mercileſs obtruſions, which for almoſt twenty years he had been forcing upon tender conſciences by all ſorts of perſecution, till through the multitude of them that were to ſuffer, it could no more *be* called a perſecution, but a plain war. From which when firſt the Scots, then the Engliſh, were conſtrained to defend themſelves, this their juſt defence is that which he calls here, "their making war upon his ſoul."

He grudges that "ſo many things are required of him, and nothing offered him in requital of thoſe favours which he had granted" What could ſatiate the deſires of this man, who being king of England, and maſter of almoſt two millions yearly *what by hook or crook*, was ſtill in want, and thoſe acts of juſtice which he was to do in duty, counts done as favours; and ſuch favours as were not done without the avaritious hope of other rewards beſides ſupreme honour, and the conſtant revenue of his place?

"This honour," he ſaith, "they did him, to put him on the giving part" And ſpake truer than he intended, it being meerly for honour's ſake that they did ſo; not that it belonged to him of right. for what can he give to a parliament, who receives all he hath from the people, and for the people's good? Yet now he brings his own conditional rights to conteſt and be preferred before the people's good, and yet unleſs it be in order to their good, he hath no rights at all, reigning by the laws of the land, not by his own; which laws are in the hands of parliament to change or abrogate as they ſhall ſee beſt for the commonwealth; even to the taking away of kingſhip itſelf, when it grows too maſterful and burdenſome. For every commonwealth is in general defined, a ſociety ſufficient of itſelf, in all things conducible to well-being and commodious life. Any of which requiſite things, if it cannot have without the gift and favour of a ſingle perſon, or without leave of his private reaſon or his conſcience, it cannot be thought ſufficient of itſelf, and by conſequence no commonwealth, nor free, but a multitude of vaſſals in the poſſeſſion and domain of one abſolute lord, and wholly obnoxious to his will. If the king have power to give or deny any thing to his parliament, he muſt do it either as a perſon ſeveral from them, or as one greater, neither of which will be allowed him. not to be conſidered ſeverally from them, for as the king of England can do no wrong, ſo neither can he do right but in his courts and by his courts; and what is legally done in them, ſhall be deemed the king's aſſent, though he as a ſeveral perſon ſhall judge or endeavour the contrary ſo that indeed without his courts, or againſt them, he is no king If therefore he obtrude upon us any public miſchief, or withhold from us any general good, which is wrong in the higheſt degree, he muſt do it as a tyrant, not as a king of England, by the known maxims of our law. Neither can he, as one greater, give aught to the parliament which is not in their

their own power, but he muſt be greater alſo than the kingdom which they repreſent: ſo that to honour him with the giving part was a meer civility, and may be well termed the courteſy of England, not the king's due.

But the " incommunicable jewel of his conſcience" he will not give, " but reſerve to himſelf." It ſeems that his conſcience was none of the crown-jewels; for thoſe we know were in Holland, not incommunicable to buy arms againſt his ſubjects. Being therefore but a private jewel, he could not have done a greater pleaſure to the kingdom than by reſerving it to himſelf But he, contrary to what is here profeſſed, would have his conſcience not an incommunicable, but a univerſal conſcience, the whole kingdom's conſcience. Thus what he ſeems to fear leſt we ſhould raviſh from him, is our chief complaint that he obtruded upon us; we never forced him to part with his conſcience, but it was he that would have forced us to part with ours.

Some things he taxes them to have offered him, " which while he had the maſtery of his reaſon, he would never conſent to." Very likely; but had his reaſon maſtered him as it ought, and not been maſtered long ago by his ſenſe and humour (as the breeding of moſt kings hath been ever ſenſual and moſt humoured) perhaps he would have made no difficulty. Mean while at what a fine paſs is the kingdom, that muſt depend in greateſt exigencies upon the fantaſy of a king's reaſon, be he wiſe or fool, who arrogantly ſhall anſwer all the wiſdom of the land, that what they offer ſeems to him unreaſonable?

He prefers his " love of truth" before his love of the people. His love of truth would have led him to the ſearch of truth, and have taught him not to lean ſo much upon his own underſtanding He met at firſt with doctrines of unaccountable prerogative, in them he reſted, becauſe they pleaſed him, they therefore pleaſed him becauſe they gave him all. and this he calls his love of truth, and prefers it before *the* love of his people's peace.

Some things they propoſed " which would have wounded the inward peace of his conſcience." The more our evil hap, that three kingdoms ſhould be thus peſtered with one conſcience, who chiefly ſcrupled to grant us that, which the parliament adviſed him to, as the chief means of our public welfare and reformation These ſcruples to many perhaps *will* ſeem pretended, to others, upon as good grounds, may ſeem real; and that it was the juſt judgment of God, that he who was ſo cruel and ſo remorſeleſs to other men's conſciences, ſhould have a conſcience within him as cruel to himſelf; conſtraining him, as he conſtrained others, and inſnaring him *in* ſuch ways and counſels as were certain to be his deſtruction.

" Other things *though* he could approve, yet in honour and policy he thought fit to deny, leſt he ſhould ſeem to dare deny nothing " By this means he will be ſure, what with reaſon, honour, policy, or punctilio's, to be found never unfurniſhed of a denial. whether it were his envy not to be overbounteous, or that the ſubmiſſneſs of our aſking ſtirred up in him a certain pleaſure of denying Good princes have thought it their chief happineſs to be always granting, if good things, for the things ſake, if things indifferent, for the people's ſake, while this man ſits calculating variety of excuſes how he may grant leaſt, as if his whole ſtrength and royalty were placed in a meer negative

Of one propoſition eſpecially he laments him much, that they would bind him " to a general and implicit conſent for whatever they deſired " Which though I find not among the nineteen, yet undoubtedly the oath of his coronation binds him to no leſs, neither is he at all by his office to interpoſe againſt a parliament in the making or not making of any law, but to take that for juſt and good legally, which is there decreed, and to ſee it executed accordingly. Nor was he ſet over us to vie wiſdom with his parliament, but to be guided by them any of whom poſſibly may as far excel him in the gift of wiſdom, as he them in place and dignity. But much nearer is it to impoſſibility that

that any king alone ſhould be wiſer than all his council; ſure enough it was not he, though no king ever before him ſo much contended to have it thought ſo. And if the *parliament ſo thought not*, but deſired *him to follow their advice and deliberation in* things of public concernment, he accounts it the ſame propoſition, as if Sampſon had been moved "to the putting out his eyes, that the Philiſtines might abuſe him." And thus out of an unwiſe *or* pretended fear, leſt others ſhould make a ſcorn of him for yielding to his parliament, he regards not to give cauſe of worſe ſuſpicion, that he made a ſcorn of his regal oath.

But "to exclude him from all power of denial ſeems an arrogance;" in the parliament he means: what in him then to deny againſt the parliament? None at all, by what he argues. for "by petitioning, they confeſs their inferiority, and that obliges them to reſt, if not ſatisfied, yet quieted with ſuch an anſwer as the will and reaſon of their ſuperior thinks fit to give." Firſt, petitioning, in better Engliſh, is no more than requeſting or requiring, and men require not favours only, but their due, and that not only from ſuperiors, but from equals, and inferiors alſo The nobleſt Romans, when they ſtood for that which was a kind of regal honour, the conſulſhip, were wont in a ſubmiſſive manner to go about, and beg that higheſt dignity of the meaneſt Plebeians, naming them man by man; which in their tongue was called Petitio conſulatus. And the parliament of England petitioned the king, not becauſe all of them were inferior to him, but becauſe he was inferior to any one of them, which they did of civil cuſtom, and for faſhion's ſake, more than of duty, for by plain law cited before, the parliament is his ſuperior.

But what law in any trial or diſpute enjoins a freeman to reſt quieted, though not ſatisfied, with the will and reaſon of his ſuperior? It were a mad law that would ſubject reaſon to ſuperiority of place. And if our higheſt conſultations and purpoſed laws muſt be terminated by the king's will, then is the will of one man our law, and no ſubtlety of diſpute can redeem the parliament and nation from being ſlaves neither can any tyrant require *more than that his will or reaſon*, though not ſatisfying, ſhould yet be reſted in, and determine all things We may conclude therefore, that when the parliament petitioned the king, it was but meerly form, let it be as "fooliſh and abſurd" as he pleaſes. It cannot certainly be ſo abſurd as what he requires, that the parliament ſhould confine their own and all the kingdom's reaſon to the will of one man, becauſe it was his hap to ſucceed his father. For neither God nor the laws have ſubjected us to his will, nor ſet his reaſon to be our ſovereign above law (which muſt needs be, if he can ſtrangle it in the birth) but ſet his perſon over us in the ſovereign execution of ſuch laws as the parliament eſtabliſh. The parliament therefore, without any uſurpation, hath had *it* always in their power to limit and confine the exorbitancy of kings, whether they call it their will, their reaſon, or their conſcience

But this above all was never expected, nor is to be indured, that a king, who is bound by law and oath to follow the advice of his parliament, ſhould be permitted to except againſt them as "young Stateſmen," and proudly to ſuſpend his following their advice, "until his ſeven years experience had ſhewn him how well they could govern themſelves." Doubtleſs the law never ſuppoſed ſo great an arrogance could be in one man, that he whoſe ſeventeen years unexperience had almoſt ruined all, ſhould ſit another ſeven years ſchoolmaſter, to tutor thoſe who were ſent by the whole realm to be his counſellors and teachers And with what modeſty can he pretend to be a ſtateſman himſelf; who with his father's king-craft and his own, did never that of his own accord which was not directly oppoſite to his profeſſed intereſt both at home and abroad; diſcontenting and alienating his ſubjects at home, weakning and deſerting his confederates abroad, and with them the common cauſe of religion; ſo that the whole courſe of his reign, by an example of his own furniſhing, hath reſembled Phaeton more than

Phœbus.

Phœbus, and forced the parliament to drive like Jehu; which omen taken from his own mouth, God hath not diverted?

And he on the other ſide might have remembred that the parliament ſit in that body, not as his ſubjects, but as his ſuperiors, called, not by him, but by the law; not only twice every year, but as oft as great affairs require, to be his counſellors and dictator, though he ſtomach it; nor to be diſſolved at his pleaſure, but when all grievances be firſt removed, all petitions heard and anſwered. This is not only reaſon, but the known law of the land.

"When he heard that propoſitions would be ſent him," he ſat conjecturing what they would propound; and becauſe they propounded what he expected not, he takes that to be a warrant for his denying them. But what did he expect? He expected that the parliament would reinforce "ſome old laws" But if thoſe laws were not a ſufficient remedy to all grievances, nay were found to be grievances themſelves, when did we loſe that other part of our freedom to eſtabliſh new? He thought "ſome injuries done by himſelf and others to the commonwealth were to be repaired." But how could that be, while he the chief offender took upon him to be ſole judge both of the injury and the reparation? "He ſtaid till the advantages of his crown conſidered, might induce him to condeſcend to the people's good." Whenas the crown itſelf with all thoſe advantages were therefore given him, that the people's good ſhould be firſt conſidered; not bargained for, and bought by inches with the bribe of more offertures and advantages to his crown. He looked "for moderate deſires of due reformation," as if any ſuch deſires could be immoderate. He looked for ſuch a reformation "both in Church and State, as might preſerve" the roots of every grievance and abuſe in both ſtill growing (which he calls "the foundation and eſſentials") and would have only the excreſcencies of evil pruned away for the preſent, as was plotted before, that they might grow faſt enough between triennial parliaments, to hinder them by work enough beſides, from ever ſtriking at the root. He alledges, "They ſhould have had regard to the laws in force, to the wiſdom and piety of former parliaments, to the ancient and univerſal practice of chriſtian churches." As if they who come with full authority to redreſs public grievances, which oft-times are laws themſelves, were to have their hands bound by laws in force, or the ſuppoſition of more piety and wiſdom in their anceſtors, or the practice of churches heretofore, whoſe fathers, notwithſtanding all theſe pretences, made as vaſt alterations to free themſelves from ancient popery. For all antiquity that adds or varies from the ſcripture, is no more warranted to our ſafe imitation, than what was done the age before at Trent. Nor was there need to have deſpaired of what could be eſtabliſhed in lieu of what was to be annulled, having before his eyes the government of ſo many churches beyond the ſeas; whoſe pregnant and ſolid reaſons wrought ſo with the parliament, as to deſire a uniformity rather with all other proteſtants, than to be a ſchiſm divided from them under a conclave of thirty biſhops, and a crew of irreligious prieſts that gaped for the ſame preferment.

And whereas he blames thoſe propoſitions for not containing what they ought, what did they mention, but to vindicate and reſtore the rights of parliament invaded by cabin councils, the courts of juſtice obſtructed, and the government of church innovated and corrupted? All theſe things he might eaſily have obſerved in them, which he affirms he could not find; but found "thoſe demanding" in parliament who were "lookt upon before as factious in the ſtate, and ſchiſmatical in the church, and demanding not only toleration for themſelves in their vanity, novelty, and confuſion, but alſo an extirpation of that government whoſe rights they had a mind to invade." Was this man ever likely to be adviſed, who with ſuch a prejudice and diſeſteem ſets himſelf againſt his choſen and appointed counſellors? likely ever to admit of reformation, who cenſures all the government of other proteſtant churches, as bad as any papiſt could have cenſured them? And what king had ever his whole kingdom in ſuch contempt, ſo to wrong

wrong and diſhonour the free elections of his people, as to judge them whom the nation thought worthieſt to ſit with him in parliament, few elſe but ſuch as were "puniſhable by the laws?" yet knowing that time was, when to be a proteſtant, to be a chriſtian, was by law as puniſhable as to be a traitor, and that our Saviour himſelf coming to reform his church, was accuſed of an intent to invade Cæſar's right, as good a right as the prelate biſhops ever had, the one being got by force, the other by ſpiritual uſurpation; and both by force upheld.

He admires and falls into an extaſy that the parliament ſhould ſend him ſuch a "horrid propoſition," as the removal of epiſcopacy But expect from him in an extaſy no other reaſons of his admiration than the dream and tautology of what he hath ſo oft repeated, law, antiquity, anceſtors, proſperity, and the like, which will be therefore not worth a ſecond anſwer, but may paſs with his own compariſon, into the common ſewer of other popiſh arguments.

"Had the two houſes ſued out their livery from the wardſhip of tumults," he could ſooner have believed them. It concerned them firſt to ſue out their livery from the unjuſt wardſhip of his encroaching prerogative. And had he alſo redeemed his overdated minority from a pupilage under biſhops, he would much leſs have miſtruſted his parliament, and never would have ſet ſo baſe a character upon them, as to count them no better than the vaſſals of certain nameleſs men, whom he charges to be ſuch as "hunt after faction with their hounds the tumults." And yet the biſhops could have told him, that Nimrod, the firſt that hunted after faction, is reputed by ancient tradition the firſt that founded monarchy, whence it appears that to hunt after faction is more properly the king's game, and thoſe hounds, which he calls the vulgar, have been often halloo'd to from court, of whom the mungrel ſort have been inticed; the reſt have not loſt their ſcent, but underſtood aright, that the parliament had that part to act which he had failed in, that truſt to diſcharge, which he had broken; that eſtate and honour to preſerve, which was far beyond his, the eſtate and honour of the commonwealth, which he had imbezzled

Yet ſo far doth ſelf-opinion or falſe principles delude and tranſport him, as to think "the concurrence of his reaſon" to the votes of parliament, not only political, but natural, "and as neceſſary to the begetting," or bringing forth of any one "compleat act of public wiſdom as the ſun's influence is neceſſary to all nature's productions." So that the parliament, it ſeems, is but a female, and without his procreative reaſon, *the laws which they can produce are but wind-eggs*. wiſdom, it ſeems, to a king is natural, to a parliament not natural, but by conjunction with the king yet he profeſſes to hold his kingly right by law, and if no law could be made but by the great council of a nation, which we now term a parliament, then certainly it was a parliament that firſt created kings, and not only made laws before a king was in being, but thoſe laws eſpecially whereby he holds his crown. He ought then to have ſo thought of a parliament, if he count it not male, as of his mother, which to civil being created both him and the royalty he wore. And if it hath been anciently interpreted the preſaging ſign of a future tyrant, but to dream of copulation with his mother, what can it be leſs than actual tyranny to affirm waking, that the parliament, which is his mother, can neither conceive or bring forth "any authoritative act" without his maſculine coition? Nay, that his reaſon is as celeſtial and life-giving to the parliament, as the ſun's influence is to the earth. what other notions but theſe or ſuch like, could ſwell up Caligula to think himſelf a God?

But to be rid of theſe mortifying propoſitions, he leaves *no* tyrannical evaſion uneſſayed; firſt, "that they are not the joint and free deſires of both houſes, or the major part," next, "that the choice of many members was carried on by faction" The former of theſe is already diſcovered to be an old device put firſt in practice by Charles the Fifth, ſince reformation. who when the proteſtants of Germany for their own defence joined themſelves in league, in his declarations and remonſtrances laid the fault only upon ſome few (for it was dangerous to take notice of too many enemies) and accuſed them that under colour of religion they had a purpoſe to invade his and the churches right; by which policy he deceived many of the German cities, and kept them divided from that league, until they ſaw themſelves brought into a ſnare. That other cavil againſt the people's choice puts us in mind rather what the court was wont to do, and how to tamper with elections: neither was there at that time any faction more potent, or more likely to do ſuch a buſineſs, than they themſelves who complain moſt

But " he muſt chew ſuch morſels as propoſitions, ere he let them down " So let him; but if the kingdom ſhall taſte nothing but after his chewing, what does he make of the kingdom, but a great baby? " The ſtreightneſs of his conſcience will not give him leave to ſwallow down ſuch camels of ſacrilege and injuſtice as others do " This is the phariſee up and down, " I am not as other men are." But what camels of injuſtice he could devour, all his three realms were witneſs, which was the cauſe that they almoſt periſhed for want of parliaments. And he that will be unjuſt to man, will be ſacrilegious to God, and to bereave a chriſtian conſcience of liberty for no other reaſon than the narrowneſs of his own conſcience, is the moſt unjuſt meaſure to man, and the worſt ſacrilege to God. That other, which he calls ſacrilege, of taking from the clergy that ſuperfluous wealth, which antiquity as old as Conſtantine, from the credit of a divine viſion, counted " poiſon in the church," hath been ever moſt oppoſed by men whoſe righteouſneſs in other matters hath been leaſt obſerved. He concludes, as his manner is, with high commendation of his own " unbiaſſed rectitude," and believes nothing to be in them that diſſent from him, but faction, innovation, and particular deſigns. Of theſe repetitions I find no end, no not in his prayer, which being founded upon deceitful principles, and a fond hope that God will bleſs him in thoſe " his errors, which he calls " honeſt," finds a fit anſwer of St James, " Ye aſk and receive not, becauſe ye aſk amiſs." As for the truth and ſincerity which he prays may be always found in thoſe his declarations to the people, the contrariety of his own actions will bear eternal witneſs, how little careful or ſolicitous he was, what he promiſed or what he uttered there.

XII. Upon the Rebellion in Ireland.

THE rebellion and horrid maſſacre of Engliſh proteſtants in Ireland, to the number of 154000 *in the province of Ulſter only, by their own computation, which added to the other three, makes up the total ſum of that ſlaughter in all likelihood four times as great*, although ſo ſudden and ſo violent, as at firſt to amaze all men that were not acceſſary, yet from whom, and from what counſels it firſt ſprung, neither was, nor could be poſſibly ſo ſecret, as the contrivers thereof, blinded with vain hope, or the deſpair that other plots would ſucceed, ſuppoſed For it cannot be imaginable that the Iriſh, guided by ſo many ſubtle and Italian heads of the Romiſh party, ſhould ſo far have loſt the uſe of reaſon, and indeed of common ſenſe, as not ſupported with other ſtrength than their own, to begin a war ſo deſperate and irreconcileable againſt both England and Scotland at once. All other nations, from whom they could expect aid, were buſied to the utmoſt in their own moſt neceſſary concernments It remains then that either ſome authority, or ſome great aſſiſtance promiſed them from England, was that whereon they chiefly truſted. And as it is not difficult to diſcern from what inducing cauſe this inſurrection firſt aroſe, ſo neither was it hard at firſt to have applied ſome effectual Remedy, though not prevention. *And yet prevention was not hopeleſs, when Strafford either believed not, or did not care to believe the ſeveral warnings and diſcoveries thereof, which more than once by Papiſts and by Friars themſelves were brought him; beſides what was brought by depoſition, diverſe months before that rebellion, to the archbiſhop of Canterbury and others of the king's council; as the declaration of "no addreſſes" declares.* But the aſſurance which they had in private, that no remedy ſhould be applied, was, it ſeems, one of the chief reaſons that drew on their undertaking. *And long it was e'er that aſſurance failed them, until the biſhops and popiſh lords, who while they ſat and voted, ſtill oppoſed the ſending aid to Ireland, were expelled the houſe.*

Seeing then the main incitement and authority for this rebellion muſt be needs derived from England, it will be next inquired, who was the prime author. The king here denounces a malediction temporal and eternal, not ſimply to the author, but to the "malicious author" of this bloodſhed. and by that limitation may exempt, not himſelf only, but perhaps the Iriſh rebels themſelves, who never will confeſs to God or man that any blood was ſhed by them maliciouſly; but either in the catholic cauſe, or common liberty, or ſome other ſpecious plea, which the conſcience from grounds both good and evil uſually ſuggeſts to itſelf thereby thinking to elude the direct force of that imputation which lies upon them.

Yet he acknowledges " it fell out as a moſt unhappy advantage of ſome mens malice againſt him " but indeed of moſt mens juſt ſuſpicion, by finding in it no ſuch wide departure or diſagreement from the ſcope of his former counſels and proceedings. And that he himſelf was the author of that rebellion, he denies both here and elſewhere, with many imprecations, but no ſolid evidence. What on the other ſide againſt his denial hath been affirmed in three kingdoms, being here briefly ſet in view, the reader may ſo judge as he finds cauſe

This is moſt certain, that the king was ever friendly to the Iriſh papiſts, and in his third year, againſt the plain advice of parliament, like a kind of pope, ſold them many indulgences for money, and upon all occaſions advancing the popiſh party, and negotiating under-hand by prieſts, who were made his agents, engaged the Iriſh papiſts in a war againſt the Scots proteſtants To that end he furniſhed them, and had them trained in arms, and kept them up, *either openly or underhand*, the only army in his three kingdoms, till the very burſt of that rebellion The ſummer before that diſmal October, a committee of moſt active papiſts, all ſince in the head of that rebellion, were in great favour at Whitehall, and admitted to many private conſultations with the king and queen And to make it evident that no mean matters were the ſubject of thoſe conferences, at their requeſt he gave away his peculiar right to more than five Iriſh counties, for the payment of an inconſiderable rent They departed not home till within two months before the rebellion; and were either from the firſt breaking out, or ſoon after, found to be the chief rebels themſelves But what ſhould move the king, beſides his own inclination to popery, and the prevalence of his queen over him, to hold ſuch frequent and cloſe meetings with a committee of Iriſh papiſts in his own houſe, while the parliament of England ſate unadviſed with, is declared by a Scots author, and of itſelf is clear enough The parliament at the beginning of that ſummer, having put Strafford to death, impriſoned others his chief favourites, and driven the reſt to fly, the king, who had in vain tempted both the Scots and the Engliſh army to come up againſt the parliament and city, finding no compliance anſwerable to his hope from the proteſtant armies, betakes himſelf laſt to the Iriſh, who had in readineſs an army of eight thouſand papiſts *which he had refuſed ſo often to diſband*, and a committee here of the ſame religion. With them, who thought the time now come, *(which to bring about they had been many years before not wiſhing only, but with much induſtry complotting to do ſome eminent ſervice for the church of Rome and their own perfidious natures againſt a puritan parliament and the hated Engliſh their maſters,)* he agrees and concludes that ſo ſoon as both armies in England *were* diſbanded, the Iriſh ſhould appear in arms, maſter all the proteſtants, and help the king againſt his parliament. And we need not doubt that thoſe five counties were given to the Iriſh for other reaſon than the four northern counties had been a little before offered to the Scots. The king in Auguſt takes a journey into Scotland, and overtaking the Scots army then on their way home, attempts the ſecond time to pervert them, but without ſucceſs. No ſooner come into Scotland, but he lays a plot, ſo ſaith the Scots author, to remove out of the way ſuch of the nobility there, as were moſt likely to withſtand, or not to further his deſigns. This being diſcovered, he ſends from his ſide one Dillon a papiſt Lord, ſoon after a chief rebel, with letters into Ireland; and diſpatches a commiſſion under the great ſeal of Scotland at that time in his own cuſtody, commanding that they ſhould forthwith, as had been formerly agreed, cauſe all the Iriſh to riſe in arms. Who no ſooner had received ſuch command, but obeyed, and began in maſſacre; for they knew no other way to make ſure the proteſtants, which was commanded them expreſly, and the way, it ſeems, left to their diſcretion He who hath a mind to read the commiſſion itſelf, and ſound reaſon added why it was not likely to be forged, beſides the atteſtation of ſo many Iriſh themſelves, may have recourſe to a book, intitled, " The Myſtery of Iniquity " *Beſides what the parliament itſelf in the declaration of " no more addreſſes" hath affirmed, that they have one copy of that commiſſion in their own hands, atteſted by the oaths of ſome that were eye-witneſſes, and had ſeen it under the ſeal. others of the principal rebels have confeſſed, that this commiſſion was the ſummer before promiſed at London to the Iriſh commiſſioners; to whom the king then diſcovered in plain words his great deſire to be revenged on the parliament of England*

After the rebellion broken out, which in words only he deteſted, but underhand favoured and promoted by all the offices of friendſhip, correſpondence, and what poſſible aid he could afford them, the particulars whereof are too many to be inſerted here, I ſuppoſe no underſtanding man could longer doubt who was " Author or Inſtigator" of that rebellion. If there be who yet doubt, I refer them eſpecially to that declaration of July 1643, *with that of " no addreſſes"* 1647, *and another full volume of examinations to be ſet out ſpeedily concerning this matter.* Againſt *all* which teſtimonies, likelihoods, evidences, and apparent actions of his own, being ſo abundant, *his* bare denial, though with imprecation, *can no way* countervail, *and leaſt of all in his own cauſe.*

As for the commiſſion granted them, he thinks to evade that by retorting, that " ſome in England fight againſt him," and yet " pretend his authority." But though a parliament by the known laws may affirm juſtly to have the king's authority, inſeparable from that court, though divided from his perſon, it is not credible that the Iriſh rebels who ſo much tendered his perſon above his authority, and were by him ſo well received at Oxford, would be ſo far from all humanity, as to ſlander him with a particular commiſſion, ſigned and ſent them by his own hand

And of his good affection to the rebels, this chapter itſelf is not without witneſs He holds them leſs in fault than the Scots, as from whom they might alledge to have fetched " their imitation;" making no difference between men that roſe neceſſarily to defend themſelves, which no proteſtant doctrine ever diſallowed, againſt them who threatned war, and thoſe who began a voluntary and cauſleſs rebellion with the maſſacre of ſo many thouſands who never meant them harm.

He falls next to flaſhes, and a multitude of words, in all which is contained no more, than what might be the plea of any guiltieſt offender · He was not the author, because " he hath the greateſt ſhare of loſs and diſhonour by what is committed " Who is there that offends God, or his neighbour, on whom the greateſt ſhare of loſs and diſhonour lights not in the end? But in the act of doing evil, men uſe not to conſider the event of their evil doing; or if they do, have then no power to curb the ſway of their own wickedneſs. ſo that the greateſt ſhare of loſs and diſhonour to happen upon themſelves, is no argument that they were not guilty. This other is as weak, that "a King's Intereſt above that of any other man, lies chiefly in the common welfare of his ſubjects;" therefore no king will do ought againſt the common welfare. For by this evaſion any tyrant might as well purge himſelf from the guilt of raiſing troubles or commotions among the people, becauſe undoubtedly his chief intereſt lies in their ſitting ſtill.

I ſaid but now that even this chapter, if nothing elſe, might ſuffice to diſcover his good affection to the rebels; which in this that follows too notoriouſly appears, imputing this inſurrection to "the prepoſterous rigour, and unreaſonable ſeverity, the covetous zeal and uncharitable fury of ſome men," (theſe "ſome men" by his continual paraphraſe are meant the parliament,) and laſtly, "to the fear of utter extirpation." If the whole Iriſhry of rebels had fee'd ſome advocate to ſpeak partially and ſophiſtically in their defence, he could have hardly dazled better: yet nevertheleſs would have proved himſelf no other than a plauſible deceiver. And perhaps, *(nay more than perhaps, for it is affirmed and extant under good evidence, that)* thoſe feigned terrors and jealouſies were either by the king himſelf, or the popiſh prieſts which were ſent by him, put into the head of that inquiſitive people, on ſet purpoſe to engage them. For who had power "to oppreſs" them, or to relieve them being oppreſſed, but the king, or his immediate deputy? This rather ſhould have made them riſe againſt the king, than againſt the parliament. Who threatned or ever thought of their extirpation, till they themſelves had begun it to the Engliſh? As for "prepoſterous rigour, covetous zeal, and uncharitable fury," they had more reaſon to ſuſpect thoſe evils firſt from his own commands, whom they ſaw uſing daily no greater argument to prove the truth of his religion than by enduring no other but his own Prelatical, and to force it upon others, made epiſcopal, ceremonial, and common-prayer book wars. But the papiſts underſtood him better than by the outſide, and knew that thoſe wars were their wars. Although if the commonwealth ſhould be afraid to ſuppreſs open idolatry, leſt the papiſts thereupon ſhould grow deſperate, this were to let them grow and become our perſecutors, while we neglected what we might have done evangelically, to be their reformers. Or to do as his father James did, who inſtead of taking heart and putting confidence in God by ſuch a deliverance as from the powder-plot, though it went not off, yet with the meer conceit of it, as ſome obſerve, was hit into ſuch a hectic trembling* between proteſtant and papiſt all his life after, that he never durſt from that time do otherwiſe than equivocate or collogue with the pope and his adherents,

He would be thought to commiſerate the ſad effects of that rebellion, and to lament that "the tears and blood ſpilt there, did not quench the ſparks of our civil" diſcord here. But who began theſe diſſenſions? and what can be more openly known than thoſe retardings and delays which by himſelf were continually deviſed, to hinder and put back the relief of thoſe diſtreſſed proteſtants? *which undoubtedly, had it not been then put back, might have ſaved many ſtreams of theſe tears and that blood whereof he ſeems here ſo ready to bewail the ſpilling. His manifold excuſes, diverſions and delays, are too well known to be recited here in particular, and too many.*

But "he offered to go himſelf in perſon upon that expedition," and reckons up many ſurmiſes why he thinks they would not ſuffer him. But mentions not that by his underdealing to debauch armies here at home, and by his ſecret intercourſe with the chief rebels, long ere that time every where known, he had brought the parliament into ſo juſt a diffidence of him, as that they durſt not leave the public arms to his diſpoſal, much leſs an army to his conduct.

* The ſecond edition has *ſhivering*.

He concludes, " That next the ſin of thoſe who began that rebellion, theirs muſt needs be who hindered the ſuppreſſing, or diverted the aids." But judgment raſhly given, ofttimes involves the judge himſelf. He finds fault with thoſe " who threatened all extremity to the rebels," and pleads much that mercy ſhould be ſhown them. It ſeems he found himſelf not ſo much concerned as thoſe who had loſt fathers, brothers, wives and children by their cruelty, whom in juſtice to retaliate, is not, as he ſuppoſes, " unevangelical," ſo long as magiſtracy and war are not laid down under the goſpel. If this his ſermon of affected mercy were not too phariſaical, how could he permit himſelf to cauſe the ſlaughter of ſo many thouſands here in England for mere prerogatives, the toys and gewgaws of his crown, for copes and ſurplices, the trinkets of his prieſts, and not perceive his own zeal, while he taxes others, to be moſt prepoſterous and unevangelical? Neither is there the ſame cauſe to deſtroy a whole city for the raviſhing of a ſiſter, not done out of villainy, and recompence offered by marriage, nor the ſame cauſe for thoſe diſciples to ſummon fire from heaven upon the whole city where they were denied lodging, and for a nation by juſt war and execution to ſlay whole families of them who ſo barbarouſly had ſlain whole families before. Did not all Iſrael do as much againſt the Benjamites for one rape committed by a few, and defended by the whole tribe? and did they not the ſame to Jabeſh Gilead for not aſſiſting them in that revenge? I ſpeak not this, that ſuch meaſure ſhould be meted rigorouſly to all the Iriſh, or as remembring that the parliament ever ſo decreed, but to ſhew that this his homily hath more craft and affectation in it, than of ſound doctrine.

But it was happy that his going into Ireland was not conſented to, for either he had certainly turned his *raiſed* forces againſt the parliament itſelf, or not gone at all, or had he gone, what work he would have made there, his own following words declare.

" He would have puniſhed ſome," no queſtion, for ſome perhaps who were of leaſt uſe, muſt of neceſſity have been ſacrificed to his reputation, and the convenience of his affairs. Others he " would have diſarmed," that is to ſay, in his own time: but " all of them he would have protected from the fury of thoſe that would have drowned them, if they had refuſed to ſwim down the popular ſtream." Theſe expreſſions are too often met, and too well underſtood for any man to doubt his meaning. By the " fury of thoſe," he means no other than the juſtice of parliament, to whom yet he had committed the whole buſineſs. Thoſe who would have refuſed to ſwim down the popular ſtream, our conſtant key tells us to be papiſts, prelates, and their faction, theſe, by his own confeſſion here, he would have protected againſt his puritan parliament. And by this who ſees not that he and the Iriſh rebels had but one aim, one and the ſame drift, and would have forthwith joined in one body againſt us?

He goes on ſtill in his tenderneſs of the Iriſh rebels, fearing leſt " our zeal ſhould be more greedy to kill the bear for his ſkin, than for any harm he hath done." This either juſtifies the rebels to have done no harm at all, or infers his opinion that the parliament is more bloody and rapacious in the proſecution of their juſtice, than thoſe rebels were in the execution of their barbarous cruelty. Let men doubt now and diſpute to whom the king was a friend moſt, to his Engliſh parliament, or to his Iriſh rebels.

With whom, that we may yet ſee further how much he was their friend, after that the parliament had brought them every where either to famine, or a low condition, he, to give them all the reſpite and advantages they could deſire, without advice of parliament, to whom he himſelf had committed the managing of that war, makes a ceſſation, in pretence to relieve the proteſtants, " overborne there with numbers," but as the event proved, to ſupport the papiſts, by diverting and drawing over the Engliſh army there, to his own ſervice here againſt the parliament. For that the proteſtants were then on the winning hand, it muſt needs be plain, who notwithſtanding the miſs of thoſe forces, which

aft

at their landing here maſtered without difficulty great part of Wales and Cheſhire, yet made a ſhift to keep their own in Ireland. But the plot of this Iriſh truce is in good part diſcovered in that declaration of September 30, 1643. And if the proteſtants were but handfuls there, as he calls them, why did he ſtop and way-lay both by land and ſea, to his utmoſt power, thoſe proviſions and ſupplies which were ſent by the parliament? How were ſo many handfuls called over, as for a while ſtood him in no ſmall ſtead, and againſt our main forces here in England?

Since therefore all the reaſons that can be given of this ceſſation appear ſo falſe and frivolous, it may be juſtly feared that the deſign itſelf was moſt wicked and pernicious. What remains then? He "appeals to God," and is caſt, likening his puniſhment to Job's trials, before he ſaw them to have Job's ending. *But how could charity herſelf believe there was at all in him any religion, ſo much as but to fear there is a God; whenas, by what is noted in the declaration of "No more addreſſes," he vowed ſolemnly to the parliament, with imprecations upon himſelf and his poſterity, if ever he conſented to the aboliſhing of thoſe laws which were in force againſt papiſts; and at the ſame time, as appeared plainly by the very date of his own letters to the queen and Ormond, conſented to the aboliſhing of all penal laws againſt them both in Ireland and England? If theſe were acts of a religious prince, what memory of man, written or unwritten, can tell us news of any prince that ever was irreligious?* He cannot ſtand "to make prolix apologies." Then ſurely thoſe long pamphlets ſet out for declarations and proteſtations in his name, were none of his; and how they ſhould be his indeed, being ſo repugnant to the whole courſe of his actions, augments the difficulty.

But he uſurps a common ſaying, "That it is kingly to do well, and hear ill." That may be ſometimes true: but far more frequently to do ill and hear well, ſo great is the multitude of flatterers, and them that deify the name of king!

Yet not content with theſe neighbours, we have him ſtill a perpetual preacher of his own virtues, and of that eſpecially, which who knows not to be Patience perforce?

He "believes it will at laſt appear that they who firſt began to embroil his other kingdoms, are alſo guilty of the blood of Ireland." And we believe ſo too, for now the ceſſation is become a peace by publiſhed articles, and commiſſion to bring them over againſt England, firſt only ten thouſand by the earl of Glamorgan*, next all of them, if poſſible, under Ormond, which was the laſt of all his tranſactions done as a public perſon. And no wonder, for he looked upon the blood ſpilt, whether of ſubjects or of rebels, with an indifferent eye, "as exhauſted out of his own veins," without diſtinguiſhing, as he ought, which was good blood and which corrupt, the not letting out whereof, endangers the whole body.

And what the doctrine is, ye may perceive alſo by the prayer, which after a ſhort ejaculation for the "poor Proteſtants," prays at large for the Iriſh rebels, that God would not give them over, or "their children, to the covetouſneſs, cruelty, fierce and curſed anger" of the parliament.

He finiſhes with a deliberate and ſolemn curſe "upon himſelf and his father's houſe." Which how far God hath already brought to paſs, is to the end that men by ſo eminent an example ſhould learn to tremble at his judgments, and not play with imprecations.

* See this fully proved in Dr Birch's *Enquiry into the ſhare, which king Charles I had in the tranſactions of the earl of Glamorgan.* The ſecond edition, 1756.

XIII. Upon

XIII. Upon the calling in of the Scots, and their coming.

IT muſt needs ſeem ſtrange, *where* men accuſtom themſelves to ponder and contemplate things in their firſt original and inſtitution, that kings, who, as all other officers of the public, were at firſt choſen and inſtalled only by conſent and ſuffrage of the people, to govern them as freemen by laws of their own making, and to be, in conſideration of that dignity and riches beſtowed upon them, the intruſted ſervants of the commonwealth, ſhould notwithſtanding grow up to that diſhoneſt encroachment, as to eſteem themſelves maſters, both of that great truſt which they ſerve, and of the people that betruſted them: counting what they ought to do, both in diſcharge of their public duty, and for the great reward of honour and revenue which they receive, as done all of meer grace and favour, as if their power over us were by nature, and from themſelves, or that God had ſold us into their hands. *Indeed, if the race of kings were eminently the beſt of men, as the breed at Tutbury is of horſes, it would in reaſon then be their part only to command, ours always to obey. But kings by generation no way excelling others, and moſt commonly not being the wiſeſt or the worthieſt by far of whom they claim to have the governing, that we ſhould yield them ſubjection to our own ruin, or hold of them the right of our common ſafety, and our natural freedom by mere gift, (as when the conduit piſſes wine at coronations) from the ſuperfluity of their royal grace and beneficence, we may be ſure was never the intent of God, whoſe ways are juſt and equal, never the intent of nature, whoſe works are alſo regular, never of any people not wholly barbarous, whom prudence, or no more but human ſenſe, would have better guided when they firſt created kings, than ſo to nullify and tread to dirt the reſt of mankind, by exalting one perſon and his lineage without other merit looked after, but the mere contingency of a begetting, into an abſolute and unaccountable dominion over them and their poſterity.* *Yet this ignorant* or wilful miſtake of the whole matter, had taken ſo deep root in the imagination of this king, that whether to the Engliſh or to the Scot, mentioning what acts of his regal office (though God knows how unwillingly) he had paſſed, he calls them, as in other places, acts of grace and bounty, ſo here "ſpecial obligations, favours, to gratify active ſpirits, and the deſires of that party." Words not only ſounding pride and lordly uſurpation, but injuſtice, partiality and corruption. For to the Iriſh he ſo far condeſcended, as firſt to tolerate in private, then to covenant openly the tolerating of popery: ſo far to the Scot, as to remove biſhops, eſtabliſh preſbytery, and the militia in their own hands, "preferring, as ſome thought, the deſires of Scotland before his own intereſt and honour." But being once on this ſide Tweed, his reaſon, his conſcience, and his honour became ſo frightened with a kind of falſe virginity, that to the Engliſh neither one nor other of the ſame demands could be granted, wherewith the Scots were gratified, as if our air and climate on a ſudden had changed the property and the nature both of conſcience, honour, and reaſon, or that he found none ſo fit as Engliſh to be the ſubjects of his arbitrary power. Ireland was as Ephraim, the ſtrength of his head; Scotland as Judah, was his lawgiver, but over England, as over Edom, he meant to caſt his ſhoe: and yet ſo many ſober Engliſhmen not ſufficiently awake to conſider this, like men inchanted with the Circæan cup of ſervitude, will not be held back from running their own heads into the yoke of bondage.

The ſum of his diſcourſe is againſt "ſettling of religion by violent means," which whether it were the Scots deſign upon England, they are beſt able to clear themſelves. But this of all may ſeem ſtrangeſt, that the king, who, while it was permitted him, never did thing more eagerly than to moleſt and perſecute the conſciences of moſt religious men, he who had made a war, and loſt all, rather than not uphold a hierarchy of perſecuting biſhops, ſhould have the confidence here to profeſs himſelf ſo much an

enemy

enemy of thoſe that force the conſcience. For was it not he, who upon the Engliſh obtruded new ceremonies, upon the Scots a new Liturgy, and with his ſword went about to engrave * a bloody Rubric on their backs? Did he not forbid and hinder all effectual ſearch of truth, nay, like a beſieging enemy, ſtopt all her paſſages both by word and writing? Yet here can talk of "fair and equal diſputations:" where notwithſtanding, if all ſubmit not to his judgment, as not being "rationally convicted," they muſt ſubmit (and he conceals it not) to his penalty, as counted obſtinate. But what if he himſelf, and thoſe his learned churchmen, were the convicted or the obſtinate part long ago; ſhould reformation ſuffer them to ſit lording over the Church in their fat biſhoprics and pluralities, like the great whore that ſitteth upon many waters, till they would vouchſafe to be diſputed out? Or ſhould we ſit diſputing, while they ſat plotting and perſecuting? Thoſe clergymen were not "to be driven into the fold like ſheep," as his ſimile runs, but to be driven out of the fold like wolves or thieves, where they ſat fleecing thoſe flocks which they never fed.

He believes "that preſbytery, though proved to be the only inſtitution of Jeſus Chriſt, were not by the ſword to be ſet up without his conſent," which is contrary both to the doctrine, and the known practice of all proteſtant churches, if his ſword threaten thoſe who of their own accord embrace it.

And although Chriſt and his apoſtles, being to civil affairs but private men, contended not with magiſtrates, yet when magiſtrates themſelves, and eſpecially parliaments, who have greateſt right to diſpoſe of the civil ſword, come to know religion, they ought in conſcience to defend all thoſe who receive it willingly, againſt the violence of any king or tyrant whatſoever. Neither is it therefore true, "that chriſtianity is planted or watered with chriſtian blood," for there is a large difference between forcing men by the ſword to turn preſbyterians, and defending thoſe who willingly are ſo, from a furious inroad of bloody biſhops, armed with the militia of a king their pupil. And if "covetouſneſs and ambition be an argument that preſbytery hath not much of Chriſt," it argues more ſtrongly againſt epiſcopacy, which from the time of her firſt mounting to an order above the preſbyters, had no other parents than covetouſneſs and ambition. And thoſe Sects, Schiſms, and Hereſies, which he ſpeaks of, "if they get but ſtrength and numbers," need no other pattern than epiſcopacy and himſelf, to "ſet up their ways by the like method of violence." Nor is there any thing that hath more marks of ſchiſm and ſectariſm than Engliſh epiſcopacy, whether we look at apoſtolic times, or at reformed Churches, for the univerſal way of church-government before," may as ſoon lead us into groſs error, as their univerſally corrupted doctrine. And Government, by reaſon of ambition, was likelieſt to be corrupted much the ſooner of the two, However, nothing can be to us catholic or univerſal in religion, but what the Scripture teaches, whatſoever without Scripture pleads to be univerſal in the Church, in being univerſal is but the more ſchiſmatical. Much leſs can particular laws and conſtitutions impart to the Church of England any power of conſiſtory or tribunal above other Churches, to be the ſole judge of what is ſect or ſchiſm, as with much rigour, and without Scripture they took upon them. Yet theſe the king reſolves here to defend and maintain to his laſt, pretending, after all thoſe conferences offered, or had with him, "not to ſee more rational and religious motives than ſoldiers carry in their knapſacks," with one thus reſolved, it was but folly to ſtand diſputing.

He imagines his "own judicious zeal to be moſt concerned in his tuition of the Church." So thought Saul when he preſumed to offer ſacrifice, for which he loſt his kingdom, ſo thought Uzziah when he went into the temple, but was thruſt out with a leproſy for his opinioned zeal, which he thought judicious. It is not the part of a king,

* The ſecond edition has *ſcore*.

becauſe he ought to defend the Church, therefore to ſet himſelf ſupreme head over the Church, or to meddle with eccleſial government, or to defend the Church otherwiſe than the Church would be defended, for ſuch defence is bondage: nor to defend abuſes, and ſtop all reformation under the name of "new moulds fancied and faſhioned to private deſigns." The holy things of Church are in the power of other keys than were delivered to his keeping. Chriſtian liberty, purchaſed with the death of our redeemer, and eſtabliſhed by the ſending of his free ſpirit to inhabit in us, is not now to depend upon the doubtful conſent of any earthly monarch. nor to be again fettered with a preſumptuous negative voice, tyrannical to the parliament, but much more tyrannical to the Church of God, which was compelled to implore the aid of parliament, to remove his force and heavy hands from off our conſciences, who therefore complains now of that moſt juſt defenſive force, becauſe only it removed his violence and perſecution. If this be a violation to his conſcience, that it was hindred by the parliament from violating the more tender conſciences of ſo many thouſand good chriſtians, let the uſurping conſcience of all tyrants be ever ſo violated!

He wonders, fox wonder! how we could ſo much "diſtruſt God's aſſiſtance," as to call in the proteſtant aid of our brethren in Scotland. why then did he, if his truſt were in God and the juſtice of his cauſe, not ſcruple to ſollicit and invite earneſtly the aſſiſtance both of papiſts and of Iriſh rebels? If the Scots were by us at length ſent home, they were not called to ſtay here always; neither was it for the people's eaſe to feed ſo many legions longer than their help was needful.

"The government of their kirk we deſpiſed not," but their impoſing of that government upon us, not preſbytery but arch-preſbytery, Claſſical, Provincial, and Diocеſan preſbytery, claiming to itſelf a lordly power and ſuperintendency both over flocks and paſtors, over perſons and congregations no way their own. But theſe debates in his judgment would have been ended better "by the beſt divines in chriſtendom in a full and free ſynod" A moſt improbable way, and ſuch as never yet was uſed, at leaſt with good ſucceſs, by any proteſtant kingdom or ſtate ſince the reformation. every true Church having wherewithal from heaven, and the aſſiſting ſpirit of Chriſt implored, to be complete and perfect within itſelf. And the whole nation is not eaſily to be thought ſo raw, and ſo perpetually a novice after all this light, as to need the help and direction of other nations, more than what they write in public of their opinion, in a matter ſo familiar as Church-government

In fine, he accuſes Piety with the want of Loyalty, and Religion with the breach of Allegiance, as if God and he were one maſter, whoſe commands were ſo often contrary to the commands of God He would perſuade the Scots that their "chief intereſt conſiſts in their fidelity to the crown" But true policy will teach them to find a ſafer intereſt in the common friendſhip of England, than in the ruins of one ejected family.

XIV. Upon the Covenant.

UPON this theme his diſcourſe is long, his matter little but repetition, and therefore ſoon anſwered First, after an abuſive and ſtrange apprehenſion of covenants, as if men "pawned their ſouls" to them with whom they covenant, he digreſſes to plead for biſhops; firſt from the antiquity of their "poſſeſſion here, ſince the firſt plantation of chriſtianity in this iſland, next from "a univerſal preſcription ſince the Apoſtles, till this laſt century" But what avails the moſt primitive antiquity againſt the plain ſenſe of Scripture? which if the laſt century have beſt followed, it ought in our eſteem to be the firſt. And yet it hath been often proved by learned men from the writings and epiſtles of moſt ancient chriſtians, that epiſcopacy crept not up into an order above the preſbyters, till many years after that the Apoſtles were deceaſed.

He next "is unſatisfied with the covenant," not only for "ſome paſſages in it referring to himſelf," as he ſuppoſes, "with very dubious and dangerous limitations," but for binding men "by oath and covenant" to the reformation of Church-diſcipline. Firſt, thoſe limitations were not more dangerous to him, than he to our liberty and religion, next, that which was there vowed, to caſt out of the Church an antichriſtian hierarchy which God had not planted, but ambition and corruption had brought in, and foſtered to the Church's great damage and oppreſſion, was no point of controverſy to be argued without end, but a thing of clear moral neceſſity to be forthwith done Neither was the "Covenant ſuperfluous, though former engagements both religious and legal bound us before" But was the practice of all Churches heretofore intending reformation All Iſrael, though bound enough before by the law of Moſes "to all neceſſary duties;" yet with Aſa their king entered into a new covenant at the beginning of a reformation And the Jews after captivity, without conſent demanded of that king who was their maſter, took ſolemn oath to walk in the commandments of God. All proteſtant Churches have done the like, notwithſtanding former engagements to their ſeveral duties. And although his aim were to ſow variance between the proteſtation and the covenant, to reconcile them is not difficult The proteſtation was but one ſtep, extending only to the doctrine of the Church of England, as it was diſtinct from Church-diſcipline, the covenant went further, as it pleaſed God to diſpenſe his light *and our encouragement* by degrees, and comprehended church-government Former with latter ſteps in the progreſs of well doing need not reconcilement Nevertheleſs he breaks through to his concluſion, "that all honeſt and wiſe men ever thought themſelves ſufficiently bound by former ties of religion," leaving Aſa, Ezra, and the whole Church of God in ſundry ages to ſhift for honeſty and wiſdom from ſome other than his teſtimony And although after-contracts abſolve not till the former be made void, yet he firſt having done that, our duty returns back, which to him was neither moral nor eternal, but conditional.

Willing to perſuade himſelf that many "good men" took the covenant, either unwarily or out of fear, he ſeems to have beſtowed ſome thoughts how theſe "good men" following his advice may keep the covenant and not keep it The firſt evaſion is, preſuming "that the chief end of covenanting in ſuch men's intentions was to preſerve religion in purity, and the kingdom's peace." But the covenant will more truly inform them that purity of religion and the kingdom's peace was not then in ſtate to be preſerved, but to be reſtored, and therefore binds them not to a preſervation of what was, but to a reformation of what was evil, what was traditional, and dangerous, whether novelty or antiquity, in church or ſtate To do this, claſhes with "no former oath" lawfully ſworn either to God or the king, and rightly underſtood.

In general, he brands all "ſuch confederations by league and covenant, as the common road uſed in all factious perturbations of ſtate and church" This kind of language reflects with the ſame ignominy upon all the proteſtant reformations that have been ſince Luther, and ſo indeed doth his whole book replenished throughout with hardly other words or arguments, than papiſts, and eſpecially popiſh kings, have uſed heretofore againſt their proteſtant ſubjects. whom he would perſuade to be "every man his own pope, and to abſolve himſelf of thoſe ties," by the ſuggeſtion of falſe or equivocal interpretations too oft repeated to be now anſwered.

The parliament he ſaith, "make their covenant like Manna, agreeable to every man's palate" This is another of his gloſſes upon the covenant, he is content to let it be Manna, but his drift is that men ſhould loath it, or at leaſt expound it by their own "reliſh," and "latitude of ſenſe," wherein leſt any one of the ſimpler ſort ſhould fail to be his crafts-maſter, he furniſhes him with two or three laxative, he terms them "general clauſes, which may ſerve ſomewhat to relieve them" againſt the covenant taken intimating, as if "what were lawful and according to the word of God," were

no

no otherwiſe ſo, than as every man fancied to himſelf. From ſuch learned explications and reſolutions as theſe upon the covenant, what marvel if no royaliſt or malignant refuſe to take it, as having learnt from theſe princely inſtructions his many " ſalvoes, cautions, and reſervations," how to be a covenanter and anticovenanter, how at once to be a Scot, and an Iriſh rebel.

He returns again to diſallow of " that Reformation which the Covenant" vows, " as being the partial advice of a few Divines " But matters of this moment, as they were not to be decided there by thoſe divines, ſo neither are they to be determined here by eſſays and curtal aphoriſms, but by ſolid proofs of ſcripture.

The reſt of his diſcourſe he ſpends, highly accuſing the parliament, " that the main reformation by" them " intended, was to rob the Church," and much applauding himſelf both for " his forwardneſs" to all due reformation, and his averſeneſs from all ſuch kind of Sacrilege. All which, with his glorious title of the " Church's Defender" we leave him to make good by " Pharaoh's divinity," if he pleaſe, for to Joſeph's Piety it will be a taſk unſuitable As for " the parity and poverty of miniſters," which he takes to be ſo ſad of " conſequence," the ſcripture reckons them for two ſpecial legacies left by our Saviour to his diſciples ; under which two primitive nurſes, for ſuch they were indeed, the church of God more truly flouriſhed than ever after, ſince the time that imparity and church-revenue ruſhing in, corrupted and belepered all the clergy with a worſe infection than Gehazi's ; ſome one of whoſe tribe, rather than a king, I ſhould take to be compiler of that unſalted and Simonical prayer annexed · although the prayer itſelf ſtrongly prays againſt them For never ſuch holy things as he means, were given to more ſwine, nor the church's bread more to Dogs, than when it fed ambitious, irreligious and dumb prelates.

XV. Upon the many Jealouſies, &c.

TO wipe off jealouſies and ſcandals, the beſt way had been by clear actions, or till actions could be cleared, by evident reaſons , but meer words we are too well acquainted with. Had " his honour and reputation been dearer to him" than the luſt of reigning, how could the parliament of either nation have laid ſo often at his door the breach of words, promiſes, acts, oaths, and execrations, as they do avowedly in many of their petitions and addreſſes to him? Thither I remit the reader And who can believe that whole parliaments, elected by the people from all parts of the land, ſhould meet in one mind and reſolution not to adviſe him, but to conſpire againſt him, in a worſe powder-plot than Cateſby's, " to blow up," as he terms it, " the people's affection towards him, and batter down their loyalty by the engines of foul aſperſions ·" Water-works rather than engines to batter with, yet thoſe aſperſions were raiſed from the foulneſs of his own actions. Whereof to purge himſelf, he uſes no other argument than a general and ſo often iterated commendation of himſelf. and thinks that court holy-water hath the virtue of expiation, at leaſt with the ſilly people ; to whom he familiarly imputes ſin where none is, to ſeem liberal of his forgiveneſs where none is aſked or needed

What ways he hath taken toward the proſperity of his people, which he would ſeem " ſo earneſtly to deſire," if we do but once call to mind, it will be enough to teach us, looking on the ſmooth inſinuations here, that tyrants are not more flattered by their ſlaves, than forced to flatter others whom they fear.

For the people's " tranquility he would willingly be the Jonah ," but leſt he ſhould be taken at his word, pretends to foreſee within ken two imaginary " winds" never heard of in the compaſs, which threaten, if he be caſt over board, " to increaſe the ſtorm ," but that controverſy divine lot hath ended

" He had rather not rule, than that his people ſhould be ruined :" and yet above theſe twenty years hath been ruining the people about the niceties of his ruling. He is accurate " to put a difference between the plague of malice, and the ague of miſtakes; the itch of novelty, and the leproſy of diſloyalty." But had he as well known how to diſtinguiſh between the venerable grey hairs of ancient religion, and the old ſcurff of ſuperſtition, between the wholeſome heat of well governing, and the feverous rage of tyrannizing, his judgment in ſtate phyſic had been of more authority

Much he propheſies, " that the credit of thoſe men who have caſt black ſcandals on him, ſhall ere long be quite blaſted by the ſame furnace of popular obloquy, wherein they ſought to caſt his name and honour." I believe not that a Romiſh gilded portraiture gives better oracle than a Babyloniſh golden image could do, to tell us truly who heated that furnace of obloquy, or who deſerves to be thrown in, Nebuchadnezzar or the three kingdoms It " gave him great cauſe to ſuſpect his own innocence," that he was oppoſed by " ſo many who profeſt ſingular piety." But this qualm was ſoon over, and he concluded rather to ſuſpect their religion than his own innocence, affirming that " many with him were both learned and religious above the ordinary ſize." But if his great ſeal without the parliament were not ſufficient to create lords, his parole muſt needs be far more unable to create learned and religious men ; and who ſhall authorize his unlearned judgment to point them out ?

He gueſſes that " many well-minded men were by popular preachers urged to oppoſe him " But the oppoſition undoubtedly proceeded and continues from heads far wiſer, and ſpirits of a nobler ſtrain , thoſe prieſt-led Herodians with their blind guides are in the ditch already , travelling, as they thought, to Sion, but moored in the Iſle of Wight

He thanks God " for his conſtancy to the proteſtant religion both abroad and at home " Abroad, his letter to the pope , at home, his innovations in the church will ſpeak his conſtancy in religion what it was, without further credit to this vain boaſt

His " uſing the aſſiſtance of ſome papiſts," as the cauſe might be, could not hurt his religion ; but in the ſettling of proteſtantiſm their aid was both unſeemly and ſuſpicious, and inferred that the greateſt part of proteſtants were againſt him and his obtruded ſettlement

But this is ſtrange indeed, that he ſhould appear now teaching the parliament what no man, till this was read, thought ever he had learned, " that difference of perſwaſion in religious matters may fall out where there is the ſameneſs of allegiance and ſubjection." If he thought ſo from the beginning, wherefore was there ſuch compulſion uſed to the puritans of England, and the whole realm of Scotland, about conforming to a liturgy ? Wherefore no biſhop no king ? Wherefore epiſcopacy more agreeable to monarchy, if different perſuaſions in religion may agree in one duty and allegiance ? Thus do court-maxims like court-minions, riſe or fall as the king pleaſes.

Not to tax him for want of elegance as a courtier, in writing Oglio for Olla the Spaniſh word, it might be well affirmed that there was a greater Medley and diſproportioning of religions, to mix papiſts with proteſtants in a religious cauſe, than to entertain all thoſe diverſified ſects, who yet were all proteſtants, one religion, though many opinions.

Neither was it any " ſhame to proteſtants," that he a declared papiſt, if his own letter to the pope, not yet renounced, belye him not, found ſo few proteſtants of his religion, as enforced him to call in both the counſel and the aid of papiſts to help eſtabliſh proteſtancy, who were led on, not " by the ſenſe of their allegiance," but by the hope of his apoſtacy to Rome, from diſputing to warring , his own voluntary and firſt appeal.

His hearkening to evil counſellors, charged upon him ſo often by the parliament, he puts off as " a device of thoſe men who were ſo eager to give him better counſel " That " thoſe men" were the parliament, and that he ought to have uſed the counſel of none

none but those, as a king, is already known. What their civility laid upon evil counsellors, he himself most commonly owned; but the event of those evil counsels "the enormities, the confusions, the miseries," he transfers from the guilt of his own civil broils to the just resistance made by parliament; and imputes what miscarriages of his they could not yet remove for his opposing, as if they were some new misdemeanors of their bringing in, and not the inveterate diseases of his own bad government, which, with a disease as bad, he falls again to magnify and commend and may all those who would be governed by his "Retractions and concessions," rather than by laws of parliament, admire his self-encomiums, and be flattered with that "Crown of patience" to which he cunningly exhorted them, that his monarchical foot might have the setting it upon their heads!

That trust which the parliament faithfully discharged in the asserting of our liberties, he calls, "another artifice to withdraw the people from him to their designs" What piece of justice could they have demanded for the people, which the jealousy of a king might not have miscalled a design to disparage his government, and to ingratiate themselves? To be more just, religious, wise, or magnanimous than the common sort, stirs up in a tyrant both fear and envy, and straight he cries out popularity, which in his account is little less than treason. The sum is, they thought to limit *or take away the remora of* his negative voice, *which, like to that little pest at sea, took upon it to arrest and stop the commonwealth steering under full sail to a reformation they thought to* share with him in the militia, both or either of which he could not possibly hold without consent of the people, and not be absolutely a tyrant. He professes "to desire no other liberty than what he envies not his subjects according to law;" yet fought with might and main against his subjects, to have a sole power over them in his hand, both against and beyond law. As for the philosophical liberty which in vain he talks of, we may conclude him very ill trained up in those free notions, who to civil liberty was so injurious.

He calls the conscience "God's sovereignty;" why then doth he contest with God about that supreme title, Why did he lay restraints, and force enlargements upon our consciences in things for which we were to answer God only and the church? God bids us "be subject for conscience sake," that is, as to a magistrate, and in the laws; not usurping over spiritual things, as Lucifer beyond his sphere. *And the same precept bids him likewise for conscience sake be subject to the parliament, both his natural and his legal superior.*

Finally, having laid the fault of these commotions, not upon his own misgovernment, but upon the "ambition of others, the necessity of some mens fortune, and thirst after novelty," he bodes himself "much honour and reputation, that like the sun shall rise and recover himself to such a splendor, as owls, bats, and such fatal birds shall be unable to bear." Poets indeed use to vapour much after this manner. But to bad kings, who without cause expect future glory from their actions, it happens as to bad poets, who sit and starve themselves with a delusive hope to win immortality by their bad lines For though men ought not to "speak evil of dignities" which are just, yet nothing hinders us to speak evil as oft as it is the truth, of those who in their dignities do evil. Thus did our Saviour himself, John the Baptist, and Stephen the Martyr. And those black veils of his own misdeeds he might be sure would ever keep "his face from shining," till he could "refute evil speaking with well doing," which grace he seems here to pray for; and his prayer doubtless as it was prayed, so it was heard. But even his prayer is so ambitious of prerogative, that it dares ask away the prerogative of Christ himself, "To become the head-stone of the corner."

XVI. Upon

XVI. Upon the Ordinance againſt the Common-Prayer Book.

WHAT to think of liturgies, both the ſenſe of ſcripture, and apoſtolical practice would have taught him better, than his human reaſonings and conjectures: nevertheleſs, what weight they have, let us conſider. If it "be no news to have all innovations uſhered in with the name of reformation," ſure it is leſs news to have all reformation cenſured and oppoſed under the name of innovation, by thoſe, who being exalted in high place above their merit, fear all change, though of things never ſo ill or ſo unwiſely ſettled. So hardly can the dotage of thoſe that dwell upon antiquity allow preſent times any ſhare of godlineſs or wiſdom.

The removing of liturgy he traduces to be done only as a "thing plauſible to the people;" whoſe rejection of it he likens, with ſmall reverence, to the crucifying of our Saviour, next, that it was done "to pleaſe thoſe men who gloried in their extemporary vein," meaning the miniſters. For whom it will be beſt to anſwer, as was anſwered for the man born blind, "They are of age, let them ſpeak for themſelves," not how they came blind, but whether it were liturgy that held them tongue tied.

"For the matter contained in that book," we need no better witneſs than king Edward the Sixth, who to the Corniſh rebels confeſſes it was no other than the old maſs-book done into Engliſh, all but ſome few words that were expunged. And by this argument which king Edward ſo promptly had to uſe againſt that irreligious rabble, we may be aſſured it was the carnal fear of thoſe divines and politicians that modelled the liturgy no farther off from the old maſs, leſt by too great an alteration they ſhould incenſe the people, and be deſtitute of the ſame ſhifts to fly to, which they had taught the young king.

"For the manner of uſing ſet forms, there is no doubt but that wholeſome" matter, and good deſires rightly conceived in the heart, wholeſome words will follow of themſelves. Neither can any true Chriſtian find a reaſon why liturgy ſhould be at all admitted, a preſcription not impoſed or practiſed by thoſe firſt founders of the church, who alone had that authority: without whoſe precept or example, how conſtantly the prieſt puts on his gown and ſurplice, ſo conſtantly doth his prayer put on a ſervile yoke of liturgy. This is evident, that they "who uſe no ſet forms of prayer," have words from their affections; while others are to ſeek affections fit and proportionable to a certain doſe of prepared words, which as they are not rigorouſly forbid to any man's private infirmity, ſo to impriſon and confine by force, into a pinfold of ſet words, thoſe two moſt unimpriſonable things, our prayers, and that divine ſpirit of utterance that moves them, is a tyranny that would have longer hands than thoſe giants who threatened bondage to heaven. What we may do in the ſame form of words is not ſo much the queſtion, as whether liturgy may be forced, as he forced it. It is true that we "pray to the ſame God," muſt we therefore always uſe the ſame words? Let us then uſe but one word, becauſe we pray to one God. "We profeſs the ſame truths," but the liturgy comprehends not all truths: "we read the ſame ſcriptures," but never read that all thoſe ſacred expreſſions, all benefit and uſe of ſcripture, as to public prayer, ſhould be denied us, except what was barrelled up in a common-prayer book with many mixtures of their own, and which is worſe, without ſalt. But ſuppoſe them ſavoury words and unmixed, ſuppoſe them Manna itſelf, yet if they ſhall be hoarded up and enjoined us, while God every morning rains down new expreſſions into our hearts, inſtead of being fit to uſe, they will be found like reſerved Manna, rather to breed worms and ſtink. "We have the ſame duties upon us, and feel the ſame wants," yet not always the ſame, nor at all times alike, but with variety of circumſtances, which aſk variety of words: whereof God hath given us plenty, not to uſe ſo copiouſly upon all other occaſions, and ſo nigardly to him

him alone in our devotions. As if chriſtians were now in a worſe famine of words fit for prayer, than was of food at the ſiege of Jeruſalem, when perhaps the prieſts being to remove the ſhew bread, as was accuſtomed, were compelled every ſabbath-day, for want of other loaves, to bring again ſtill the ſame. If the "Lord's Prayer" had been the "warrant or the pattern of ſet liturgies," as is here affirmed, why was neither that prayer, nor any other ſet form ever after uſed, or ſo much as mentioned by the Apoſtles, much leſs commended to our uſe? Why was their care wanting in a thing ſo uſeful to the church? ſo full of danger and contention to be left undone by them to other men's penning, of whoſe authority we could not be ſo certain? Why was this forgotten by them, who declare that they have revealed to us the whole counſel of God? who as he left our affections to be guided by his ſanctifying ſpirit, ſo did he likewiſe our words to be put into us without our premeditation *; not only thoſe cautious words to be uſed before gentiles and tyrants, but much more thoſe filial words, of which we have ſo frequent uſe in our acceſs with freedom of ſpeech to the throne of grace. Which to lay aſide for other outward dictates of men, were to injure him and his perfect gift, who is the ſpirit, and the giver of our ability to pray; as if his miniſtration were incompleat, and that to whom he gave affections, he did not alſo afford utterance to make his gift of prayer a perfect gift, *to them eſpecially whoſe office in the church is to pray publicly.*

And although the gift were only natural, yet voluntary prayers are leſs ſubject to formal and ſuperficial tempers than ſet forms for in thoſe, at leaſt for words and matter, he who prays muſt conſult firſt with his heart, which in likelihood may ſtir up his affections, in theſe, having both words and matter ready made to his lips, which is enough to make up the outward act of prayer, his affections grow lazy, and come not up eaſily at the call of words not their own, the prayer alſo having leſs intercourſe and ſympathy with a heart wherein it was not conceived, ſaves itſelf the labour of ſo long a journey downward, and flying up in haſte on the ſpecious wings of formality, if it fall not back again headlong, inſtead of a prayer which was expected, preſents God with a ſet of ſtale and empty words

No doubt but "oſtentation and formality" may taint the beſt duties; we are not therefore to leave duties for no duties, and to turn prayer into a kind of lurry. Cannot unpremeditated bablings be rebuked, and reſtrained in whom we find they are, but the ſpirit of God muſt be forbidden in all men? But it is the cuſtom of bad men and hypocrites to take advantage at the leaſt abuſe of good things, that under that covert they may remove the goodneſs of thoſe things, rather than the abuſe And how unknowingly, how weakly is the uſing of ſet forms attributed here to "conſtancy," as if it were conſtancy in the cuckoo to be always in the ſame liturgy

Much leſs can it be lawful that an Engliſhed maſs-book, compoſed, for aught we know, by men neither learned, nor godly, ſhould juſtle out, or at any time deprive us the exerciſe of that heavenly gift, which God by ſpecial promiſe pours out daily upon his church, that is to ſay, the ſpirit of prayer. Whereof to help thoſe many infirmities, which he reckons up, "Rudeneſs, Impertinency, Flatneſs," and the like, we have a remedy of God's finding out, which is not liturgy, but his own free ſpirit. Though we know not what to pray as we ought, yet he with ſighs unutterable by any words, much leſs by a ſtinted liturgy, dwelling in us makes interceſſion for us, according to the mind and will of God, both in private, and in the performance of all eccleſiaſtical duties For it is his promiſe alſo, that where two or three gathered together in his name ſhall agree to aſk him any thing, it ſhall be granted, for he is there in the midſt of them If *then* ancient churches, to remedy the infirmities of prayer, or rather the infections of Arian and Pelagian hereſies, neglecting that ordained and promiſed help of the ſpirit, betook them almoſt four hundred years after Chriſt to liturgy, (their own invention,)

* The promiſe of the Spirit's aſſiſtance here alluded to, was extraordinary, and belonged only to the firſt age ſo that the author's argument is in this part inconcluſive.

we are not to imitate them; nor to diſtruſt God in the removal of that truant-help to our devotion, which by him never was appointed. And what is ſaid of liturgy, is ſaid alſo of directory, if it be impoſed: although to forbid the ſervice-book there be much more reaſon, as being of itſelf ſuperſtitious, offenſive, and indeed, though Engliſhed, yet ſtill the maſs-book: and public places ought to be provided of ſuch as need not the help of liturgies or directories continually, but are ſupported with miniſterial gifts anſwerable to their calling

Laſtly, that the common-prayer book was rejected becauſe it "prayed ſo oft for him," he had no reaſon to object for what large and laborious prayers were made for him in the pulpits, if he never heard, it is doubtful they were never heard in heaven. We might now have expected that his own following prayer ſhould add much credit to ſet forms, but on the contrary we find the ſame imperfections in it, as in moſt before, which he lays here upon extemporal. Nor doth he aſk of God to be directed whether liturgies be lawful, but preſumes, and in a manner would perſuade him that they be ſo, praying "that the church and he may never want them" What could be prayed worſe extempore? *unleſs he mean by wanting, that they may never need them.*

XVII. Of the differences in point of Church-Government.

THE government of church by biſhops hath been ſo fully proved from the ſcriptures to be vicious and uſurped, that whether out of piety or policy maintained, it is not much material for piety grounded upon error, can no more juſtify king Charles, than it did queen Mary, in the ſight of God or man. This however muſt not be let paſs without a ſerious obſervation; God having ſo diſpoſed the author in this chapter as to confeſs and diſcover more of myſtery and combination between tyranny and falſe religion, than from any other hand would have been credible Here we may ſee the very dark roots of them both turned up, and how they twine and interweave one another in the earth, tho' above ground ſhooting up in two ſeveral branches We may have learnt both from ſacred *hiſtory*, and times of reformation, that the kings of this world have both ever hated, and inſtinctively feared the church of God Whether it be for that their doctrine ſeems much to favour two things to them ſo dreadful, liberty and equality; or becauſe they are the children of that kingdom, which, as ancient prophecies have foretold, ſhall in the end break to pieces and diſſolve all their great power and dominion. And thoſe kings and potentates who have ſtrove moſt to rid themſelves of this fear, by cutting off or ſuppreſſing the true church, have drawn upon themſelves the occaſion of their own ruin, while they thought with moſt policy to prevent it Thus Pharaoh, when once he began to fear and wax jealous of the Iſraelites, leſt they ſhould multiply and fight againſt him, and that his fear ſtirred him up to afflict and keep them under, as the only remedy of what he feared, ſoon found that the evil which before ſlept, came ſuddenly upon him, by the prepoſterous way he took to prevent * it. Paſſing by examples between, and not ſhutting wilfully our eyes, we may ſee the like ſtory brought to paſs in our own land. This king, more than any before him, except perhaps his father, from his firſt entrance to the crown, harbouring in his mind a ſtrange fear and ſuſpicion of men moſt religious, and their doctrine, which in his own language he here acknowledges, terming "it the ſeditious exorbitancy" of miniſters tongues, and doubting "leſt they," as he not chriſtianly expreſſes it, "ſhould with the keys of heaven let out peace and loyalty from the people's hearts," though they never preached or attempted aught that might juſtly raiſe in him ſuch thoughts,† he could not reſt, or think himſelf ſecure, ſo long as they remained

* The ſecond edition has to *ſhun* it

† The ſecond edition has *apprehenſions.*

in any of his three kingdoms unrooted out. But outwardly professing the same religion with them, he could not presently use violence as Pharaoh did, and that course had with others before but ill succeeded. He chooses therefore a more mystical way, a newer method of antichristian fraud, to the church more dangerous: and like to Balac the son of Zippor, against a nation of prophets thinks it best to hire other esteemed prophets, and to undermine and wear out the true church by a false ecclesiastical policy. To this drift he found the government of bishops most serviceable; an order in the church, as by men first corrupted, so mutually corrupting them who receive it, both in judgment and manners. He, by conferring bishoprics and great livings on whom he thought most pliant to his will, against the known canons and universal practice of the ancient church, whereby those elections were the people's right, sought, as he confesses, to have "greatest influence upon Church-men." They on the other side finding themselves in a high dignity, neither founded by scripture, nor allowed by reformation, nor supported by any spiritual gift or grace of their own, knew it their best course to have dependance only upon him · and wrought his fancy by degrees to that degenerate and unkingly persuasion of "No bishop, no King." Whenas on the contrary all prelates in their own subtle sense are of another mind; according to that of Pius the fourth, remembered in the history of Trent,* that bishops then grow to be most vigorous and potent, when princes happen to be most weak and impotent Thus when both interests of tyranny and episcopacy were incorporate into each other, the king, whose principal safety and establishment consisted in the righteous execution of his civil power, and not in bishops and their wicked counsels, fatally driven on, set himself to the *extirpating* of those men whose doctrine and desire of church-discipline he so feared would be the undoing of his monarchy. And because no temporal law could touch the innocence of their lives, he begins with the persecution of their consciences, laying scandals before them; and makes that the argument to inflict his unjust penalties both on their bodies and estates. In this war against the church, if he *hath* sped so, as other haughty monarchs whom God heretofore hath hardened to the like enterprize, we ought to look up with praises and thanksgiving to the author of our deliverance, to whom victory and power, majesty, honour and dominion belongs for ever.

In the mean while, from his own words we may perceive easily, that the special motives which he had to endear and deprave his judgment to the favouring and utmost defending of episcopacy, are such as here we represent them: and how unwillingly, and with what mental reservation he condescended against his interest to remove it out of the peers house, hath been shewn already. The reasons, which he affirms wrought so much upon his judgment, shall be so far answered as they be urged.

Scripture he *reports, but distinctly* produces none; and next the "constant practice of all christian churches, till of late years tumult, faction, pride, and covetousness, invented new models under the title of Christ's government." Could any papist have spoke more scandalously against all reformation? Well may the parliament and best-affected people not now be troubled at his calumnies and reproaches, since he binds them in the same bundle with all other the reformed churches; who also may now further see, besides their own bitter experience, what a cordial and well-meaning helper they had of him abroad, and how true to the protestant cause

As for Histories to prove bishops, the bible, if we mean not to run into errors, vanities, and uncertainties, must be our only history. Which informs us that the apostles were not properly bishops; next, that bishops were not successors of apostles, in the function of apostleship: and that if they were apostles, they could not be precisely bishops; if bishops, they could not be apostles; this being universal, extraordinary, and immediate from God; that being an ordinary, fixed, and particular charge, the continual inspection over a certain flock. And although an ignorance and deviation

* The second edition has in the *Trentine story*

of the ancient churches afterward, may with as much reaſon and charity be ſuppoſed as ſudden in point of prelaty, as in other manifeſt corruptions, yet that " no example ſince the firſt age for 1500 years can be produced of any ſettled church, wherein were many miniſters and congregations, which had not ſome biſhops above them;" the eccleſiaſtical ſtory, to which he appeals for want of ſcripture, proves clearly to be a falſe and over-confident aſſertion. Sozomenus, who wrote above twelve hundred years ago, in his ſeventh book, relates from his own knowledge, that in the churches of Cyprus and Arabia (places near to Jeruſalem, and with the firſt frequented by apoſtles) they had biſhops in every village; and what could thoſe be more than preſbyters? The like he tells of other nations; and that epiſcopal churches in thoſe days did not condemn them. I add, that many weſtern churches, eminent for their faith and good works, and ſettled above four hundred years ago in France, in Piemont and Bohemia, have both taught and practiſed the ſame doctrine, and not admitted of epiſcopacy among them. And if we may believe what the papiſts themſelves have written of theſe churches, which they call Waldenſes, I find it in a book written almoſt four hundred years ſince, and ſet forth in the Bohemian hiſtory, that thoſe churches in Piemont * have held the ſame doctrine and government, ſince the time that Conſtantine with his miſchievous donations poiſoned Sylveſter and the whole church. Others affirm they have ſo continued there ſince the apoſtles: and Theodorus Belvederenſis in his relation of them, confeſſeth that thoſe hereſies, as he names them, were from the firſt times of chriſtianity in that place. For the reſt I refer me to that famous teſtimony of Jerom, who upon † that very place which he cites here, the epiſtle to Titus, declares openly that biſhop and preſbyter were one and the ſame thing, till by the inſtigation of Satan, partialities grew up in the church, and that biſhops rather by cuſtom than any ordainment of Chriſt, were exalted above preſbyters: whoſe interpretation we truſt ſhall be received before this intricate ſtuff tattled here of Timothy and Titus, and I know not whom their ſucceſſors, far beyond court element, and as far beneath true edification. Theſe are his " fair grounds both from ſcripture-canons and eccleſiaſtical examples," how undivine-like written, and how like a worldly goſpeller that underſtands nothing of theſe matters, poſterity no doubt will be able to judge; and will but little regard what he calls Apoſtolical, who in his letter to the pope calls apoſtolical the Roman religion.

Nor let him think to plead, that therefore " it was not policy of ſtate," or obſtinacy in him which upheld epiſcopacy, becauſe the injuries and loſſes which he ſuſtained by ſo doing were to him " more conſiderable than epiſcopacy itſelf," for all this might Pharaoh have had to ſay in his excuſe of detaining the Iſraelites, that his own and his kingdom's ſafety, ſo much endangered by his denial, was to him more dear than all their building labours could be worth to Egypt. But whom God hardens, them alſo he blinds

He endeavours to make good epiſcopacy not only in " religion, but from the nature of all civil government, where parity breeds confuſion and faction." But of faction and confuſion, to take no other than his own teſtimony, where hath more been ever bred than under the imparity of his own monarchical government? of which to make at this time longer diſpute, and from civil conſtitutions and human conceits to debate and queſtion the convenience of divine ordinations, is neither wiſdom nor ſobriety: and to confound Moſaic Prieſthood with evangelic preſbytery againſt expreſs inſtitution, is as far from warrantable. As little to purpoſe is it, that we ſhould ſtand polling the reformed churches, whether they equalize in number " thoſe of his three kingdoms;" of whom ſo lately the far greater part, what they have long deſired to do, have now quite thrown off epiſcopacy.

* *We have a moſt curious hiſtory of theſe churches, written by* Samuel Morland *eſq, who went commiſſioner extraordinary from* O Cromwel, *for relief of the proteſtants in the valleys of* Piemont, *It was publiſhed in folio,* 1658

† The ſecond edition has it thus, *who upon this very place which he only roves at here.*

Nei-

Neither may we count it the language or religion of a protestant, so to vilify the best reformed churches (for none of them but Lutherans retain bishops) as to fear more the scandalizing of papists, because more numerous, than of our protestant brethren, because a handful. It will not be worth the while to say what "Schismatics or Heretics" have had no bishops; yet, lest he should be taken for a great reader, he who prompted him, if he were a doctor, might have remembered the forementioned place in Sozomenus; which affirms, that besides the Cyprians and Arabians who were counted orthodoxal, the Novatians also, and Montanists in Phrygia had no other bishops than such as were in every village: and what presbyter hath a narrower diocese? As for the Aërians we know of no heretical opinion justly fathered upon them, but that they held bishops and presbyters to be the same. Which he in this place not obscurely seems to hold a heresy in all the reformed churches, with whom why the church of England desired conformity, he can find no reason, with all his "charity, but the coming in of the Scots army;" such a high esteem he had of the English!

He tempts the clergy to return back again to bishops, from the fear of "tenuity and contempt," and the assurance of better "thriving under the favour of princes;" against which temptations if the clergy cannot arm themselves with their own spiritual armour, they are indeed as "poor a carcass" as he terms them.

Of secular honours and great revenues added to the dignity of prelates, since the subject of that question is now removed, we need not spend time: But this perhaps will never be unseasonable to bear in mind out of Chrysostom, that when ministers came to have lands, houses, farms, coaches, horses, and the like lumber, then religion brought forth riches in the church, and the daughter devoured the mother.

But if his judgment in episcopacy may be judged by the goodly choice he made of bishops, we need not much amuse ourselves with the consideration of those evils which, by his foretelling, will "necessarily follow" their pulling down, until he prove that the apostles, having no certain diocese or appointed place of residence, were properly "bishops over those presbyters whom they ordained, or churches they planted;" wherein oft-times their labours were both joint and promiscuous: Or that the apostolic power must "necessarily descend to bishops, the use and end" of either function being so different. And how the church hath flourished under episcopacy, let the multitude of their ancient and gross errors testify, and the words of some learnedest and most zealous bishops among them; Nazianzen in a devout passion wishing prelaty had never been, Bazil terming them the slaves of slaves; Saint Martin, the enemies of Saints, and confessing that after he was made a bishop, he found much of that grace decay in him which he had before.

Concerning his "Coronation-Oath," what it was, and how far it bound him, already hath been spoken. This we may take for certain, that he was never sworn to his own particular conscience and reason, but to our conditions as a free people, which required him to give us such laws as ourselves * should chuse. This the Scots could bring him to, and would not be baffled with the pretence of a coronation-oath, after that episcopacy had for many years been settled there. Which concession of his to them, and not to us, he seeks here to put off with evasions that are ridiculous. And to omit no shifts, he alledges that the presbyterian manners gave him no encouragement to like their Modes of government. If that were so, yet certainly those men are in most likelihood nearer to amendment, who seek a stricter church-discipline than that of episcopacy, under which the most of them learned their manners. If estimation were to be made of God's law by their manners, who leaving Egypt, received it in the wilderness, it could reap from such an inference as this, nothing but rejection and disesteem.

For the prayer wherewith he closes, it had been good some safe liturgy, which he so commends, had rather been in his way; it would perhaps in some measure have performed the end for which they say liturgy was first invented, and have hindered him both here, and at other times, from turning his notorious errors into his prayers.

* The second edition has *shall* chuse.

XVIII. Upon the Uxbridge Treaty, &c.

"IF the way of treaties be looked upon" in general, "as retiring" from beftial force to human reafon, his firft aphorifm here is in part deceived. For men may treat like beafts as well as fight. If fome fighting were not manlike, then either fortitude were no virtue, or no fortitude in fighting: And as politicians oft-times through dilatory purpofes and emulations handle the matter, there hath been no where found more beftiality than in treating; which hath no more commendation in it, than from fighting to come to undermining, from violence to craft; and when they can no longer do as lions, to do as foxes.

The fincereft end of treating after war once proclaimed, is either to part with more, or to demand lefs than was at firft fought for, rather than to hazard more lives, or worfe mifchiefs. What the parliament in that point were willing to have done, when firft after the war begun, they petitioned him at Colebrook to vouchfafe a treaty, is not unknown. For after he had taken God to witnefs of his continual readinefs to treat, or to offer treaties to the avoiding of bloodfhed, *had named Windfor the place of treaty, and paffed his royal word not to advance further, 'till commiffioners by fuch a time were fpeeded towards him*; taking the advantage of a *thick mift, which fell that evening, weather that foon invited him to a defign no lefs treacherous and obfcure*; he follows at the heels thofe meffengers of peace with a train of covert war; and with a bloody furprize falls on our fecure forces which lay quartering at Brentford in the thoughts and expectation of a treaty. And although in them who make a trade of war, and againft a natural enemy, fuch an onfet might in the rigour of martial* law have been excufed, while arms were not yet by agreement fufpended; yet by a king, who feemed fo heartily to accept of treating *with his fubjects*, and profeffes here, "he never wanted either defire or difpofition to it, profeffes to have greater confidence in his reafon than in his fword, and as a chriftian to feek peace and enfue it," fuch bloody and deceitful advantages would have been forborne one day at leaft, if not much longer; in whom there had not been a thirft rather than a deteftation of civil war and blood, *and a defire to fubdue rather than to treat*.

In the midft of a fecond treaty not long after, fought by the parliament, and after much ado obtained with him at Oxford, what fubtle and unpeaceable defigns he then had in chace, his own letters difcovered: What attempts of treacherous hoftility fuccefsful and unfuccefsful he made againft Briftol, Scarborough, and other places, the proceedings of that treaty will foon put us in mind: and how he was fo far from granting more of reafon after fo much of blood, that he denied then to grant, what before he had offered, making no other ufe of treaties pretending peace, than to gain advantages that might enable him to continue war: What marvel then if "he thought it no diminution of himfelf," as oft as he faw his time, "to be importunate for treaties," when he fought them only, as by the upfhot appeared, "to get opportunities?" *And once to a moft cruel purpofe, if we remember May* 1643. *And that meffenger of peace from Oxford, whofe fecret meffage and commiffion, had it been effected, would have drowned the innocence of our treating, in the blood of a defigned maffacre. Nay, when treaties from the parliament fought out him, no lefs than feven times, (oft enough to teftify the willingnefs of their obedience, and too oft for the majefty of a parliament to court their fubjection) he, in the confidence of his own ftrength, or of our divifions, returned us nothing back but denials, or delays, to their moft neceffary demands, and being at loweft, kept up ftill and fuftained his almoft famifhed hopes with the hourly expectation of raifing up himfelf the higher, by the greater heap which he fat promifing himfelf of our fudden ruin through diffention.*

* The fecond edition has *military*.

But

But he infers, as if the parliament would have compelled him to part with ſomething of "his honour as a king." What honour could he have, or call his, joined not only with the offence or diſturbance, but with the bondage and deſtruction of three nations? whereof, though he be careleſs and improvident, yet the parliament, by our laws and freedom, ought to judge, and uſe prevention; our laws elſe were but cobweb laws. And what were all his moſt rightful honours, but the people's gift, and the inveſtment of that luſtre, majeſty and honour, which for the public good, and no otherwiſe, redounds from a whole nation into one perſon? So far is any honour from being his to a common miſchief and calamity. Yet ſtill he talks on equal terms with the grand repreſentative of that people, for whoſe ſake he was a king; as if the general welfare, and his ſubſervient rights were of equal moment or conſideration. His aim indeed hath ever been to magnify and exalt his borrowed rights and prerogatives above the parliament and kingdom, of whom he holds them. But when a king ſets himſelf to bandy againſt the higheſt court and reſidence of all his regal power, he then, in the ſingle perſon of a man, fights againſt his own majeſty and kingſhip, and then indeed ſets the firſt hand to his own depoſing.

"The treaty at Uxbridge," he ſaith, "gave the faireſt hopes of a happy compoſure;" faireſt indeed, if his inſtructions to bribe our commiſſioners with the promiſe of Security, Rewards, and Places, were fair: What other hopes it gave, no man can tell. There being but three main heads whereon to be treated, Ireland, epiſcopacy, and the militia; the firſt was anticipated and foreſtalled by a peace at any rate to be haſtened with the Iriſh rebels, ere the treaty could begin, that he might pretend his word and honour paſt againſt "the ſpecious and popular arguments" (he calls them no better) which the parliament would urge upon him for the continuance of that juſt war. Epiſcopacy he bids the queen be confident he will never quit; which informs us by what patronage it ſtood: And the ſword he reſolves to clutch as faſt, as if God with his own hand had put it into his. This was the "moderation which he brought," this was "as far as reaſon, honour, conſcience," and the queen, who was his regent in all theſe, "would give him leave." Laſtly, for "compoſure," inſtead of happy, how miſerable it was more likely to have been, wiſe men could then judge; when the Engliſh, during treaty, were called rebels, the Iriſh, good and catholic ſubjects; and the parliament beforehand, though for faſhion's ſake called a parliament, yet by a jeſuitical ſlight not acknowledged, though called ſo; but privately in the council-books inrolled no parliament. that if accommodation had ſucceeded, upon what terms ſoever, ſuch a deviliſh fraud was prepared, that the king in his own eſteem had been abſolved from all performance, as having treated with rebels and no parliament; and they on the other ſide, inſtead of an expected happineſs, had been brought under the hatchet Then no doubt "war had ended," that maſſacre and tyranny might begin Theſe jealouſies, however raiſed, let all men ſee whether they be diminiſhed or allayed, by the letters of his own cabinet opened. And yet the breach of this treaty is laid all upon the parliament and their commiſſioners, with odious names of "Pertinacy, hatred of Peace, Faction, and Covetouſneſs," nay his own brat "Superſtition" is laid to their charge; notwithſtanding his here profeſſed reſolution to continue both the Order, Maintenance, and Authority, of prelates, as a truth of God.

And who "were moſt to blame in the unſucceſsfulneſs of that treaty," his appeal is to God's deciſion; believing to be very excuſable at that tribunal. But if ever man gloried in an unflexible ſtiffneſs, he came not behind any, and that grand maxim, always to put ſomething into his treaties, which might give colour to refuſe all that was in other things granted, and to make them ſignify nothing, was his own [illegible] particular inſtructions to his commiſſioners. Yet all, by [illegible] ſtructed Reaſon in the king, and depraved temper in the parliament

That the "higheſt tide of ſucceſs," with theſe principles and deſigns, "ſet him not above a treaty," no great wonder. *And yet if that be ſpoken to his praiſe, the parliament therein ſurpaſſed him; who, when he was their vanquiſhed and their captive, his forces utterly broken and diſbanded, yet offered him three ſeveral times no worſe propoſals or demands, than when he ſtood fair to be their conqueror. But that imprudent ſurmize that his loweſt ebb could not ſet him "below a fight," was a preſumption that ruined him.*

He preſaged the future "unſucceſsfulneſs of treaties by the unwillingneſs of ſome men to treat;" and could not ſee what was preſent, that their unwillingneſs had good cauſe to proceed from the continual experience of his own obſtinacy and breach of word.

His prayer therefore of forgiveneſs to the guilty of "that treaty's breaking," he had good reaſon to ſay heartily over, as including no man in that guilt ſooner than himſelf

As for that proteſtation following in his prayer, "how oft have I entreated for peace, but when I ſpeak thereof they make them ready to war;" unleſs he thought himſelf ſtill in that perfidious miſt between Colebrook and Hounſlow, and thought that miſt could hide him from the eye of heaven as well as of man, after ſuch a bloody recompence given to our firſt offers of peace, how could this in the ſight of heaven without horrors of conſcience be uttered?

XIX. Upon the various events of the War.

IT is no new or unwonted thing, for bad men to claim as much part in God as his beſt ſervants; to uſurp and imitate their words, and appropriate to themſelves thoſe properties which belong only to the good and righteous. This not only in Scripture is familiarly to be found, but here alſo in this chapter of Apocrypha He tells us much, why "it pleaſed God" to ſend him victory or loſs (although what in ſo doing was the intent of God, he might be much miſtaken as to his own particular) but we are yet to learn what real good uſe he made thereof in his practice.

Thoſe numbers which he grew to "from ſmall beginnings," were not ſuch as out of love came to protect him, for none approved his actions as a king, except courtiers and prelates, but were ſuch as fled to be protected by him from the fear of that reformation which the pravity of their lives would not bear. Such a ſnow-ball he might eaſily gather by rolling through thoſe cold and dark provinces of ignorance and lewdneſs, where on a ſudden he became ſo numerous. He imputes that to God's "protection," which, to them who perſiſt in a bad cauſe, is either his long-ſuffering, or his hardening, and that to wholeſome "chaſtiſement," which were the gradual beginnings of a ſevere puniſhment. For if neither God nor nature put civil power in the hands of any whomſoever, but to a lawful end, and commands our obedience to the authority of law only, not to the tyrannical force of any perſon, and if the laws of our land have placed the ſword in no man's *ſingle* hand, ſo much as to unſheath againſt a foreign enemy, much leſs upon the native people; but have placed it in that elective body of the parliament, to whom the making, repealing, judging, and interpreting of law itſelf was alſo committed, as was fitteſt, ſo long as we intended to be a free nation, and not the ſlaves of one man's will, then was the king himſelf diſobedient and rebellious to that law by which he reigned. and by authority of parliament to raiſe arms againſt him in defence of law and liberty, we do not only think, but believe and know was juſtifiable both "by the word of God, the laws of the land, and all lawful oaths," and they who ſided with him, fought againſt all theſe.

The ſame allegations which he uſes for himſelf and his party, may as well fit any tyrant in the world: for let the parliament be called a faction when the king pleaſes, and that no law muſt be made or changed, either civil or religious, becauſe no law will content

content all ſides, then muſt be made or changed no law at all, but what a tyrant, be he proteſtant or papiſt, thinks fit. Which tyrannous aſſertion forced upon us by the ſword, he who fights againſt, and dies fighting, if his other ſins outweigh not, dies a Martyr undoubtedly both of the faith and of the commonwealth: and I hold it not as the opinion, but as the full belief and perſuaſion of far holier and wiſer men than Paraſitic Preachers: Who, without their dinner-doctrine, know that neither King, Law, civil Oaths, or Religion, was ever eſtabliſhed without the parliament: and their power is the ſame to abrogate as to eſtabliſh: neither is any thing to be thought eſtabliſhed, which that houſe declares to be aboliſhed. Where the parliament ſits, there inſeparably ſits the king, there the laws, there our oaths, and whatſoever can be civil in religion. They who fought for the parliament, in the trueſt ſenſe fought for all theſe; who fought for the king divided from his parliament, fought for the ſhadow of a king againſt all theſe; and for things that were not, as if they were eſtabliſhed. It were a thing monſtrouſly abſurd and contradictory to give the parliament a legiſlative power, and then to upbraid them for tranſgreſſing old eſtabliſhments.

But the king and his party having loſt in this quarrel their heaven upon earth, begin to make great reckoning of eternal life, and at an eaſy rate in forma pauperis canonize one another into heaven; he them in his book, they him in the portraiture before his book: but as was ſaid before, ſtage-work will not do it, much leſs the "juſtneſs of their cauſe," wherein moſt frequently they died in a brutiſh fierceneſs, with oaths and other damning words in their mouths; as if ſuch had been all "the only oaths" they fought for: which undoubtedly ſent them full ſail on another voyage than to heaven. In the mean while they to whom God gave victory, never brought to the king at Oxford the ſtate of their Conſciences, that he ſhould preſume without confeſſion, more than a pope preſumes, to tell abroad what "conflicts and accuſations," men whom he never ſpoke with, have "in their own thoughts." We never read of any Engliſh king but one that was a confeſſor, and his name was Edward; yet ſure it paſſed his ſkill to know thoughts, as this king takes upon him. But they who will not ſtick to ſlander men's inward conſciences, which they can neither ſee nor know, much leſs will care to ſlander outward actions, which they pretend to ſee, though with ſenſes never ſo vitiated.

To judge of "his condition conquered," and the manner of "dying" on that ſide, by the ſober men that choſe it, would be his ſmall advantage. it being moſt notorious, that they who were hotteſt in his cauſe, the moſt of them were men oftener drunk, than by their good-will ſober, and very many of them ſo fought and ſo died*

And that the Conſcience of any man ſhould grow ſuſpicious, or be now convicted by any pretenſions in the parliament, which are now proved falſe and unintended, there can be no juſt cauſe. For neither did they ever pretend to eſtabliſh his throne without our liberty and religion, nor religion without the word of God, nor to judge of laws by their being eſtabliſhed, but to eſtabliſh them by their being good and neceſſary.

He tells the world "he often prayed that all on his ſide might be as faithful to God and their own ſouls, as to him." But kings, above all other men, have in their hands not to pray only, but to do. To make that prayer effectual, he ſhould have governed as well as prayed. To pray and not to govern, is for a monk, and not a king. Till then he might be well aſſured they were more faithful to their luſt and rapine than to him.

In the wonted predication of his own virtues he goes on to tell us, that to "conquer he never deſired, but only to reſtore the laws and liberties of his people." It had been happy then he had known at laſt, that by force to reſtore laws abrogated by the legi-

* Hear what deſcription an hiſtorian of that party gives of thoſe on the royal ſide. *Never had any good undertaking ſo many unworthy attendants, ſuch horrid blaſphemers and wicked wretches as ours hath had: I quake to think, much more to ſpeak, what mine ears have heard from ſome of their lips: but to diſcover them is not my preſent buſineſs.* Symmon's Defence of King Charles I. p. 165.

lative

lative parliament, is to conquer abſolutely both them and law itſelf. And for our liberties, none ever oppreſſed them more, both in peace and war; firſt like a maſter by his arbitrary power, next as an enemy by hoſtile invaſion.

And if his beſt friends feared him, and "he himſelf, in the temptation of an abſolute conqueſt," it was not only pious but friendly in the parliament, both to fear him and reſiſt him, ſince their not yielding, was the only means to keep him out of that temptation wherein he doubted his own ſtrength.

He takes himſelf to be "guilty in this war of nothing elſe, but of confirming the power of ſome men:" Thus all along he ſignifies the parliament, whom to have ſettled by an act he counts to be his only guiltineſs. So well he knew that to continue a parliament, was to raiſe a war againſt himſelf; what were his actions then, and his government the while? For never was it heard in all our ſtory, that parliaments made war on their kings, but on their tyrants; whoſe modeſty and gratitude was more wanting to the parliament, than theirs to any of ſuch kings.

What he yielded was his fear; what he denied was his obſtinacy. Had he yielded more, fear might perchance have ſaved him; had he granted leſs, his obſtinacy had perhaps the ſooner delivered us.

"To review the occaſions of this war," will be to them never too late, who would be warned by his example from the like evils: but to wiſh only a happy concluſion, will never expiate the fault of his unhappy beginnings. It is true, on our ſide the ſins of our lives not ſeldom fought againſt us: but on their ſide, beſides thoſe, the grand ſin of their cauſe.

How can it be otherwiſe, when he deſires here moſt unreaſonably, and indeed ſacrilegiouſly, that we ſhould be ſubject to him, though not further, yet as far as all of us may be ſubject to God, to whom this expreſſion leaves no precedency? He who deſires from men as much obedience and ſubjection, as we may all pay to God, deſires not leſs than to be a God: a ſacrilege far worſe than meddling with the Biſhop's lands, as he eſteems it.

His prayer is a good prayer and a glorious; but glorying is not good, if it know not that a little leven levens the whole lump. It ſhould have purged out the leven of untruth, in telling God that the blood of his ſubjects by him ſhed, was in his juſt and neceſſary defence. Yet this is remarkable; God hath here ſo ordered his prayer, that as his own lips acquitted the parliament, not long before his death, of all the blood ſpilt in this war, ſo now his prayer unwittingly draws it upon himſelf. For God imputes not to any man the blood he ſpills in a juſt cauſe, and no man ever begged his not imputing of that, which he in his juſtice could not impute. ſo that now, whether purpoſely, or unaware, he hath confeſſed both to God and man the blood-guiltineſs of all this war to lie upon his own head.

XX. Upon the Reformation of the Times.

THIS chapter cannot punctually be anſwered without more repetitions than now can be excuſable: which perhaps have already been more humoured than was needful. As it preſents us with nothing new, ſo with his exceptions againſt reformation pitifully old, and tattered with continual uſing; not only in his book, but in the words and writings of every papiſt and popiſh king. On the ſcene he thruſts out firſt an antimaſque of two bugbears, Novelty and Perturbation; that the ill looks and noiſe of thoſe two, may as long as poſſible drive off all endeavours of a reformation. Thus ſought pope Adrian, by repreſenting the like vain terrors, to divert and diſſipate the zeal of thoſe reforming princes of the age before in Germany. And if we credit Latimer's ſermons, our papiſts here in England pleaded the ſame dangers and inconveni-

encies

encies againſt that which was reformed by Edward the Sixth. Whereas if thoſe fears had been available, chriſtianity itſelf had never been received Which Chriſt foretold us, would not be admitted without the cenſure of novelty and many great commotions. These therefore are not to deter us.

He grants reformation to be "a good work", and confeſſes "what the indulgence of times and corruption of manners might have depraved." So did the fore-mentioned pope, and our grandſire papiſts in this realm Yet all of them agree in one ſong with this here, that "they are ſorry to ſee ſo little regard had to laws eſtabliſhed, and the religion ſettled."

"Popular compliance, diſſolution of all order and government in the church, ſchiſms, opinions, undecencies, confuſions, ſacrilegious invaſions, contempt of the clergy and their liturgy, diminution of princes," all theſe complaints are to be read in the meſſages and ſpeeches almoſt of every legate from the pope to thoſe ſtates and cities which began reformation. From whence he either learned the ſame pretences, or had them naturally in him from the ſame ſpirit. Neither was there ever ſo ſincere a reformation that hath eſcaped theſe clamours.

He offered a "Synod or convocation rightly choſen." So offered all thoſe popiſh kings heretofore, a courſe the moſt unſatisfactory, as matters have been long carried, and found by experience in the church liable to the greateſt fraud and packing; no ſolution, or redreſs of evil, but an increaſe rather; deteſted therefore by Nazianzen, and ſome other of the fathers. And let it be produced, what good hath been done by ſynods from the firſt times of reformation.

Not to juſtify what enormities the vulgar may commit in the rudeneſs of their zeal, we need but only inſtance how he bemoans "the pulling down of croſſes" and other ſuperſtitious monuments, as the effect "of a popular and deceitful Reformation" How little this ſavours of a proteſtant, is too eaſily perceived

What he charges in defect of "piety, charity, and morality," hath been alſo charged by papiſts upon the beſt reformed churches; not as if they the accuſers were not tenfold more to be accuſed, but out of their malignity to all endeavour of amendment; as we know who accuſed to God the ſincerity of Job, an accuſation of all others the moſt eaſy, whenas *there* lives not any mortal man ſo excellent, who in theſe things is not always deficient But the infirmities of beſt men, and the ſcandals of mixed hypocrites in all times of reforming, whoſe bold intruſion covets to be ever ſeen in things moſt ſacred as they are moſt ſpecious, can lay no juſt blemiſh upon the integrity of others, much leſs upon the purpoſe of reformation itſelf. Neither can the evil doings of ſome be the excuſe of our delaying or deſerting that duty to the church, which for no reſpect of times or carnal policies can be at any time unſeaſonable

He tells with great ſhew of piety what kind of perſons public Reformers ought to be, and what they ought to do It is ſtrange that in above twenty years, the church growing ſtill worſe and worſe under him, he could neither be as he bids others be, nor do, as he pretends here ſo well to know, nay, which is worſt of all, after the greateſt part of his reign ſpent in neither knowing nor doing aught toward a reformation either in church or ſtate, ſhould ſpend the reſidue in hindring thoſe by a ſeven years war, whom it concerned, with his conſent or without it, to do their parts in that great performance.

'Tis true that the "method of reforming" may well ſubſiſt without "perturbation of the ſtate," but that it falls out otherwiſe for the moſt part, is the plain text of ſcripture And if by his own rule he had allowed us to "fear God firſt," and the king in due order, our allegiance might have ſtill followed our religion in a fit ſubordination But if Chriſt's kingdom be taken for the true diſcipline of the church, and by "his Kingdom" be meant the violence he uſed againſt it, and to uphold an antichriſtian hierarchy, then ſure enough it is, that Chriſt's kingdom could not be ſet up without pulling down his: and they were beſt chriſtians who were leaſt ſubject to him. "Chriſt's Government," out of queſtion meaning it prelatical, he thought would confirm his: and this was that which overthrew it.

He profeſſes "to own his kingdom from Chriſt, and to deſire to rule for his glory, and the church's good." The pope and the king of Spain profeſs every where as much, and both his practice and all his reaſonings, all his enmity againſt the true church we ſee hath been the ſame with theirs, ſince the time that in his letter to the pope he aſſured them both of his full compliance. "But evil beginnings never bring forth good concluſions." they are his own words, and he ratified them by his own ending. To the pope he engaged himſelf to hazard life and eſtate for the Roman religion, whether in compliment he did it, or in earneſt; and God, who ſtood nearer than he for complimenting minded, writ down thoſe words; that according to his reſolution, ſo it ſhould come to paſs. He prays againſt "his hypocriſy and phariſaical waſhings," a prayer to him moſt pertinent, but choaks it ſtreight with other words which pray him deeper into his old errors and deluſions.

XXI. Upon his Letters taken and divulged.

THE king's letters taken at the battle of Naſeby, being of greateſt importance to let the people ſee what faith there was in all his promiſes and ſolemn proteſtations, were tranſmitted to public view by ſpecial order of the parliament. They diſcovered his good affection to papiſts and Iriſh rebels, the ſtrict * intelligence he held, the pernicious and diſhonourable peace he made with them, not ſollicited, but rather ſolliciting, which by all invocations that were holy he had in public abjured. They revealed his endeavours to bring in foreign forces, Iriſh, French, Dutch, Lorrainers, and our old invaders the Danes upon us, beſides his ſubtleties and myſterious arts in treating: to ſum up all, they ſhewed him governed by a woman. All which, though ſuſpected vehemently before, and from good grounds believed, yet by him and his adherents peremptorily denied, were, by the opening of that cabinet, viſible to all men under his own hand.

The parliament therefore, to clear themſelves of aſperſing him without cauſe, and that the people might no longer be abuſed and cajoled, as they call it, by falſities and court-impudence, in matters of ſo high concernment; to let them know on what terms their duty ſtood, and the kingdom's peace, conceived it moſt expedient and neceſſary that thoſe letters ſhould be made public. This the king affirms was by them done without "honour and civility" words, which if they contain not in them, as in the language of a courtier moſt commonly they do not, more of ſubſtance and reality than compliment, ceremony, court-fawning and diſſembling, enter not I ſuppoſe further than the ear into any wiſe man's conſideration. Matters were not then between *the* parliament and a king their enemy, in that ſtate of trifling, as to obſerve thoſe ſuperficial vanities. But if honour and civility mean, as they did of old, diſcretion, honeſty, prudence, and plain truth, it will be then maintained againſt any ſect of thoſe Cabaliſts, that the parliament in doing what they did with thoſe letters, could ſuffer in their honour and civility no diminution. The reaſons are already heard

And that it is with none more familiar than with kings, to tranſgreſs the bounds of all honour and civility, there ſhould not want examples good ſtore, if brevity would permit; in point of letters, this one ſhall ſuffice The Dutcheſs of Burgundy, and heir of Duke Charles, had promiſed to her ſubjects that ſhe intended no otherwiſe to govern, than by advice of the three eſtates; but to Lewis the French king had written letters, that ſhe had reſolved to commit wholly the managing of her affairs to four perſon,

* The ſecond edition has the old word *ſtraight*.

ſons, whom ſhe named. The three eſtates, not doubting the ſincerity of her princely word, ſend embaſſadors to Lewis, who then beſieged Arras belonging to the duke of Burgundy. The king, taking hold of this occaſion to ſet them at diviſion among themſelves, queſtioned their credence: which when they offered to produce with their inſtructions, he not only ſhews them the private letter of their dutcheſs, but gives it them to carry home, wherewith to affront her; which they did, ſhe denying it ſtoutly; till they, ſpreading it before her face in a full aſſembly, convicted her of an open lye. Which, although Comines the hiſtorian much blames, as a deed too harſh and diſhonourable in them who were ſubjects, and not at war with their princeſs, yet to his maſter Lewis, who firſt divulged thoſe letters, to the open ſhaming of that young governeſs, he imputes no incivility or diſhonour at all, although betraying a certain confidence repoſed by that letter in his royal ſecreſy.

With much more reaſon then may letters not intercepted only, but won in battle from an enemy, be made public to the beſt advantages of them that win them, to the diſcovery of ſuch important truth or falſhood Was it not more diſhonourable in himſelf to feign ſuſpicions and jealouſies, which we firſt found among thoſe letters, touching the chaſtity of his mother, thereby to gain aſſiſtance from the king of Denmark, as in vindication of his ſiſter? The damſel of Burgundy at ſight of her own letter was ſoon blank, and more ingenuous than to ſtand out-facing, but this man, whom nothing will convince, thinks by talking world without end, to make good his integrity and fair dealing, contradicted by his own hand and ſeal They who can pick nothing out of them but phraſes, ſhall be counted bees: they that diſcern further both there and here, that conſtancy to his wife is ſet in place before laws and religion, are in his naturalities no better than Spiders.

He would work the people to a perſuaſion, that " if he be miſerable, they cannot be happy." What ſhould hinder them? Were they all born twins of Hippocrates with him and his fortune, one birth, one burial? It were a nation miſerable indeed, not worth the name of a nation, but a race of idiots, whoſe happineſs and welfare depended upon one man The happineſs of a nation conſiſts in true religion, piety, juſtice, prudence, temperance, fortitude, and the contempt of avarice and ambition. They in whomſoever theſe virtues dwell eminently, need not kings to make them happy, but are the architects of their own happineſs; and whether to themſelves or others are not leſs than kings. But in him, which of theſe virtues were to be found, that might extend to the making happy, or the well governing of ſo much as his own houſhold, which was the moſt licentious and ill-governed in the whole land?

But the opening of his letters was deſigned by the parliament " to make all Reconciliation deſperate." Are the lives of ſo many good and faithful men that died for the freedom of their country, to be ſo ſlighted, as to be forgotten in a ſtupid reconcilement without juſtice done them? What he fears not by war and ſlaughter, ſhould we fear to make deſperate by opening his letters? Which fact he would parallel with Cham's revealing of his father's nakedneſs: when he at that time could be no way eſteemed the Father of his Country, but the deſtroyer, nor had he ever before merited that former title.

" He thanks God he cannot only bear this with patience, but with charity forgive the doers " Is not this meer mockery, to thank God for what he can do, but will not? For is it patience to impute Barbariſm and Inhumanity to the opening of an enemy's letter, or is it charity to clothe them with curſes in his prayer, whom he hath forgiven in his diſcourſe? In which prayer, to ſhew how readily he can return good for evil to the parliament, and that if they take away his coat, he can let them have his cloak alſo, for the diſmantling of his letters he wiſhes " they may be covered with the cloak of confuſion " Which I ſuppoſe they do reſign with much willingneſs, both livery, badge and cognizance, to them who choſe rather to be *the ſlaves and vaſſals of his will,*

 than

than to ſtand againſt him, as men by nature free; born and created with a better title to their freedom, than any king hath to his crown.

XXII. Upon his going to the Scots.

THE king's coming in, whether to the Scots or Engliſh, deſerved no thanks: for Neceſſity was his Counſellor; and that he hated them both alike, his expreſſions every where manifeſt. Some ſay his purpoſe was to have come to London, till hearing how ſtrictly it was proclaimed, that no man ſhould conceal him, he diverted his courſe. But that had been a frivolous excuſe: and beſides, he himſelf rehearſing the conſultations had, before he took his journey, ſhews us clearly that he was determined to adventure "upon their loyalty who firſt began his troubles." And that the Scots had notice of it before, hath been long ſince brought to light. What prudence there could be in it, no man can imagine, malice there might be, by raiſing new jealouſies to divide friends. For beſides his diffidence of the Engliſh, it was no ſmall diſhonour that he put upon them, when rather than yield himſelf to the parliament of England, he yielded to a hireling army of Scots in England, paid for their ſervice here, not in Scotch coin, but in Engliſh ſilver; nay, who from the *firſt* beginning of theſe troubles, what with brotherly aſſiſtance, and what with monthly pay, have defended their own liberty and conſciences at our charge. However, it was a hazardous and raſh journey taken, "to reſolve riddles in mens loyalty," who had more reaſon to miſtruſt the riddle of ſuch a diſguiſed yielding; and to put himſelf in their hands whoſe loyalty was a riddle to him, was not the courſe to be reſolved of it, but to tempt it. What Providence denied to force, he thought it might grant to fraud, which he ſtiles Prudence: but providence was not cozened with diſguiſes, neither outward nor inward.

To have known "his greateſt danger in his ſuppoſed ſafety, and his greateſt ſafety in his ſuppoſed danger" was to him a fatal riddle never yet reſolved, wherein rather to have employed his main ſkill, had been much more to his preſervation.

Had he "known when the game was loſt," it might have ſaved much conteſt, but the way to give over fairly, was not to ſlip out of open war into a new diſguiſe. He lays down his arms, but not his wiles; nor all his arms, for in obſtinacy he comes no leſs armed than ever, Cap a-pè. And what were they but wiles, continually to move for treaties, and yet to perſiſt the ſame man, and to fortify his mind before-hand, ſtill purpoſing to grant no more than what ſeemed good to that violent and lawleſs triumvirate within him, under the falſified names of his reaſon, honour, and conſcience, the old circulating dance of his ſhifts and evaſions?

The words of a king, as they are full of power, in the authority and ſtrength of law, ſo like Sampſon without the ſtrength of that Nazarites's lock, they have no more power in them than the words of another man.

He adores reaſon as Domitian did Minerva, and calls her the "Divineſt power," thereby to intimate as if at reaſoning, as at his own weapon, no man were ſo able as himſelf. Might we be ſo happy as to know where theſe monuments of his reaſon may be ſeen, for in his actions and his writing they appear as thinly as could be expected from the meaneſt parts, bred up in the midſt of ſo many ways extraordinary to know ſomething. He who reads his talk, would think he had left Oxford not without mature deliberation: yet his prayer confeſſes that "he knew not what to do." Thus is verified that pſalm, "he poureth contempt upon princes, and cauſeth them to wander in the wilderneſs where there is no way." Pſal. 107.

XXIII. Upon the Scots delivering the King to the Engliſh.

THAT the Scots in England ſhould "ſell their king," as he himſelf here affirms, and for a "price ſo much above that," which the covetouſneſs of Judas was contented with to ſell our Saviour, is ſo foul an infamy and diſhonour caſt upon them, as befits none to vindicate but themſelves. And it were but friendly counſel to wiſh them beware the ſon, who comes among them with a firm belief that they ſold his father. The reſt of this chapter he ſacrifices to the echo of his conſcience, out-babling creeds and ave's; glorying in his reſolute obſtinacy, and as it were triumphing how "evident it is now, that not evil counſellors," but he himſelf hath been the author of all our troubles. Herein only we ſhall diſagree to the world's end, while he who ſought ſo manifeſtly to have annihilated all our laws and liberties, hath the confidence to perſuade us that he hath fought and ſuffered all this while in their defence.

But he who neither by his own letters and commiſſions under hand and ſeal, nor by his own actions held as in a mirror before his face, will be convinced to ſee his faults, can much leſs be won upon by any force of words, neither he, nor any that take after him, who in that reſpect are no more to be diſputed with, than they who deny principles. No queſtion then, but the parliament did wiſely in their decree at laſt, to make no more addreſſes For how unalterable his will was, that would have been our Lord, how utterly averſe from the parliament and reformation during his confinement, we may behold in this chapter. But to be ever anſwering fruitleſs repetitions, I ſhould become liable to anſwer for the ſame myſelf. He borrows David's pſalms, as he charges the aſſembly of divines in his twentieth diſcourſe, "To have ſet forth old catechiſms and confeſſions of faith new dreſt." had he borrowed David's heart, it had been much the holier theft For ſuch kind of borrowing as this, if it be not bettered by the borrower, among good authors is accounted Plagiary. However, this was more tolerable than Pamela's prayer, ſtolen out of Sir Philip.

XXIV. Upon the denying him the attendance of his chaplains.

A Chaplain is a thing ſo diminutive and inconſiderable, that how he ſhould come here among matters of ſo great concernment, to take ſuch room up in the diſcourſes of a prince, if it be not wondered, is to be ſmiled at. Certainly by me, ſo mean an argument ſhall not be written, but I ſhall huddle him, as he does prayers The ſcripture owns no ſuch order, no ſuch function in the church, and the church not owning them, they are left, for aught I know, to ſuch a further examining as the ſons of Sceva the Jew met with Biſhops or preſbyters we know, and deacons we know, but what are chaplains? In ſtate perhaps they may be liſted among the upper ſervingmen of ſome great houſhold, and be admitted to ſome ſuch place, as may ſtile them the ſewers, or the yeomen uſhers of devotion, where the maſter is too reſty, or too rich to ſay his own prayers, or to bleſs his own table Wherefore ſhould the parliament then take ſuch implements of the court cup-board into their conſideration? They knew them to have been the main corrupters at the king's elbow, they knew the king to have been always their moſt attentive ſcholar and imitator, and of a child to have ſucked from them and their cloſet work all his impotent principles of tyranny and ſuperſtition. While therefore they had any hope left of his reclaiming, theſe ſowers of malignant tares they kept aſunder from him, and ſent to him ſuch of the miniſters and other zealous perſons as they thought were beſt able to inſtruct him, and to convert him What could religion herſelf have done more, to the ſaving of a ſoul? But when they found him paſt cure, and that he to himſelf was grown the

moſt

moſt evil counſellor of all, they denied him not his chaplains, as many as were fitting, and ſome of them attended him, or elſe were at his call to the very laſt. Yet here he makes more lamentation for the want of his chaplains, than ſuperſtitious Micah did to the Danites, who had taken away his houſhold prieſt: " Ye have taken away my Gods which I made, and the prieſt, and what have I more?" And perhaps the whole ſtory of Micah might ſquare not unfitly to this argument: " Now know I," ſaith he, " that the Lord will do me good, ſeeing I have a Levite to my prieſt." Micah had as great a care that his prieſt ſhould be Moſaical, as the king had that his ſhould be Apoſtolical, yet both in an error touching their prieſts. Houſhold and private orifons were not to be officiated by prieſts; for neither did public prayer appertain only to their office. Kings heretofore, David, Solomon, and Jehoſophat, who might not touch the prieſthood, yet might pray in public, yea in the temple, while the prieſts themſelves ſtood and heard. What ailed this king then, that he could not chew his own mattins without the prieſt's Ore tenus? Yet is it like he could not pray at home, who can here publiſh a whole prayer-book of his own, and ſignifies in ſome part of this chapter, almoſt as good a mind to be a prieſt himſelf, as Micah had to let his ſon be! There was doubtleſs therefore ſome other matter in it, which made him ſo deſirous to have his chaplains about him, who were not only the contrivers, but very oft the inſtruments alſo of his deſigns.

The miniſters which were ſent him, no marvel he endured not, for they preached repentance to him: the others gave him eaſy confeſſion, eaſy abſolution, nay ſtrengthened his hands, and hardened his heart, by applauding him in his wilful ways. To them he was an Ahab, to theſe a Conſtantine; it muſt follow then, that they to him were as unwelcome as Eliah was to Ahab, theſe as dear and pleaſing as Amaziah the prieſt of Bethel was to Jeroboam These had learnt well the leſſon that would pleaſe, " Prophecy not againſt Bethel, for it is the king's chapel, the king's court;" and had taught the king to ſay of thoſe miniſters which the parliament had ſent, " Amos hath conſpired againſt me, the land is not able to bear all his words "

Returning to our firſt parallel, *this* king looked upon his prelates, " as orphans under the ſacrilegious eyes of many rapacious reformers " and there was as great fear of ſacrilege between Micah and his mother, till with their holy treaſure, about the loſs whereof there was ſuch curſing, they made a graven and a molten image, and got a prieſt of their own. To let go his criticizing about the " ſound of prayers, imperious, rude, or paſſionate," modes of his own deviſing, we are in danger to fall again upon the flats and ſhallows of liturgy. Which if I ſhould repeat again, would turn my anſwers into Reſponſories, and beget another liturgy, having too much of one already

This only I ſhall add, that if the heart, as he alledges, cannot ſafely " join with another man's extemporal ſufficiency," becauſe we know not ſo exactly what they mean to ſay, then thoſe public prayers made in the temp'e by thoſe forenamed kings, and by the apoſtles in the congregation, and by the ancient chriſtians for above three hundred years before liturgies came in, were with the people made in vain

After he hath acknowledged that kings heretofore prayed without chaplains, even publicly in the temple itſelf, and that every " private believer is inveſted with a royal prieſthood," yet like one that reliſhed not what he " taſted of the heavenly gift, and the good word of God," whoſe name he ſo confidently takes into his mouth, he frames to himſelf impertinent and vain reaſons, why he ſhould rather pray by the officiating mouth of a cloſet-chaplain. " Their prayers," ſaith he, " are more prevalent, they flow from minds more enlightened, from affections leſs diſtracted " Admit this true, which is not, this might be ſomething ſaid as to their prayers for him, but what avails it to their praying with him? If his own mind " be incumbered with ſecular affairs," what helps it his particular prayer, though the mind of his chaplain be not wandring, either after new preferment, or his dinner? The fervency of one man in prayer, cannot

not ſupererogate for the coldneſs of another; neither can his ſpiritual defects in that duty be made out, in the acceptance of God, by another man's abilities. Let him endeavour to have more light in himſelf, and not to walk by another man's lamp, but to get oil into his own. Let him caſt from him, as in a chriſtian warfare, that ſecular incumbrance which either diſtracts or overloads him; his load elſe will never be the leſs heavy, becauſe another man's is light. Thus theſe pious flouriſhes and colours examined throughly, are like the apples of Aſphaltis, appearing goodly to the ſudden eye, but look well upon them, or at leaſt but touch them, and they turn into cinders.

In his prayer he remembers what "voices of joy and gladneſs" there were in his chappel, "God's houſe," in his opinion, between the ſinging-men and the organs; and this was "unity of ſpirit in the bond of peace," the vanity, ſuperſtition, and miſdevotion of which place, was a ſcandal far and near: Wherein ſo many things were ſung, and prayed in thoſe ſongs, which were not underſtood; and yet he who makes a difficulty how the people can join their hearts to extemporal prayers, though diſtinctly heard and underſtood, makes no queſtion how they ſhould join their hearts in unity to ſongs not underſtood!

I believe that God is no more moved with a prayer elaborately penned, than men truly charitable, are moved with the penned ſpeech of a beggar.

Finally, O ye miniſters, *ye pluraliſts, whoſe lips preſerve not knowlege, but the way ever open to your bellies*, read here what work he makes among your *wares*, *your* gally-pots, your Balms and Cordials, *in print*; and not only your ſweet Sippets in widows houſes, but the huge gobbets wherewith he charges you to have devoured houſes and all; the "houſes of your brethren, your king, and your God." Cry him up for a ſaint in your pulpits, while he cries you down for atheiſts into hell!

XXV. Upon his penitential Meditations and Vows at Holmby.

IT is not hard for any man who hath a Bible in his hands, to borrow good words and holy ſayings in abundance; but to make them his own, is a work of grace only from above. He borrows here many penitential verſes out of David's pſalms. So did many among thoſe Iſraelites, who had revolted from the true worſhip of God, "invent to themſelves inſtruments of muſic like David," and probably pſalms alſo like his; and yet the prophet Amos complains heavily againſt them. But to prove how ſhort this is of true repentance, I will recite the penitence of others who have repented in words not borrowed, but their own, and yet by the doom of Scripture itſelf are judged reprobates.

"Cain ſaid unto the Lord, My iniquity is greater than I can bear. behold thou haſt driven me this day from the face of the earth, and from thy face ſhall I be hid.

"And when Eſau heard the words of his father, he cried with an exceeding bitter cry, and ſaid, Bleſs me, even me alſo, O my father; yet found no place of repentance, though he ſought it carefully with tears. Heb 12.

"And Pharaoh ſaid to Moſes, the Lord is righteous, I and my people are wicked; I have ſinned againſt the Lord your God, and againſt you.

"And Balaam ſaid, Let me die the death of the righteous, and let my laſt end be like his.

"And Saul ſaid to Samuel, I have ſinned, for I have tranſgreſſed the commandment of the Lord, yet honour me now, I pray thee, before the elders of my people.

"And when Ahab heard the words of Eliah, he rent his clothes, and put ſackcloth upon his fleſh, and faſted, and lay in ſackcloth, and went ſoftly.

"Jehoram,

" Jehoram alſo rent his clothes, and the people looked, and behold he had ſackcloth upon his fleſh," yet in the very act of his humiliation he could ſay, " God do ſo, and more alſo to me, if the head of Eliſha ſhall ſtand on him this day.

" Therefore, ſaith the Lord, they have not cried unto me with their heart, when they howled upon their beds. They return, but not to the moſt high. Hoſea vii.

" And Judas ſaid, I have ſinned, in that I have betrayed innocent blood.

" And Simon Magus ſaid, Pray ye to the Lord for me, that none of theſe things come upon me."

All theſe took the pains both to confeſs and to repent in their own words, and many of them in their own tears, not in David's. But tranſported with the vain oſtentation of imitating David's language, not his life, obſerve, how he brings a curſe upon himſelf and his father's houſe (God ſo diſpoſing it) by his uſurped and ill-imitated prayer, " Let thy anger I beſeech thee be againſt me and my father's houſe; as for theſe ſheep, what have they done?" For if David indeed ſinned in numbring the people, of which fault he in earneſt made that confeſſion, and acquitted the whole people from the guilt of that ſin; then doth this king, uſing the ſame words, bear witneſs againſt himſelf to be the guilty perſon, and either in his ſoul and conſcience here acquits the parliament and the people, or elſe abuſes the words of David, and diſſembles groſly to the *very* face of God, which is apparent in the next line; wherein he accuſes even the church itſelf to God, as if ſhe were the church's enemy, for having overcome his tyranny by the powerful and miraculous might of God's manifeſt arm: For to other ſtrength in the midſt of our diviſions and diſorders, who can attribute our victories? Thus had this miſerable man no worſe enemies to ſollicit and mature his own deſtruction, from the haſtened ſentence of divine juſtice, than the obdurate curſes which proceeded againſt himſelf out of his own mouth.

Hitherto his meditations, now his vows; which as the vows of hypocrites uſe to be, are moſt commonly abſurd, and ſome wicked. Jacob vowed that God ſhould be his God, if he granted him but what was neceſſary to perform that vow, life and ſubſiſtence, but the obedience proffered here is nothing ſo cheap. He who took ſo heinouſly to be offered nineteen propoſitions from the parliament, capitulates here with God almoſt in as many articles.

" If he will continue that light," or rather that darkneſs of the goſpel, which is among his prelates, ſettle their luxuries, and make them gorgeous biſhops,

If he will " reſtore" the grievances and miſchiefs of thoſe obſolete and popiſh laws, which the parliament without his conſent hath abrogated, and will ſuffer juſtice to be executed according to his ſenſe,

" If he will ſuppreſs the many ſchiſms in church," to contradict himſelf in that which he hath foretold muſt and ſhall come to paſs, and will remove reformation as the greateſt ſchiſm of all, and factions in ſtate, by which he means in every leaf the parliament;

If he will " reſtore him" to his negative voice and the militia, as much as to ſay, to arbitrary power, which he wrongfully avers to be the " Right of his Predeceſſors,"

" If he will turn the hearts of his people" to their old cathedral and parochial ſervice in the liturgy, and their paſſive obedience to the king,

" If he will quench" the army, and withdraw our forces from withſtanding the piracy of Rupert, and the plotted Iriſh invaſion;

" If he will bleſs him with the freedom" of Biſhops again in the houſe of peers, and of fugitive delinquents in the houſe of commons, and deliver the honour of parliament into his hands, from the moſt natural and due protection of the people, that entruſted them with the dangerous enterprize of being faithful to their country againſt the rage and malice of his tyrannous oppoſition,

" If

" If he will keep him from that great offence" of following the counſel of his parliament, and enacting what they adviſe him to, which in all reaſon, and by the known law, and oath of his coronation he ought to do, and not to call that Sacrilege which neceſſity through the continuance of his own civil war hath compelled them to, neceſſity, which made David eat the ſhew-bread, made Ezekiah take all the ſilver which was found in God's houſe, and cut off the gold which overlaid thoſe doors and pillars, and give it to Senacherib; neceſſity, which oft times made the primitive church to ſell her ſacred utenſils, even to the communion-chalice;

" If he will reſtore him to a capacity of glorifying him by doing" that both in church and ſtate, which muſt needs diſhonour and pollute his name,

" If he will bring him again with peace, honour and ſafety to his chief city," without repenting, without ſatisfying for the blood ſpilt, only for a few politic conceſſions, which are as good as nothing;

" If he will put again the ſword into his hand, to puniſh" thoſe that have delivered us, and to protect delinquents againſt the juſtice of parliament,

Then, if it be poſſible to reconcile contradictions, he will praiſe him by diſpleaſing him, and ſerve him by diſſerving him.

" His glory," in the gaudy copes and painted windows, mitres, rochets, altars, and the chanted ſervice-book, " ſhall be dearer to him" than the eſtabliſhing his crown in righteouſneſs, and the ſpiritual power of religion.

" He will pardon thoſe that have offended him in particular," but there ſhall want no ſubtle ways to be even with them upon another ſcore of their ſuppoſed offences againſt the commonwealth; whereby he may at once affect the glory of a ſeeming juſtice, and deſtroy them pleaſantly, while he feigns to forgive them as to his own particular, and outwardly bewails them.

Theſe are the conditions of his treating with God, to whom he bates nothing of what he ſtood upon with the parliament: as if commiſſions of array could deal with him alſo.

But of all theſe conditions, as it is now evident in our eyes, God accepted none, but that final petition which he ſo oft, no doubt but by the ſecret judgment of God, importunes againſt his own head; praying God, " That his mercies might be ſo toward him, as his reſolutions of truth and peace were toward his people." It follows then, God having cut him off, without granting any of theſe mercies, that his reſolutions were as feigned, as his vows were fruſtrate.

XXVI. Upon the Army's ſurpriſal of the King at Holmby.

TO give account to royaliſts what was done with their vanquiſhed king, yielded up into our hands, is not to be expected from them whom God hath made his conquerors. And for brethren to debate and rip up their falling out in the ear of a common enemy, thereby making him the judge, or at leaſt the well-pleaſed auditor of their diſagreement, is neither wiſe nor comely. To the king therefore, were he living, or to his party yet remaining, as to this action, there belongs no anſwer. Emulations, all men know, are incident among military men, and are, if they exceed not, pardonable. But ſome of the former army, eminent enough for their own martial deeds, and prevalent in the houſe of commons, touched with envy to be ſo far outdone by a new model which they contemned, took advantage of preſbyterian and independent names, and the virulence of ſome miniſters, to raiſe diſturbance. And the war being then ended, though ſlightly to have diſcarded them, who had faithfully done the work, without their due pay, and the reward of their invincible valour. But they who had the ſword yet in their hands, diſdaining to be made the firſt objects of ingratitude and oppreſſion, after all that expence of their blood for juſtice and the common liberty, ſeized upon the king their priſoner, whom nothing but their matchleſs deeds had brought ſo low as to ſurrender up his perſon: though he, to ſtir up new diſcord, choſe rather to give up himſelf a captive to his own country-men, who leſs had won him. This in likelihood might have grown to ſome height of miſchief; partly through the ſtrife which was kindling between our elder and our younger warriors, but chiefly through the ſeditious tongues of ſome falſe miniſters, more zealous againſt ſchiſms, than againſt their own ſimony and pluralities, or watchful of the common enemy, whoſe ſubtle inſinuations had got ſo far in among them, as with all diligence to blow the coals. But it pleaſed God not to embroil and put to confuſion his whole people for the perverſeneſs of a few. The growth of our diſſention was either prevented, or ſoon quieted: the enemy ſoon deceived of his rejoicing, and the king eſpecially diſappointed of not the meaneſt morſel that his hope preſented him, to ruin us by our diviſion. And being now ſo nigh the end, we may the better be at leiſure to ſtay a while, and hear him commenting upon his own captivity.

He ſaith of his ſurpriſal, that it was a "motion eccentric and irregular." What then? his own alluſion from the celeſtial bodies, puts us in mind that irregular motions may be neceſſary on earth ſometimes, as well as conſtantly in heaven. That is not always beſt which is moſt regular to written law. Great worthies heretofore, by diſobeying law, oft-times have ſaved the commonwealth, and the law afterward by firm decree hath approved that planetary motion, that unblameable exorbitancy in them.

He means no good to either independent or preſbyterian, and yet his parable like that of Balaam, is over-ruled to portend them good, far beſide his intention. Thoſe Twins that ſtrove encloſed in the womb of Rebecca, were the ſeed of Abraham; the younger undoubtedly gained the heavenly birth right, the elder, though ſupplanted in his ſimile, ſhall yet no queſtion find a better portion than Eſau found, and far above his uncircumciſed prelates.

He cenſures, and in cenſuring ſeems to hope it will be an ill omen, that they who build Jeruſalem divide their tongues and hands. But his hope failed him with his example, for that there were diviſions both of tongues and hands at the building of Jeruſalem, the ſtory would have certified him, and yet the work proſpered and if God will, ſo may this, notwithſtanding all the craft and malignant wiles of Sanballat and Tobiah, adding what fuel they can to our diſſentions, or the indignity of his compariſon, that likens us to thoſe ſeditious Zealots whoſe inteſtine fury brought deſtruction to the laſt Jeruſalem.

It being now no more in his hand to be revenged on his oppoſers, he ſeeks to ſatiate his fancy with the imagination of ſome revenge upon them from above, and like one who in a drowth obſerves the ſky, *he* ſits and watches when any thing will drop, that might ſolace him with the likeneſs of a puniſhment from heaven upon us; which he ſtrait expounds how he pleaſes. No evil can befal the parliament or city, but he poſitively interprets it a judgment upon them for his ſake; as if the very manuſcript of God's judgments had been delivered to his cuſtody and expoſition. But his reading declares it well to be a falſe copy which he uſes: diſpenſing often to his own bad deeds and ſucceſſes the teſtimony of divine favour, and to the good deeds and ſucceſſes of other men, divine wrath and vengeance. But to counterfeit the hand of God, is the boldeſt of all forgery: And he who without warrant, but his own fantaſtic ſurmiſe, takes upon him perpetually to unfold the ſecret and unſearchable myſteries of high providence, is likely for the moſt part to miſtake and ſlander them; and approaches to the madneſs of thoſe reprobate thoughts, that would wreſt the ſword of juſtice out of God's hand, and employ it more juſtly in their own conceit. It was a ſmall thing to contend with the parliament about ſole power of the militia, when we ſee him doing little leſs than laying hands on the weapons of God himſelf, which are his judgments, to wield and manage them

by

by the ſway and bent of his own frail cogitations. Therefore "they that by tumults firſt occaſioned the raiſing of armies," in his doom muſt needs "be chaſtened by their own army for new tumults."

Firſt, note here his confeſſion, that thoſe tumults were the firſt occaſion of raiſing armies, and by conſequence that he himſelf raiſed them firſt, againſt thoſe ſuppoſed tumults: But who occaſioned thoſe tumults, or who made them ſo, being at firſt nothing more than the unarmed and peaceable concourſe of people, hath been diſcuſſed already. And that thoſe pretended tumults were chaſtized by their own army for new tumults, is not proved by a game at tic-tac with words; "tumults and armies, armies and tumults," but ſeems more like the method of a juſtice irrational than divine.

If the city were chaſtened by the army for new tumults, the reaſon is by himſelf ſet down evident and immediate, "their new tumults" With what ſenſe can it be referred then to another far-fetched and imaginary cauſe that happened ſo many years before, and in his ſuppoſition only as a cauſe? Manlius defended the capitol and the Romans from their enemies the Gauls: Manlius for ſedition afterward was by the Romans thrown headlong from the capitol; therefore Manlius was puniſhed by divine juſtice for defending the capitol, becauſe in that place puniſhed for ſedition, and by thoſe whom he defended. This is his logic upon divine juſtice; and was the ſame before upon the death of Sir John Hotham. And here again, "ſuch as were content to ſee him driven away by unſuppreſſed tumults, are now forced to fly to an army." Was this a judgment? was it not a mercy rather, that they had a noble and victorious army ſo near at hand to fly to?

From God's juſtice, he comes down to man's juſtice. Thoſe few of both houſes, who at firſt withdrew with him from the vain pretence of tumults, were counted deſerters; therefore thoſe many muſt be alſo deſerters who withdrew afterwards from real tumults: as if it were the place that made a parliament, and not the end and cauſe. Becauſe it is denied that thoſe were tumults from which the king made ſhew of being driven, is it therefore of neceſſity implied, that there could be never any tumults for the future? If ſome men fly in craft, may not other men have cauſe to fly in earneſt? But mark the difference between their flight and his, they ſoon returned in ſafety to their places, he not till after many years, and then a captive to receive his puniſhment. So that their flying, whether the cauſe be conſidered or the event, or both, neither juſtified him, nor condemned themſelves.

But he will needs have vengeance to purſue and overtake them; though to bring it in, it coſt him an inconvenient and obnoxious compariſon, "As the mice and rats overtook a German biſhop" I would our mice and rats had been as orthodoxal here, and had ſo purſued all his biſhops out of England, then vermin had rid away vermin, which now hath loſt the lives of too many thouſand honeſt men to do.

"He cannot but obſerve this divine juſtice, yet with ſorrow and pity." But ſorrow and pity in a weak and over-maſtered enemy, is looked upon no otherwiſe than as the aſhes of his revenge burnt out upon itſelf: or as the damp of a cooled fury when we ſay, it gives. But in this manner to ſit ſpelling and obſerving divine juſtice upon every accident and ſlight diſturbance that may happen humanly to the affairs of men, is but another fragment of his broken revenge; and yet the ſhrewdeſt and the cunningeſt obloquy that can be thrown upon their actions. For if he can perſuade men that the parliament and their cauſe is purſued with divine vengeance, he hath attained his end, to make all men forſake them, and think the worſt that can be thought of them.

Nor is he only content to ſuborn divine juſtice in his cenſure of what is paſt, but he aſſumes the perſon of Chriſt himſelf to prognoſticate over us what he wiſhes would come. So little is any thing or perſon ſacred from him, no not in heaven, which he will not uſe, and put on, if it may ſerve him plauſibly to wreck his ſpleen, or eaſe his mind upon the parliament. Although, if ever fatal blindneſs did both attend and puniſh wilfulneſs, if ever any enjoyed not comforts for neglecting counſel belonging to their peace, it was in none more *conſpicuouſly* brought to paſs than in himſelf: and his predictions againſt the parliament and their adherents have for the moſt part been verified upon his own head, and upon his chief counſellors.

He concludes with high praiſes of the army. But praiſes in an enemy are ſuperfluous, or ſmell of craft; and the army ſhall not need his praiſes, nor the parliament fare worſe for his accuſing prayers that follow. Wherein, as his charity can be no way comparable to that of Chriſt, ſo neither can his aſſurance that they whom he ſeems to pray for, in doing what they did againſt him, "knew not what they did." It was but arrogance therefore, and not charity, to lay ſuch ignorance to others in the ſight of God, till he himſelf had been infallible, like him whoſe peculiar words he overweeningly aſſumes.

XXVII. Intitled to the Prince of Wales.

WHAT the king wrote to his ſon, as a father, concerns not us, what he wrote to him as a king of England, concerns not him; God and the parliament having now otherwiſe diſpoſed of England. But becauſe I ſee it done with ſome artifice and labour, to poſſeſs the people that they might amend their preſent condition, by his or by his ſon's reſtorement, I ſhall ſhew point by point, that although the king had been re-inſtalled to his deſire, or that his ſon admitted, ſhould obſerve exactly all his father's precepts, yet that this would be ſo far from conducing to our happineſs, either as a remedy to the preſent diſtempers, or a prevention of the like to come, that it would inevitably throw us back again into all our paſt and fulfilled miſeries; would force us to fight over again all our tedious wars, and put us to another fatal ſtruggling for liberty and life, more dubious than the former. In which, as our ſucceſs hath been no other than our cauſe, ſo it will be evident to all poſterity, that his misfortunes were the mere conſequence of his perverſe judgment

Firſt, he argues from the experience of thoſe troubles which both he and his ſon have had, to the improvement of their piety and patience: and by the way bears witneſs in his own words, that the corrupt education of his youth, which was but glanced at only in ſome former paſſages of this anſwer, was a thing neither of mean conſideration, nor untruly charged upon him or his ſon · himſelf confeſſing here, that "court-delights are prone either to root up all true virtue and honour, or to be contented only with ſome leaves and withering formalities of them, without any real fruits tending to the public good." Which preſents him ſtill in his own words another Rehoboam, ſoftened by a far worſe court than Solomon's, and ſo corrupted by flatteries, which he affirms to be unſeparable, to the overturning of all peace, and the loſs of his own honour and kingdoms. That he came therefore thus bred up and nurtured to the throne, far worſe than Rehoboam, unleſs he be of thoſe who equalized his father to king Solomon, we have here his own confeſſion And how voluptuouſly, how idly reigning in the hands of other men, he either tyrannized or trifled away thoſe ſeventeen years of peace, without care or thought, as if to be a king had been nothing elſe in his apprehenſion, but to eat and drink, and have his will, and take his pleaſure; though there be who can relate his domeſtic life to the exactneſs of a diary, there ſhall be here no mention made This yet we might have then foreſeen, that he who ſpent his leiſure ſo remiſsly and ſo corruptly to his own pleaſing, would one day or other be worſe buſied and employed to our ſorrow. And that he acted in good earneſt what Rehoboam did but threaten, to make his little finger heavier than his father's loins, and to whip us with his two-twiſted ſcorpions, both temporal and ſpiritual tyranny, all his kingdoms have felt. What good uſe he made afterward of his adverſity, both his impenitence and obſtinacy to the end (for he was no Manaſſeh) and the ſequel of theſe his meditated reſolutions, abundantly expreſs, retaining, commending, teaching to his ſon all thoſe putrid and pernicious documents both of

ſtate

ſtate and of religion, inſtilled by wicked doctors, and received by him as in a veſſel nothing better ſeaſoned, which were the firſt occaſion both of his own and all our miſeries. And if he, in the beſt maturity of his years and underſtanding, made no better uſe to himſelf or others of his ſo long and manifold afflictions, either looking up to God, or looking down upon the reaſon of his own affairs; there can be no probability that his ſon, bred up, not in the ſoft effeminacies of a court only, but in the rugged and more boiſterous licence of undiſciplined camps and garriſons, for years unable to reflect with judgment upon his own condition, and thus ill inſtructed by his father, ſhould give his mind to walk by any other rules than theſe, bequeathed him as on *his father's death-bed*, and as the choiceſt of all that experience, which his moſt ſerious obſervation and retirement in good or evil days had taught him. David indeed, by ſuffering without juſt cauſe, learned that meekneſs and that wiſdom by adverſity, which made him much the fitter man to reign. But they who ſuffer as oppreſſors, tyrants, violaters of law, and perſecutors of reformation, without appearance of repenting; if they once get hold again of that dignity and power which they had loſt, are but whetted and enraged by what they ſuffered, againſt thoſe whom they look upon as them that cauſed their ſufferings.

How he hath been "ſubject to the ſceptre of God's word and ſpirit," though acknowledged to be the beſt government, and what his diſpenſation of civil power hath been, with what juſtice, and what honour to the public peace, it is but looking back upon the whole catalogue of his deeds, and that will be ſufficient to remember us. "The cup of God's phyſic," as he calls it, what alteration it wrought in him to a firm healthfulneſs from any ſurfeit, or exceſs whereof the people generally thought him ſick, if any man would go about to prove, we have his own teſtimony following here, that it wrought none at all.

Firſt, he hath the ſame fixed opinion and eſteem of his old Epheſian goddeſs, called the Church of England, as he had ever; and charges ſtrictly his ſon after him to perſevere in that anti-papal ſchiſm (for it is not much better) as that which will be neceſſary both for his ſoul's and the kingdom's peace. But if this can be any foundation of the kingdom's peace, which was the firſt cauſe of our diſtractions, let common ſenſe be judge. It is a rule and principle worthy to be known by chriſtians, that no ſcripture, no nor ſo much as any ancient creed, binds our faith, or our obedience to any Church whatſoever, denominated by a particular name, far leſs, if it be diſtinguiſhed by a ſeveral government from that which is indeed catholic. No man was ever bid be ſubject to the Church of Corinth, Rome, or Aſia, but to the Church without addition, as it held faithful to the rules of Scripture, and the government eſtabliſhed in all places by the Apoſtles, which at firſt was univerſally the ſame in all churches and congregations; not differing or diſtinguiſhed by the diverſity of countries, territories, or civil bounds That Church, that from the name of a diſtinct place, takes authority to ſet up a diſtinct faith or government, is a ſchiſm and faction, not a Church It were an injury to condemn the papiſt of abſurdity and contradiction, for adhering to his catholic Romiſh religion, if we, for the pleaſure of a king and his politic conſiderations, ſhall adhere to a catholic Engliſh.

But ſuppoſe the Church of England were as it ought to be, how is it to us the ſafer by being ſo named and eſtabliſhed, whenas that very name and eſtabliſhment, by his contriving, or approbation, ſerved for nothing elſe but to delude us and amuſe us, while the Church of England *inſenſibly* was almoſt changed and tranſlated into the Church of Rome. Which as every man knows in general to be true, ſo the particular treaties and tranſactions tending to that concluſion, are at large diſcovered in a book intitled the "*Engliſh Pope*" But when the people, diſcerning theſe abuſes, began to call for reformation, in order to which the parliament demanded of the king to un-eſtabliſh that prelatical government, which without Scripture had uſurped over us, ſtrait, as Pharaoh accuſed of idleneſs the Iſraelites that ſought leave to go and ſacrifice to God, he lays faction to their charge And that we may not hope to have ever any thing reformed in the Church either by him or his ſon, he forewarns him, "that the devil of rebellion doth most commonly turn himself into an angel of reformation:" and says enough to make him hate it, as the worst of evils, and the bane of his crown: nay he counsels him to "let nothing seem little or despicable to him, so as not speedily and effectually to suppress errors and schisms." Whereby we may perceive plainly that our consciences were destined to the same servitude and persecution, if not worse than before, whether under him, or if it should so happen, under his son; who count all protestant Churches erroneous and schismatical, which are not episcopal. His next precept is concerning our civil liberties; which by his sole voice and predominant will must be circumscribed, and not permitted to extend a hand's breadth further than his interpretation of the laws already settled. And although all human laws are but the offspring of that frailty, that fallibility, and imperfection which was in their authors, whereby many laws, in the change of ignorant and obscure ages, may be found both scandalous, and full of grievance to their posterity that made them, and no law is further good than mutable upon just occasion; yet if the removing of an old law, or the making of a new would save the kingdom, we shall not have it, unless his arbitrary voice will so far slacken the stiff curb of his prerogative, as to grant it us; who are as freeborn to make our own laws, as our fathers were who made these we have Where are then the English liberties which we boast to have been left us by our progenitors? To that he answers, that "our liberties consist in the enjoyment of the fruits of our industry, and the benefit of those laws to which we ourselves have consented." First, for the enjoyment of those fruits which our industry and labours have made our own upon our own, what privilege is that above what the Turks, Jews and Moors enjoy under the Turkish monarchy? For without that kind of justice, which is also in Algiers, among thieves and pirates between themselves, no kind of government, no society, just or unjust, could stand; no combination or conspiracy could stick together. Which he also acknowledges in these words: "that if the crown upon his head be so heavy as to oppress the whole body, the weakness of inferior members cannot return any thing of strength, honour, or safety to the head; but that a necessary debilitation must follow" So that this liberty of the subject concerns himself and the subsistence of his own regal power in the first place, and before the consideration of any right belonging to the subject. We expect therefore something more, that must distinguish free government from slavish. But instead of that, this king, though ever talking and protesting as smooth as now, suffered it in his own hearing to be preached and pleaded without controul or check, by them whom he most favoured and upheld, that the subject had no property of his own goods, but that all was the king's right

Next, for the "benefit of those laws to which we ourselves have consented," we never had it under him; for not to speak of laws ill executed, when the parliament, and in them the people, have consented to divers laws, and, according to our ancient rights, demanded them, he took upon him to have a negative will, as the transcendent and ultimate law above all our laws, and to rule us forcibly by laws to which we ourselves did not consent, but complained of Thus these two heads, wherein the utmost of his allowance here will give our liberties leave to consist, the one of them shall be so far only made good to us, as may support his own interest and crown from ruin or debilitation; and so far Turkish vassals enjoy as much liberty under Mahomet and the Grand Signior · the other we neither yet have enjoyed under him, nor were ever like to do under the tyranny of a negative voice, which he claims above the unanimous consent and power of a whole nation virtually in the parliament

In which negative voice to have been cast by the doom of war, and put to death by those who vanquished him in their own defence, he reckons to himself more than a negative Martyrdom. But martyrs bear witness to the truth, not to themselves. If I bear witness of myself, saith Christ, my witness is not true. He who writes himself Martyr by his own inscription, is like an ill painter, who by writing on the shapeless picture which

which he hath drawn, is fain to tell paſſengers what ſhape it is, which elſe no man could imagine: no more than how a martyrdom can belong to him, who therefore dies for his religion becauſe it is eſtabliſhed. Certainly if Agrippa had turned chriſtian, as he was once turning, and had put to death Scribes and Phariſees for obſerving the law of Moſes, and refuſing chriſtianity, they had died a truer martyrdom. For thoſe laws were eſtabliſhed by God and Moſes, theſe by no warrantable authors of religion, whoſe laws in all other beſt reformed churches are rejected. And if to die for an eſtabliſhment of religion be martyrdom, then Romiſh prieſts executed for that, which had ſo many hundred years been eſtabliſhed in this land, are no worſe martyrs than he. Laſtly, if to die for the teſtimony of his own conſcience, be enough to make him martyr, what heretic dying for direct blaſphemy, as ſome have done conſtantly, may not boaſt a martyrdom? As for the conſtitution or repeal of civil laws, that power lying only in the parliament, which he by the very law of his coronation was to grant them, not to debar them, nor to preſerve a leſſer law with the contempt and violation of a greater; it will conclude him not ſo much as in a civil and metaphorical ſenſe to have died a martyr of our laws, but a plain tranſgreſſor of them. And ſhould the parliament, endued with legiſlative power, make our laws, and be after to diſpute them piece-meal with the reaſon, conſcience, humour, paſſion, fancy, folly, obſtinacy, or other ends of one man, whoſe ſole word and will ſhall baffle and unmake what all the wiſdom of a parliament hath been deliberately framing; what a ridiculous and contemptible thing a parliament would ſoon be and what a baſe unworthy nation we, who boaſt our freedom and ſend them with the maniſeſt peril of their lives to preſerve it, they who are not marked by deſtiny for ſlaves, may apprehend! In this ſervile condition to have kept us ſtill under hatches, he both reſolves here to the laſt, and ſo inſtructs his ſon.

As to thoſe offered condeſcenſions of "charitable connivance, or toleration," if we conſider what went before, and what follows, they moulder into nothing. For, what with not ſuffering ever ſo little to ſeem a deſpicable ſchiſm, without effectual ſuppreſſion, as he warned him before, and what with no oppoſition of law, government, or eſtabliſhed religion to be permitted, which is his following proviſo, and wholly within his own conſtruction; what a miſerable and ſuſpected toleration, under ſpies and haunting promooters we ſhould enjoy, is apparent. Beſides that it is ſo far beneath the honour of a parliament and free nation, to beg and ſupplicate the godſhip of one frail man, for the bare and ſimple toleration of what they all conſent to be both juſt, pious, and beſt pleaſing to God, while that which is erroneous, unjuſt and miſchievous in the church or ſtate, ſhall by him alone againſt them all be kept up and eſtabliſhed, and they cenſured the while for a covetous, ambitious, and ſacrilegious faction.

Another bait to allure the people, is the charge he lays upon his ſon to be tender of them. Which if we ſhould believe in part, becauſe they are his herd, his cattle, the ſtock upon his ground, as he accounts them, whom to waſte and deſtroy would undo himſelf, yet the inducement which he brings to move him, renders the motion itſelf ſomething ſuſpicious. For if princes need no palliations, as he tells his ſon, wherefore is it that he himſelf hath ſo often uſed them? Princes, of all other men, have not more change of raiment in their wardrobes, than variety of ſhifts and palliations in their ſolemn actings and pretences to the people.

To try next if he can enſnare the prime men of thoſe who have oppoſed him, whom, more truly than his meaning was, he calls the "patrons and vindicators of the people," he gives out Indemnity, and offers Acts of Oblivion. But they who with a good conſcience and upright heart did their civil duties in the ſight of God, and in their ſeveral places, to reſiſt tyranny and the violence of ſuperſtition banded both againſt them, he may be ſure will never ſeek to be forgiven that, which may be juſtly attributed to their immortal praiſe; nor will aſſent ever to the guilty blotting out of thoſe actions before men,

men, by which their faith aſſures them they chiefly ſtand approved, and are had in remembrance before the throne of God.

He exhorts his ſon "not to ſtudy revenge" But how far he, or at leaſt they about him intend to follow that exhortation, was ſeen lately at the Hague, *and now latelieſt at Madrid; where to execute in the baſeſt manner, though but the ſmalleſt part of that ſavage and barbarous revenge which they do nothing elſe but ſtudy and contemplate, they cared not to let the world know them for profeſſed traitors and aſſaſſinators of all law both divine and human, even of that laſt and moſt extenſive law kept inviolable to public perſons among all fair enemies in the midſt of uttermoſt defiance and hoſtility. How implacable therefore they would be, after any terms of cloſure or admittance for the future, or any like opportunity given them hereafter,* it will be wiſdom and our ſafety to believe rather, and prevent, than to make trial. And it will concern the multitude, though courted here, to take heed how they ſeek to hide or colour their own fickleneſs and inſtability with a bad repentance of their well-doing, and their fidelity to the better cauſe, to which at firſt ſo chearfully and conſcientiouſly they joined themſelves

He returns again to extol the Church of England, and again requires his ſon by the joint authority of "a Father and a King, not to let his heart receive the leaſt check or diſaffection againſt it" And not without cauſe, for by that means having ſole influence upon the clergy, and they upon the people, "after long ſearch and many diſputes," he could not poſſibly find a more compendious and politic way to uphold and ſettle tyranny, than by ſubduing firſt the conſciences of vulgar men, with the inſenſible poiſon of their ſlaviſh doctrine: for then the body and beſotted mind without much reluctancy was likelieſt to admit the yoke.

He commends alſo "parliaments held with freedom and with honour" But I would aſk how that can be, while he only muſt be the ſole free perſon in that number, and would have the power with his unaccountable denial, to diſhonour them by rejecting all their counſels, to confine their law-giving power, which is the foundation of our freedom, and to change at his pleaſure the very name of a parliament into the name of a faction.

The concluſion therefore muſt needs be quite contrary to what he concludes; that nothing can be more unhappy, more diſhonourable, more unſafe for all, than when a wiſe, grave, and honourable parliament ſhall have laboured, debated, argued, conſulted, and, as he himſelf ſpeaks, "contributed" for the public good all their counſels in common, to be then fruſtrated, diſappointed, denied and repulſed by the ſingle whiff of a negative, from the mouth of one wilful man, nay, to be blaſted, to be ſtruck as mute and motionleſs as a parliament of tapeſtry in the hangings, or elſe after all their pains and travel to be diſſolved, and caſt away like ſo many noughts in arithmetic, unleſs it be to turn the O of their inſignificance into a lamentation with the people, who had ſo vainly ſent them. For this is not "to enact all things by public conſent," as he would have us be perſuaded, this is to enact nothing but by the private conſent and leave of one not negative tyrant, this is miſchief without remedy, a ſtifling and obſtructing evil that hath no vent, no out-let, no paſſage through grant him this, and the parliament hath no more freedom than if it ſate in his nooſe, which when he pleaſes to draw together with one twitch of his negative, ſhall throttle a whole nation, to the wiſh of Caligula in one neck. This with the power of the militia in his own hands over our bodies and eſtates, and the prelates to enthrall our conſciences either by fraud or force, is the ſum of that happineſs and liberty we were to look for, whether in his own reſtitution, or in theſe precepts given to his ſon. Which unavoidably would have ſet us in the ſame ſtate of miſery, wherein we were before, and have either compelled us to ſubmit like bond-ſlaves, or put us back to a ſecond wandering over that horrid wilderneſs of diſtraction and civil ſlaughter, which, not without the ſtrong and miraculous hand of God aſſiſting us, we have meaſured out, and ſurvived.

And

And who knows, if we make ſo ſlight of this incomparable deliverance, which God hath beſtowed upon us, but that we ſhall, like thoſe fooliſh Iſraelites, who depoſed God and Samuel to ſet up a king, "cry out" one day, "becauſe of our king," which we have been mad upon; and then God, as he foretold them, will no more deliver us.

There remains now but little more of his diſcourſe, whereof yet to take a ſhort view will not be amiſs. His words make ſemblance as if he were magnanimouſly exerciſing himſelf, and ſo teaching his ſon, "To want as well as to wear a crown;" and would ſeem to account it "not worth taking up or enjoying, upon ſordid, diſhonourable, and irreligious terms;" and yet to his very laſt did nothing more induſtriouſly than ſtrive to take up and enjoy again his ſequeſtered crown, upon the moſt ſordid, diſloyal, diſhonourable, and irreligious terms, not of making peace only, but of joining and incorporating with the murderous Iriſh, formerly by himſelf declared againſt, for "wicked and deteſtable rebels, odious to God and all good men." And who but thoſe rebels now, are the chief ſtrength and confidence of his ſon? *While* the preſbyter Scot that woos and ſollicits him, is neglected and put off, as if no terms were to him ſordid, irreligious and diſhonourable, but the Scottiſh and preſbyterian, *never to be complied with, till the fear of inſtant periſhing ſtarve him out at length to ſome unſound and hypocritical agreement.*

He bids his ſon "keep to the true principles of piety, virtue, and honour, and he ſhall never want a kingdom." And I ſay, people of England! keep ye to thoſe principles, and ye ſhall never want a king. Nay, after ſuch a fair deliverance as this, with ſo much fortitude and valour ſhewn againſt a tyrant, that people that ſhould ſeek a king, claiming what this man claims, would ſhew themſelves to be by nature ſlaves, and arrant beaſts; not fit for that liberty which they cried out and bellowed for, but fitter to be led back again into their old *ſervitude*, like a ſort of clamouring and fighting brutes, broke looſe *from their copy-holds*, that know not how to uſe or poſſeſs the liberty which they fought for, *but with the fair words and promiſes of an old exaſperated foe, are ready to be ſtroaked and tamed again, into the wonted and well pleaſing ſtate of their true Norman villenage, to them beſt agreeable.*

The laſt ſentence, whereon he ſeems to venture the whole weight of *all* his former reaſons and argumentations, "That religion to their God, and loyalty to their king, cannot be parted, without the ſin and infelicity of a people," is contrary to the plain teaching of Chriſt, that "No man can ſerve two maſters; but, if he hold to the one, he muſt reject and forſake the other. If God then, and earthly kings be for the moſt part not ſeveral only, but oppoſite maſters, it will as oft happen, that they who will ſerve their king muſt forſake their God; and they who will ſerve God, muſt forſake their king; which then will neither be their ſin, nor their infelicity; but their wiſdom, their piety, and their true happineſs: as to be deluded by theſe unſound and ſubtle oſtentations here, would be their miſery, *and in all likelihood much greater than what they hitherto have undergone: if now again intoxicated and moaped with theſe royal, and therefore ſo delicious becauſe royal rudiments of bondage, the cup of deception, ſpiced and tempered to their bane, they ſhould deliver up themſelves to theſe glozing words and illuſions of him, whoſe rage and utmoſt violence they have ſuſtained, and overcome ſo nobly.*

XXVIII. Intitled Meditations upon Death.

IT might be well thought by him who reads no further than the title of this laſt eſſay, that it required no anſwer. For all other human things are diſputed, and will be variouſly thought of to the world's end. But this buſineſs of death is a plain caſe, and admits no controverſy: in that centre all opinions meet. Nevertheleſs, ſince out of thoſe few mortifying hours that ſhould have been intireſt to themſelves, and moſt at peace from all paſſion and diſquiet, he can afford ſpare time to inveigh bitterly againſt that juſtice which was done upon him; it will be needful to ſay ſomething in defence of thoſe proceedings, though briefly, in regard ſo much on this ſubject hath been written lately.

It happened once, as we find in Eſdras and Joſephus, authors not leſs believed than any under ſacred, to be a great and ſolemn debate in the court of Darius, what thing was to be counted ſtrongeſt of all other. He that could reſolve this, in reward of his excelling wiſdom, ſhould be clad in purple, drink in gold, ſleep on a bed of gold, and ſit next Darius. None but they doubtleſs *who* were reputed wiſe, had the queſtion propounded to them who after ſome reſpite given them by the king to conſider, in full aſſembly of all his lords and graveſt counſellors, returned ſeverally what they thought. The firſt held, that wine was ſtrongeſt, another that the king was ſtrongeſt. But Zorobabel prince of the captive Jews, and heir to the crown of Judah, being one of them, proved women to be ſtronger than the king, for that he himſelf had ſeen a concubine take his crown from off his head to ſet it upon her own. and others beſides him have lately ſeen the like feat done, and not in jeſt Yet he proved on, and it was ſo yielded by the king himſelf, and all his ſages, that neither wine, nor women, nor the king, but truth of all other things was the ſtrongeſt. For me, though neither aſked, nor in a nation that gives ſuch rewards to wiſdom, I ſhall pronounce my ſentence ſomewhat different from Zorobabel, and ſhall defend, that either truth and juſtice are all one, (for truth is but juſtice in our knowledge, and juſtice is but truth in our practice, and he indeed ſo explains himſelf, in ſaying that with truth is no accepting of perſons, which is the property of juſtice) or elſe if there be any odds, that juſtice, though not ſtronger than truth, yet by her office is to put forth and exhibit more ſtrength in the affairs of mankind. For truth is properly no more than contemplation; and her utmoſt efficiency is but teaching but juſtice in her very eſſence is all ſtrength and activity, and hath a ſword put into her hand, to uſe againſt all violence and oppreſſion on the earth She it is moſt truly, who accepts no perſon, and exempts none from the ſeverity of her ſtroke She never ſuffers injury to prevail, but when falſhood firſt prevails over truth; and that alſo is a kind of juſtice done on them who are ſo deluded. Though wicked kings and tyrants counterfeit her ſword, as ſome did that buckler, fabled to fall from heaven into the capitol, yet ſhe communicates her power to none but ſuch as like herſelf are juſt, or at leaſt will do juſtice For it were extreme partiality and injuſtice, the flat denial and overthrow of herſelf, to put her own authentic ſword into the hand of an unjuſt and wicked man, or ſo far to accept and exalt one mortal perſon above his equals, that he alone ſhall have the puniſhing of all other men tranſgreſſing, and not receive like puniſhment from men, when he himſelf ſhall be found the higheſt tranſgreſſor

We may conclude therefore, that juſtice, above all other things, is and ought to be the ſtrongeſt ſhe is the ſtrength, the kingdom, the power, and majeſty of all ages Truth herſelf would ſubſcribe to this, though Darius and all the monarchs of the world ſhould deny And if by ſentence thus written, it were my happineſs to ſet free the minds of Engliſhmen from longing to return poorly under that captivity of kings, from which the ſtrength and ſupreme ſword of juſtice hath delivered them, I ſhall have done a work not much inferior to that of Zorobabel who by well praiſing and extolling the force of truth, in that contemplative ſtrength conquered Darius, and freed his country and the people of God from the captivity of Babylon Which I ſhall yet not deſpair to do, if they in this land whoſe minds are yet captive, be but as ingenuous to acknowledge the ſtrength and ſupremacy of juſtice, as that heathen king was to confeſs the ſtrength of truth or let them but as he did, grant that, and they will ſoon perceive that truth reſigns all her outward ſtrength to juſtice juſtice therefore muſt needs be ſtrongeſt,

Loth

both in her own and in the ſtrength of truth. But if a king may do among men whatſoever is his will and pleaſure, and notwithſtanding be unaccountable to men, then contrary to his magnified wiſdom of Zorobabel, neither truth nor juſtice, but the king is ſtrongeſt of all other things: which that Perſian monarch himſelf in the midſt of all his pride and glory durſt not aſſume.

Let us ſee therefore what this king hath to affirm, why the ſentence of juſtice and the weight of that ſword which ſhe delivers into the hands of men, ſhould be more partial to him offending, than to all others of human race. Firſt he pleads that "no law of God or man gives to ſubjects any power of judicature without or againſt him." Which aſſertion ſhall be proved in every part to be moſt untrue The firſt expreſs law of God given to mankind, was that to Noah, as a law, in general, to all the ſons of men. And by that moſt ancient and univerſal law, "Whoſoever ſheddeth man's blood, by man ſhall his blood be ſhed," we find here no exception. If a king therefore do this, to a king, and that by men alſo, the ſame ſhall be done. This in the law of Moſes, which came next, ſeveral times is repeated, and in one place remarkably, Numb xxxv. "Ye ſhall take no ſatisfaction for the life of a murderer, but he ſhall ſurely be put to death: the land cannot be cleanſed of the blood that is ſhed therein," but by the blood of him that ſhed it. This is ſo ſpoken as that which concerned all Iſrael, not one man alone, to ſee performed, and if no ſatisfaction were to be taken, then certainly no exception. Nay the king, when they ſhould ſet up any, was to obſerve the whole law, and not only to ſee it done, but to "do it; that his heart might not be lifted up above his brethren," to dream of vain and reaſonleſs prerogatives or exemptions, whereby the law itſelf muſt needs be founded in unrighteouſneſs.

And were that true, which is moſt falſe, that all kings are the Lord's anointed, it were yet abſurd to think that the anointment of God ſhould be, as it were, a charm againſt law, and give them privilege, who puniſh others, to ſin themſelves unpuniſhably. The high-prieſt was the Lord's anointed as well as any king, and with the ſame conſecrated oil: yet Solomon had put to death Abiathar, had it not been for other reſpects than that anoinment. If God himſelf ſay to kings, "Touch not mine anointed," meaning his choſen people, as is evident in that pſalm, yet no man will argue thence, that he protects them from civil laws if they offend, then certainly, though David as a private man, and in his own cauſe, feared to lift his hand againſt the Lord's anointed, much leſs can this forbid the law, or diſarm juſtice from having legal power againſt any king. No other ſupreme magiſtrate, in what kind of government ſoever, lays claim to any ſuch enormous privilege; wherefore then ſhould any king, who is but one kind of magiſtrate, and ſet over the people for no other end than they?

Next in order of time to the laws of Moſes, are thoſe of Chriſt, who declares profeſſedly his judicature to be ſpiritual, abſtract from civil managements, and therefore leaves all nations to their own particular laws, and way of government Yet becauſe the church hath a kind of juriſdiction within her own bounds, and that alſo, though in proceſs of time much corrupted and plainly turned into a corporal judicature, yet much approved by this king, it will be firm enough and valid againſt him, if ſubjects, by the laws of church alſo, be "inveſted with a power of judicature" both without and againſt their king, though pretending, and by them acknowledged "next and immediately under Chriſt ſupreme head and governor" Theodoſius, *one of the beſt chriſtian emperors*, having made a ſlaughter of the Theſſalonians for ſedition, but too cruelly, was excommunicated to his face by St. Ambroſe, who was his ſubject, and excommunion is the utmoſt of eccleſiaſtical judicature, a ſpiritual putting to death But this, ye will ſay, was only an example. Read then the ſtory; and it will appear, both that Ambroſe avouched it for the law of God, and Theodoſius confeſt it of his own accord to be ſo, "and that the law of God was not to be made void in him, for any reverence to his imperial power" From hence, not to be tedious, I ſhall paſs into our own land of Britain; and ſhow that ſubjects here have exerciſed the utmoſt of ſpiritual judicature, and more than ſpiritual againſt their kings, his predeceſſors. Vortiger, for committing inceſt with his daughter, was by St. German, at that time his ſubject, curſed and condemned in a Britiſh council about the year 448; and thereupon ſoon after was depoſed. Mauricus, a king in Wales, for breach of oath and the murder of Cynetus, was excommunicated and curſt, with all his offſpring, by Oudoceus biſhop of Llandaff in full ſynod, about the year 560; and not reſtored till he had repented. Morcant, another king in Wales, having ſlain Frioc his uncle, was fain to come in perſon, and receive judgment from the ſame biſhop and his clergy; who upon his penitence acquitted him, for no other cauſe than leſt the kingdom ſhould be deſtitute of a ſucceſſor in the royal line. Theſe examples are of the primitive, Britiſh, and epiſcopal church; long ere they had any commerce or communion with the church of Rome. What power afterward of depoſing kings, and ſo conſequently of putting them to death, was aſſumed and practiſed by the canon law, I omit, as a thing generally known Certainly, if whole councils of the Romiſh church have in the midſt of their dimneſs diſcerned ſo much of truth, as to decree at Conſtance, and at Baſil, and many of them to avouch at Trent alſo, that a council is above the pope, and may judge him, though by them not denied to be the vicar of Chriſt, we in our clearer light may be aſhamed not to diſcern further, that a parliament is by all equity and right above a king, and may judge him, whoſe reaſons and pretenſions to hold of God only, as his immediate vicegerent, we know how far fetched they are, and inſufficient.

As for the laws of man, it would aſk a volume to repeat all that might be cited in this point againſt him from all antiquity. In Greece, Oreſtes, the ſon of Agamemnon, and by ſucceſſion king of Argos, was in that country judged and condemned to death for killing his mother: whence eſcaping, he was judged again, though a ſtranger, before the great council of Areopagus in Athens. And this memorable act of judicature, was the firſt that brought the juſtice of that grave ſenate into fame and high eſtimation over all Greece for many ages after. And in the ſame city, tyrants were to undergo legal ſentence by the laws of Solon. The kings of Sparta, though deſcended lineally from Hercules, eſteemed a God among them, were often judged, and ſometimes put to death by the moſt juſt and renowned laws of Lycurgus; who, though a king, thought it moſt unequal to bind his ſubjects by any law, to which he bound not himſelf In Rome the laws made by Valerius Publicola, *ſoon after the expelling of Tarquin and his race, expelled without a written law, the law being afterward written*; and what the ſenate decreed againſt Nero, that he ſhould be judged, and puniſhed according to the laws of their anceſtors, and what in like manner was decreed againſt other emperors, is vulgarly known, *as it was known to thoſe heathen, and found juſt by nature ere any law mentioned it And that the chriſtian civil law warrants, like power of judicature to ſubjects againſt tyrants, is written clearly by the beſt and famouſeſt civilians* For if it was decreed by Theodoſius, and ſtands yet firm in the code of Juſtinian, that the law is above the emperor, then certainly the emperor being under law, the law may judge him; and if judge him, may puniſh him, proving tyrannous how elſe is the law above him, or to what purpoſe? Theſe are neceſſary deductions, and thereafter hath been done in all ages and kingdoms, oftner than to be here recited.

But what need we any further ſearch after the law of other lands, for that which is ſo fully and ſo plainly ſet down lawful in our own? Where ancient books tell us, Bracton, Fleta, and others, that the king is under law, and inferior to his court of parliament, that although his place "to do juſtice" be higheſt, yet that he ſtands as liable "to receive juſtice," as the meaneſt of his kingdom. Nay, Alfred the moſt worthy king, and by ſome accounted firſt abſolute monarch of the Saxons here, ſo ordained; as is cited out of an ancient law-book called "the Mirror;" in "Rights of the kingdom," p. 31. where it is complained on, "as the ſovereign abuſe of all," that "the king ſhould be deemed above the law, whereas he ought to be ſubject to it by his oath." Of which oath, anciently it was the laſt clauſe, that the king "ſhould be as liable, and obedient to ſuffer right, as others of his people." And indeed it were but fond and ſenſeleſs, that the king ſhould be accountable to every petty ſuit in leſſer courts, as we all know he was, and not be ſubject to the judicature of parliament in the main matters of our common ſafety or deſtruction; that he ſhould be anſwerable in the ordinary courſe of law for any wrong done to a private perſon, and not anſwerable in court of parliament for deſtroying the whole kingdom. By all this, and much more that might be added, as in an argument over-copious rather than barren, we ſee it manifeſt that all laws, both of God and man are made without exemption of any perſon whomſoever; and that if kings preſume to over-top the law by which they reign for the public good, they are by law to be reduced into order, and that can no way be more juſtly, than by thoſe who exalted them to that high place. For who ſhould better underſtand their own laws, and when they are tranſgreſt, than they who are governed by them, and whoſe conſent firſt made them? And who can have more right to take knowledge of things done within a free nation, than they within themſelves?

Thoſe objected oaths of allegiance and ſupremacy we ſwore, not to his perſon, but as it was inveſted with his authority; and his authority was by the people firſt given him conditionally, in law, and under law, and under oath alſo for the kingdom's good, and not otherwiſe; the oaths then were interchanged, and mutual; ſtood and fell together, he ſwore fidelity to his truſt; (not as a deluding ceremony, but as a real condition of their admitting him for king; and the conqueror himſelf ſwore it oftner than at his crowning:) they ſwore homage and fealty to his perſon in that truſt. There was no reaſon why the kingdom ſhould be further bound by oaths to him, than he by his coronation-oath to us, which he hath every way broken. and having broken, the ancient crown-oath of Alfred above mentioned, conceals not his penalty.

As for the covenant, if that be meant, certainly no diſcreet perſon can imagine it ſhould bind us to him in any ſtricter ſenſe than thoſe oaths formerly. The acts of hoſtility which we received from him, were no ſuch dear obligements that we ſhould owe him more fealty and defence for being our enemy, than we could before when we took him only for a king They were accuſed by him and his party to pretend liberty and reformation, but to have no other end than to make themſelves great, and to deſtroy the king's perſon and authority. For which reaſon they added that third article, teſtifying to the world, that as they were reſolved to endeavour firſt a reformation in the church, to extirpate prelacy, to preſerve the rights of parliament, and the liberties of the kingdom, ſo they intended, ſo far as it might conſiſt with the preſervation and defence of theſe, to preſerve the king's perſon and authority; but not otherwiſe. As far as this comes to, they covenant and ſwear in the ſixth article, to preſerve and defend the perſons and authority of one another, and all thoſe that enter into that league, ſo that this covenant gives no unlimitable exemption to the king's perſon, but gives to all as much defence and preſervation as to him, and to him as much as to their own perſons, and no more, that is to ſay, in order and ſubordination to thoſe main ends for which we live and are a nation of men joined in ſociety either chriſtian, or at leaſt human. But if the covenant were made abſolute, to preſerve and defend any one whomſoever, without reſpect had, either to the true religion, or thoſe other ſuperior things to be defended and preſerved however, it cannot then be doubted, but that the covenant was rather a moſt fooliſh, haſty, and unlawful vow, than a deliberate and well-weighed covenant; ſwearing us into labyrinths and repugnances, no way to be ſolved or reconciled, and therefore no way to be kept; as firſt offending againſt the law of God, to vow the abſolute preſervation, defence, and maintaining of one man, though

in

in his sins and offences never so great and heinous against God or his neighbour; and to except a person from justice, whereas his law excepts none. Secondly, it offends against the law of this nation, wherein, as hath been proved, kings in receiving justice, and undergoing due trial, are not differenced from the meanest subject. Lastly, it contradicts and offends against the covenant itself, which vows in the fourth article to bring to open trial and condign punishment all those that shall be found guilty of such crimes and delinquencies, whereof the king by his own letters and other undeniable testimonies not brought to light till afterward, was found and convicted to be chief actor in what they thought him, at the time of taking that covenant, to be over-ruled only by evil counsellors; and those, or whomsoever they should discover to be principal, they vowed to try, either by their own supreme judicatories," (for so even then they called them,) " or by others having power from them to that effect." So that to have brought the king to condign punishment hath not broke the covenant, but it would have broke the covenant to have saved him from those judicatories, which both nations declared in that covenant to be supreme against any person whatsoever. *And besides all this, to swear in covenant the bringing of his evil counsellors and accomplices to condign punishment, and not only to leave unpunished and untouched the grand offender, but to receive him back again from the accomplishment of so many violences and mischiefs, dipt from head to foot, and stained over with the blood of thousands that were his faithful subjects, forced to their own defence against a civil war by him first raised upon them; and to receive him thus, in this gory pickle, to all his dignities and honours, covering the ignominious and horrid purple robe of innocent blood that sat so close about him, with the glorious purple of royalty and supreme rule, the reward of highest excellence and virtue here on earth, were not only to swear and covenant the performance of an unjust vow, the strangest and most impious to the face of God, but were the most unwise and unprudential act as to civil government For so long as a king shall find by experience, that, do the worst he can, his subjects, overawed by the religion of their own covenant, will only prosecute his evil instruments, not dare to touch his person, and that whatever hath been on his part offended or transgressed, he shall come off at last with the same reverence to his person, and the same honour as for well doing, he will not fail to find them work; seeking far and near, and inviting to his court all the concourse of evil counsellors, or agents, that may be found who, tempted with preferments and his promise to uphold them, will hazard easily their own heads, and the chance of ten to one but they shall prevail at last, over men so quelled and fitted to be slaves by the false conceit of a religious covenant. And they in that superstition neither wholly yielding, nor to the utmost resisting, at the upshot of all their foolish war and expence, will find to have done no more but fetched a compass only of their miseries, ending at the same point of slavery, and in the same distractions wherein they first begun. But when kings themselves are made as liable to punishment as their evil counsellors, it will be both as dangerous from the king himself as from his parliament, to those that evil counsel him and they, who else would be his readiest agents in evil, will then not fear to dissuade or to disobey him, not only in respect of themselves and their own lives, which for his sake they would not seem to value, but in respect of that danger which the king himself may incur, whom they would seem to love and serve with greatest fidelity. On all these grounds therefore of the covenant itself, whether religious or political, it appears likeliest, that both the English parliament and the Scotch commissioners, thus interpreting the covenant, (as indeed at that time they were the best and most authentical interpreters joined together) answered the king unanimously, in their letter dated January the 13th, 1645, that till security and satisfaction first given to both kingdoms for the blood spilled, for the Irish rebels brought over, and for the war in Ireland by him fomented, they could in no wise yield their consent to his return. Here was satisfaction, full two years and upward after the covenant taken, demanded of the king by both nations in parliament for crimes at least capital, wherewith they charged him. And what satisfaction could be given for so much blood, but justice upon him that spilled it? Till which done, they neither took themselves bound to grant him the exercise of his regal office*

by

by any meaning of the covenant which they then declared (tho' other meanings have been ſince contrived) nor ſo much regarded the ſafety of his perſon, as to admit of his return among them from the midſt of thoſe whom they declared to be his greateſt enemies; nay from himſelf as from an actual enemy, not as from a king, they demanded ſecurity. But if the covenant, all this notwithſtanding, ſwore otherwiſe to preſerve him than in the preſervation of true religion and our liberties, againſt which he fought, if not in arms, yet in reſolution to his dying day, and now after death ſtill fights againſt in this his book, the covenant was better broken than he ſaved. And God hath teſtified by all propitious and *the moſt* evident ſign, whereby in theſe latter times he is wont to teſtify what pleaſes him, that ſuch a ſolemn and for many ages unexampled act of due puniſhment, was no mockery of juſtice, but a moſt grateful and well-pleaſing ſacrifice. Neither was it to cover their Perjury, as he accuſes, but to uncover his perjury to the oath of his coronation.

The reſt of his diſcourſe quite forgets the title, and turns his meditations upon death into obloquy and bitter vehemence againſt his "Judges and Accuſers;" imitating therein, not our Saviour, but his grandmother Mary queen of Scots, as alſo in the moſt of his other ſcruples, exceptions and evaſions; and from whom he ſeems to have learnt, as it were by heart, or elſe by kind, that which is thought by his admirers to be the moſt virtuous, moſt manly, moſt chriſtian, and moſt martyr-like, both of his words and ſpeeches here, and of his anſwers and behaviour at his trial

"It is a ſad fate," he ſaith, "to have his enemies both accuſers, parties, and judges." Sad indeed, but no ſufficient plea to acquit him from being ſo judged. For what malefactor might not ſometimes plead the like? If his own crimes have made all men his enemies, who elſe can judge him? They of the powder-plot againſt his father, might as well have pleaded the ſame Nay, at the reſurrection it may as well be pleaded, that the ſaints who then ſhall judge the world, are "both enemies, judges, parties, and accuſers."

So much he thinks to abound in his own defence, that he undertakes an unmeaſurable taſk, to beſpeak "the ſingular care and protection of God over all kings," as being the greateſt patrons of law, juſtice, order, and religion on earth But what patrons they be, God in the ſcripture oft enough hath expreſt, and the earth itſelf hath too long groaned under the burden of their injuſtice, diſorder, and irreligion. Therefore "to bind their kings in chains, and their nobles with links of Iron," is an honour belonging to his ſaints; not to build Babel, (which was Nimrod's work, the firſt king, and the beginning of his kingdom was Babel,) but to deſtroy it, eſpecially that ſpiritual Babel and firſt to overcome thoſe European kings, which receive their power, not from God, but from the beaſt; and are counted no better than his ten horns. "Theſe ſhall hate the great whore," and yet "ſhall give their kingdoms to the beaſt that carries her; they ſhall commit fornication with her," and yet "ſhall burn her with fire," and yet "ſhall lament the fall of Babylon," where they fornicated with her. *Revelations* 17 *and* 18, *chap*.

Thus ſhall they be to and fro, doubtful and ambiguous in all their doings, until at laſt, "joining their armies with the beaſt," whoſe power firſt raiſed them, they ſhall periſh with him by the "King of Kings," againſt whom they have rebelled, and "the fowls ſhall eat their fleſh" This is their doom written, *Revel* xix and the utmoſt that we find concerning them in theſe latter days; which we have much more cauſe to believe, than his unwarranted revelation here, propheſying what ſhall follow after his death, with the ſpirit of enmity, not of St John

He would fain bring us out of conceit with the good Succeſs which God hath vouchſafed us We meaſure not our cauſe by our ſucceſs, but our ſucceſs by our cauſe. Yet certainly in a good cauſe, ſucceſs is a good confirmation; for God hath promiſed it to good men almoſt in every leaf of ſcripture If it argue not for us, we are ſure it argues

not

not againſt us; but as much or more for us, than ill ſucceſs argues for them; for to the wicked God hath denounced ill ſucceſs in all they take in hand.

He hopes much of thoſe "ſofter tempers," as he calls them, and "leſs advantaged by his ruin, that their conſciences do already" gripe them. 'Tis true, there be a ſort of moody, hot-brained, and always unedified conſciences; apt to engage their leaders into great and dangerous affairs paſt retirement, and then upon a ſudden qualm and ſwimming of their conſcience, to betray them baſely in the midſt of what was chiefly undertaken for their ſakes.* Let ſuch men never meet with any faithful parliament to hazard for them; never with any noble ſpirit to conduct and lead them out, but let them live and die in ſervile condition and their ſcrupulous queaſineſs, if no inſtruction will confirm them! Others there be in whoſe conſciences the loſs of gain, and thoſe advantages they hoped for, hath ſprung a ſudden leak. Theſe are they that cry out, the Covenant broken! and to keep it better, ſlide back into neutrality, or join actually with incendiaries and malignants. But God hath eminently begun to puniſh thoſe, firſt, in Scotland, then in Ulſter, who have provoked him with the moſt hateful kind of mockery, to break his covenant under pretence of ſtricteſt keeping it; and hath ſubjected them to thoſe malignants, with whom they ſcrupled not to be aſſociates. In God therefore we ſhall not fear what their falſe fraternity can do againſt us.

He ſeeks again with cunning words to turn our ſucceſs into our ſin. But might call to mind, that the ſcripture ſpeaks of thoſe alſo, who "when God ſlew them, then ſought him;" yet did but "flatter him with their mouth, and lyed to him with their tongues; for their heart was not right with him" And there was one, who in the time of his affliction treſpaſſed more againſt God. This was that king Ahaz."

He glories much in the forgiveneſs of his enemies; ſo did his grandmother at her death. Wiſe men would ſooner have believed him, had he not ſo often told us ſo. But he hopes to erect "the trophies of his charity over us." And trophies of charity no doubt will be as glorious as trumpets before the alms of hypocrites; and more eſpecially the trophies of ſuch an aſpiring charity as offers in his prayer to ſhare victory with God's compaſſion, which is over all his works. Such prayers as theſe may *haply* catch the people, as was intended. but how they pleaſe God, is to be much doubted, though prayed in ſecret, much leſs written to be divulged. Which perhaps may gain him after death a ſhort, contemptible, and ſoon fading reward; not what he aims at, to ſtir the conſtancy and ſolid firmneſs of any wiſe man, or to unſettle the conſcience of any knowing chriſtian, (if he could ever aim at a thing ſo hopeleſs, and above the genius of his Cleric elocution,) but to catch the worthleſs approbation of an inconſtant, irrational, and image-doting rabble; *that like a credulous and hapleſs herd, begotten to ſervility, and inchanted with theſe popular inſtitutes of tyranny, ſubſcribed with a new device of the king's picture at his prayers, hold out both their ears with ſuch delight and raviſhment to be ſtigmatized and bored through, in witneſs of their own voluntary and beloved baſeneſs.* The reſt, whom perhaps ignorance without malice, or ſome error, leſs than fatal, hath for the time miſled, on this ſide ſorcery or obduration, may find the grace and good guidance to bethink themſelves and recover.

* A ſevere rebuke this, to the *Preſbyterians*

CPSIA information can be obtained at www.ICGtesting.com
Printed in the USA
BVOW01s1515070214

344280BV00007B/262/P

9 781171 185383